Bonded Labour in Pakistan

*Oxford in Pakistan Readings in Sociology
and Social Anthropology*

SERIES EDITOR: ALI KHAN

BONDED LABOUR IN PAKISTAN

Edited by
AYAZ QURESHI
ALI KHAN

OXFORD
UNIVERSITY PRESS

OXFORD

UNIVERSITY PRESS

Oxford University Press is a department of the University of Oxford.
It furthers the University's objective of excellence in research, scholarship,
and education by publishing worldwide. Oxford is a registered trade mark of
Oxford University Press in the UK and in certain other countries

Published in Pakistan by
Ameena Saiyid, Oxford University Press
No.38, Sector 15, Korangi Industrial Area,
PO Box 8214, Karachi-74900, Pakistan

ISBN 978-0-19-940389-9

Typeset in Adobe Garamond Pro
Printed on 80gsm Local Offset paper

Printed by Mas Printers, Karachi

Contents

Introduction

Among more than 20 million bonded labourers in the world, around 85 per cent are in South Asia, mostly in India, Pakistan and Nepal (Kara 2014). The commonest pattern for bonded labour is for a landlord or an employer to extend a loan to labourers, in advance of the work done, on the understanding that this advance payment or *peshgi* would be paid back by providing labour. Although in theory the loan is repayable over a period of time, in practice borrowers often cannot pay it back, despite their efforts, and become trapped in a vicious cycle of debt and forced labour. Also known as debt-bondage, it has been internationally recognized as a form of slavery. The *UN Supplementary Convention on Abolition of Slavery, the Slave Trade and Institutions and Practices Similar to Slavery* of 1956 defined debt-bondage as 'where a debtor pledges his personal services or those of a person under his control as security for a debt, if the reasonable value of those services is not applied towards the payment of the debt or if the length and nature of these services are not limited or defined'.[1]

Bonded labour has existed in many parts of the world under various forms throughout history. From Egyptian and Roman civilizations to medieval Europe and the Indian sub-continent of the Mughal era, landless peasants and serfs have been exploited as unpaid labour by their masters and feudal lords. However, today, four out of five bonded labourers are found in South Asia alone (Kara 2014). Some forms of bonded labour persist in the developed countries of Western Europe and North America, most notably among migrant domestic servants (Wittenburg, 2008). However, debt-bondage in South Asia is most obviously feudal, which sometimes involves extreme forms of violence. Newer forms of debt bondage are also evolving in certain sectors where the growth of capitalistic modes of production have altered traditional relations.

Pakistan ranks third, after China and India, in the list of countries with the highest number of people caught in modern forms of slavery, including debt-bondage, human trafficking and forced domestic and child labour. According to the Global Slavery Index, approximately 2.1 million individuals in Pakistan are enslaved in one or the other of these forms of slavery. The most common form is debt-bondage in agriculture and the brick industry. Landlords or kiln owners exercise exclusive rights over the labour power of those who are indebted to them. They restrict labourers from taking up extra work elsewhere and control or manipulate other spheres of their lives as well. For example, if a family of bonded labourers has to visit relatives in a different town for a wedding, they may be required to leave behind at least one adult member at the kiln as a guarantee that the family would return to resume work. In extreme cases a landlord will decide on his workers' marriages, the education (or not) of their children, and will exert the kind of control that a master had over his slave but with the added advantage of not having to make the initial investment of purchasing an individual. The Human Rights Commission of Pakistan has reported that some bonded labourers in brick kilns are 'either kept in captivity by armed guards or their family members become virtual hostages' (HRCP 2012: 7). It is not only in brick kilns, but as this book demonstrates, also in other sectors that bonded labourers are subjected to exploitation, torture and incarceration.

This book is explicitly comparative. It brings together case studies of bonded labour across different sectors in contemporary Pakistan, contributed by authors with different disciplinary backgrounds, with a small number of key social scientific and legal overvixews.

In bringing together these cases, this book allows us to identify, for the first time, the salient parameters of differentiation in bonded labour in Pakistan. In this introduction, we draw explicit comparisons between the case studies so as to be able to link individual cases of bonded labour to wider debates, and draw out the questions raised by our cases for academic and policy work on bonded labour in Pakistan and beyond.

The introduction proceeds as follows. After introducing the international and Pakistani legislative context, we isolate the following axes of differentiation: the significance of *biradari*, kinship and ancestral ties; variation between industries and regions; incentive structures for employers and labourers; ethnic, religious, caste and gender dimensions. We conclude by discussing the existence of apologist discourses about bonded labour in Pakistan, and offer our response to them, before drawing out the pressing wider questions that remain.

BONDED LABOUR AS SLAVERY

The condition of bonded labourers in Pakistan appears to satisfy the United Nation's definition of slavery as 'the status or condition of a person over whom any or all of the powers attaching to the right of ownership are exercised' (UNHR 2015). The 1973 Pakistan constitution, under article 11 (1), declared that slavery is nonexistent and forbidden in Pakistan. Although the constitution explicitly denies the existence of bonded labour in Pakistan, in 1992, under pressure both internationally and from within Pakistan, the country passed the Bonded Labour System (Abolition) Act. This piece of legislation set ambitious targets to root out bonded labour in all sectors by establishing vigilance committees and putting legal sanctions on the perpetrators. It was further strengthened in 1995 in a subsequent piece of legislation which defined the rules for implementation, laid out the scope for the involvement of non-governmental organizations and set up a fund for the legal and financial assistance of bonded labourers. Although the targets were ambitious, the legal provisions were a significant achievement. Nonetheless, in the cases that made it into the judicial system, the implementation of these provisions could not move beyond 'setting bonded labourers at liberty' by perfunctory court orders, which did not have a substantial impact on the continuation of bonded labour at large (see Qazilbash, this volume).

Typically entire families of bonded labourers in agriculture, brick making and fishing work for the same landlord or employer to try and pay back the debt on the whole family. In brick kilns, for example, once a member of a family of bonded labourers has worked as a kiln labourer, he or she cannot work elsewhere at his or her own discretion while the debt remains outstanding. Even when the kiln is shut down in the off-season or during the rains, a member of the bonded labourer's family must seek permission from the kiln owner if he or she wants to work elsewhere. In some cases, family debt is transferred from one generation to the next even if the main earner has died or suffered permanent disability due to the hazardous nature of the work. Juveniles have been documented working as main earners to pay off the debt their dead or incapacitated elders had taken (see Ercelawn and Nauman, this volume). Where they are not the main earners, children are made to work alongside their parents and older siblings as part of the family of labourers, especially where wages are calculated at piece-rate.

Owners also control and manipulate decisions about whether to send the children to school or how to plan their future (see Martin, this volume). In some cases, landlords, their male family members, and foremen sexually molest women bonded labourers. Due to their vulnerability to further violence, women often do not speak out against such atrocities and the men also keep their silence or feign ignorance (see Ahmad, this volume). Bonded labour is clearly no different than slavery because the control exercised over men, women, and children of bonded labourers amounts to 'ownership rights' for the landlord or employer. In the case of agriculture, and to an extent brick making, the control exerted by the 'employer' is significantly increased because workers and their families often live 'on site' and are therefore not only constantly vulnerable to abuse but also face the threat of eviction, leading to a loss of living space.

BIRADARI, KINSHIP AND ANCESTRAL TIES

Bonded labour is often conflated with the system of advance payments or *peshgi*, especially in the brick kiln sector. However, it is important to clarify that these are two different forms of relations between employers and workers. The *peshgi* system is neither a precondition for, nor does it always lead to, bonded labour. The chapters of this volume demonstrate that the role played by the *peshgi* system in bonded labour varies among various sectors across different regions of Pakistan. For example, in the football-stitching and bangle-making industries in Sialkot and Hyderabad respectively, *peshgis* are taken regularly but do not lead to debt-bondage. This despite the fact these two industries have all the usual characteristics of the industries that would be likely to have widespread bonded labour— labour intensive sectors, sub-contracting, seasonality, and a decentralized and informal structure with an outwardly formal appearance. What makes a difference, however, is the presence of the common background, shared histories and kinship ties between workers and their employers. These factors mitigate the chances of extreme forms of exploitation between the employers and workers (see Khan, this volume, on the link between debt and *peshgi*). In Sialkot, a sentiment of commonality arises from the fact that many of the employers originated from the ranks of the workers. These are seen to be inspirational individuals who have worked their way up to become small entrepreneurs and owners of factories. The football industry itself is imagined as 'Sialkoti' by everyone involved in it, thus giving them a sense of shared pride.

In the bangle-making industry of Hyderabad, similarly, the majority of workers and employers come from a *biradari* (extended kin group) of artisans who migrated from Hyderabad in India and brought with them their traditional skills. This common kinship tie works to prevent the development of debt-bondage despite the widespread practice of *peshgis*. Thus, a sense of common origin and the place/people-centred identity of an industry shape the relationship between the employers and the labourers. The absence of a clear link between the *peshgi* system and bonded labour should not lead to the conclusion that there is little exploitation of the labourers in industries such as football-stitching and bangle-making. In fact, the very notions of common origin, shared pride, and the inspirational life stories of successful entrepreneurs might be used tactfully by employers to achieve ideological domination over the labourers, yielding a labour force that is willing to accept low wages to keep 'their' industry going or to save an ancestral skill from dying out. Labourers may feel indebted to the benevolent employer, who comes from amongst themselves, for his generosity in sparing monies for them in advance of the work done, and meeting their unforeseen needs for cash to spend on an illness or an accident. Whilst the amount of debt on a labourer may start to mount due to recurrent *peshgis*, possibly because of frequent illnesses or other emergencies in the family, thus straining the relationship with the employer, any attempt at dissension against the employer is judged negatively by the entire community. This happens in other sectors as well, where bonded labourers face social sanctions from the wider group for foot-dragging or badmouthing the landlord or the owner. Thus hegemony sometimes achieves for the employers a degree of compliance (and amounts of profit, one may add) that the most naked forms of physical coercion cannot.

VARIATIONS BETWEEN INDUSTRIES AND REGIONS

Bonded labour exists not only on brick kilns or agricultural farms, as it is commonly suggested by the media images carried on World Labour Days, but also, to a varying degree, in other sectors of the economy such as fishing, mining, carpet-weaving and other small industries. The largest numbers of bonded labourers in Pakistan are to be found in agriculture, where the tenant-landlord relationship is often hereditary, stretching back to many generations of landowning and landless castes. Children are born into bondage and women married into it. The already existing patron-client relationship between the landlord and tenants is further strengthened by advancing *peshgi* to the tenants, thus giving further leverage to the landlord. This form of recruitment into debt-bondage is most prevalent in Sindh and southern Punjab. In areas of Punjab and Khyber Pakhtunkhwa where commercial agriculture is widely practiced and self-cultivation has pushed tenants off the land, the traditional landowner-tenant bond has been substantially weakened or has disappeared altogether. Here *peshgi* plays a different role; it forms new ties rather than consolidating the already existing ones. The nature of bondage is now contractual rather than customary or what Breman (2007) has termed 'neo-bondage'. However, despite this 'contractual' nature of bondage, the influence of traditional hierarchies and caste privileges remain strong. In other words, even though the relation between the employers and employees is premised on capitalist methods of labour management (so as to achieve the control of labour and compression of costs), the vertical ties of subordination are rooted in the consciousness of both the employers and the workers as historically given and socially acceptable (see also Servet 2007).

Many landowning castes have ventured into setting up industries and have taken with them their client castes to work for them in factories. This is particularly striking in the case of the Christian *patheras* (moulders) in the brick making sector and *chamars* in tanneries (see Khan, this volume, on recruitment and wages). The employers also use sub-contractors or middlemen to recruit additional labourers for them. This is inextricably linked to the informality and decentralized operation of industries where bonded labour is most prevalent. For example, middlemen are the main channels of requirement in the mining sector where the majority of labourers are long-distance migrants, usually from northern districts of Khyber Pakhtunkhwa and Azad Kashmir. They live at the mining sites in camps or shabby quarters hundreds of miles away from their native villages. The middlemen are usually former migrant labourers who have worked their way up to become sub-contractors. They recruit workers from their own villages and adjoining areas by extending *peshgi* and thus binding them to work at mines which are usually located away from major towns. The fact that the labourers cannot escape the middleman because he is a co-villager or even a kinsman, coupled with being a long distance from home, keeps the workers at the mines.

Forced labour in the mining sector is characterized by extremes. The power balance is strongly skewed against the labourers who have multiple vulnerabilities—illiteracy, migrant status, extreme poverty. The mines often lack necessary safety equipment and the labourers are forced to work in extremely hazardous conditions with no insurance. Large amounts of *peshgis* to attract migrants appears to lead to substantial bondage, which may involve the worst conditions experienced across sectors—namely the use of physical violence, incarceration in private 'jails' and the tracking down of those who are non-compliant. Occupational hazards further lead to a heavy burden of disease, which in turn often leads to workers taking out additional advances to treat the very illnesses that arise from the work that they undertake, thus creating a vicious cycle of debt-bondage (see Saleem, this volume). All these conditions are further exacerbated by the remoteness of the mines and the fact that the majority of workers are long-distance migrants.

Tactics such as falsifying accounts, delaying wage payments, demanding rapid repayment and withholding or reducing periodic advances are used across all sectors to strengthen the grip of the employer and his men over bonded labourers. Violence or the threat of violence towards the individual worker and their families with verbal and physical abuse are also used to extract work from 'lazy' labourers and to prevent any attempts to escape. Even if a labourer does not directly experience physical abuse from his employer, the possibility of violence is part of his consciousness due to widely circulated stories about punishments meted out to defaulters and renegades. These stories detail how workers who attempted to flee were tracked down with the help of police and influential local politicians, were forced to return to work, and physically abused for their disobedience. The police, on the behest of the owners, sometimes register false cases of theft against the rebellious labourers and lock them up to 'teach them a lesson' (see Ercelawn and Nauman, this volume). Thus the only redemption for bonded labourers facing extreme violence is to find another employer who would be willing to buy off their debt from the current employer.

INCENTIVES FOR EMPLOYERS AND LABOURERS

There are huge variations in the amount of *peshgi* given and the mode of its payment across various sectors. However, large amounts of *peshgi* play a central role in the retention of labourers in bondage. Brick kiln owners speak keenly of the importance of *peshgi* in providing a degree of predictability and regularity to both parties. It ensures a stable supply of a disciplined labour force to the employer and regular employment to the labourers. In a context of high unemployment and precariousness it is, thus, the security of employment that the labourers, according to the kiln owners, willingly trade for their freedom and the owners risk their capital in order to ensure future supply of labour (see Khan, Bushra and Sultan, this volume). Therefore, it would make perfect sense for not only the employer to keep mounting the debt on the labourers but also the labourer to avoid clearing it completely, which might result in losing guaranteed employment. The *peshgi*, therefore, is a way of tying not only the labourer to the employer but also vice versa. Some even argue that, contrary to the classic accounts of bonded labour, in some cases it is the employee rather than the employer who is the net creditor. The worker may accept an advance from the employer but he is remunerated towards the end of the contract period which makes him, rather than his employer, the creditor in a strictly economic sense (see Gazdar, this volume).

A related argument is made for explaining debt-bondage in the agriculture sector. While acknowledging the inevitability of an antagonistic relation between landlords and workers, this perspective posits that while entering debt-bondage, the workers 'choose' to sacrifice freedom for the security and other benefits that come with patronage—access to loans, to the police, courts, schools, and hospitals. The implication, again, is that this relationship is mutually beneficial for the landlord and the worker. For example, in southern Punjab and Sindh—where historically the power of the landlords has been very strong, with reports of tenant beating, private jails, physical and sexual abuse and a clear hierarchy between landowning castes and landless menial and artisan castes—the introduction of newer, commercial forms of agriculture, greater urbanization and diversification of employment afford the workers a chance to break away from the 'old slavery' (Bales 2000). These new developments give them access to higher wages, greater mobility and more freedom. However, with this freedom comes greater insecurity due to seasonal employment, unavailability of loans for lumpy expenditures, unfamiliarity with urban employers, and problems in the enforcement of contracts with powerful employers. For the rural labourers, then, this leads to maintaining a kind of 'attachment' with the traditional patron, the local landlord (see Martin, this volume). Maintaining this attachment gives access to loans and other forms of patronage, but it also restricts freedoms and resurrects long-term debt-bondage, physical violence and abuse.

The case studies in this volume therefore intervene in a wider debate about the 'double coincidence of wants' that results in a mutually advantageous contract of *peshgi* from the rich in return for the labour from the poor, as advocated by the economist Bardhan (1991). According to this perspective, the expectation from the poor is to honour the debt that they received voluntarily on the understanding that they would pay it back with their labour. It implies that the labourers should be grateful for much needed credit and secure employment under this system and that it works equally well for the employers who need cheap labour and low turnover. Therefore, both parties are better off by tying labour to credit.

Kiln owners, according to this perspective, must be appreciated as lenders of last resort given the 'imperfections' of the market and the government in countries like Pakistan. Where the markets and the state fail them, work obtained through the *peshgi* system, with their labour as the only collateral against the loans, promises the bonded labourers job security, earnings and shelter.

Brass (1994) has trenchantly critiqued this perspective. The studies in this volume complicate such self-serving economistic accounts by exploring, from the subjective positions of employers and labourers, the incentive structures that keep both sides locked into, and perpetuating, the system of debt-bondage (see Ercelawn and Nauman; Khan, Bushra, and Sultan; Gazdar; and Martin, this volume).

ETHNIC, RELIGIOUS, AND CASTE DIMENSIONS

Extreme poverty and unequal distribution of wealth have rightly been blamed for a high prevalence of bonded labour in Pakistan and across South Asia. Yet there are ethnic, religious, and caste dimensions of this problem which often go unexplored. For example, in Pakistan's Sindh province, most of the bonded labourers in the agriculture sector are Hindu *haris* (see Ahmed, this volume). The bonded labourers in fishing along the stretches of Indus River in South Punjab are Sindhi *looray*, who are ethnically distinct from their employers and the rest of the local population (see Qureshi, this volume). Begging and domestic work in Sindh and Punjab are organized around caste lines (see Gazdar, this volume). Those who work in brick kilns in Punjab and KPK are mostly either Christians or Afghan migrants, and the migratory brick moulder (*patheras*) traditionally originates from the impoverished and ethnically distinct southern districts of Punjab (see Ercelawn and Nauman's chapter). In central Punjab, there is a clear distinction between landlords and bonded labourers along lines of caste (see Martin, and Gazdar, this volume). These differences of religion, ethnicity, region, and caste are not neutral in labour relations. The powerful role played by these factors becomes clearer when contrasted with the relations between employers and workers in the football-stitching and bangle-making industries, where commonalities of kinship and locality seem to mitigate extreme forms of exploitation (see Khan, this volume).

GENDER

Women experience bonded labour differently than men. Under the patriarchal social system women labourers are exploited not only by the employers but also by their husbands who demand productive and reproductive labour from them (see Ahmed, this volume). The notion of 'honour', attached to the protection or violation of the female body, turns their bodies, at once, into sites of vigilance and control by their male family members and objects of abuse by the landlords and their men. Landlords have been reported to sexually assault and abuse women in order to shame entire families into submission and to continue the bondage. The intersecting vulnerabilities of women in bonded labour result in often hidden multiple burdens. The threat or actual use of sexual violence or other forms of violence against women is an effective tool in the hands of the powerful and keeps bonded labourers under their control. In addition to the everyday physical violence that women have to endure or the threat of which that looms large, there is the structural violence of patriarchy which remains invisible, often internalized as a cultural value and unchallenged at multiple levels.

APOLOGISTS FOR BONDED LABOUR

This internalization, however, does not stop at patriarchy nor does it end with the men and women trapped in debt-bondage. Bonded labour enjoys a degree of cultural acceptance at a much broader level. There have been accounts of judges in the higher judiciary admonishing labourers for not honouring their debts (see Ercelawn and Nauman, and Qazilbash, this volume) and some academics condoning the system of patron-clientism as fundamental to Pakistani society (see for example Lyon 2004 and Lieven 2011). Then there are others who justify these arrangements in terms of the poor households' needs for credit and regular employment combined with the absence of other viable sources (e.g. Bardhan 1991). Such authors reproduce the employers' discourse about the excessive debts that land labourers into debt-bondage, resulting from their own greed and conspicuous consumption rather than any unfairness on the part of the employer. The occurrence of coercion and physical abuse are brushed aside as statistically insignificant, something that happens in extreme cases and is a consequence of the laziness and dishonesty of a few labourers.

Whether in the garb of traditional patron-clientism or in its more naked form of 'contracts', the practice of debt-bondage continues to thrive on the highly skewed distribution of political and economic power between the rich and the poor. Advance payments may be seen as a response to the needs of the labourer for lumpy expenditures such as treatment of an unexpected illness or the need to spend on weddings—expenditure that can neither be met by their meagre savings from very low incomes, nor delayed for another time. However, meeting these sudden needs of the labourers does not absolve the owners from the charge of using economic inequalities and the desperate poverty of the labourers to lock them into labour supply for themselves. Neither do the claims about patron-clientism as some form of social safety net in the absence of a 'perfect' market or state, or the absurd logic of the coincidence of wants, justify the inhuman conditions in which bonded labourers are entrenched.

QUESTIONS RAISED FOR STUDIES OF BONDED LABOUR IN PAKISTAN AND BEYOND

We would like to conclude this introduction by emphasizing that for us, the question about the status of bonded labour as a form of slavery is settled. Even if a labourer, by his own account, does not feel bonded because of the full knowledge and 'voluntary' acceptance of the 'contract' or 'patronage', and even if violence in the relationship between the owner and worker is not all too obvious, the extraction of labour in lieu of a debt by controlling the labour power of the workers until the debt is redeemed, is debt-bondage, hence a form of slavery. Two further issues emerge from this collection. First, the notion of *peshgi* needs to be complicated to get a better understanding of the actual practices that are problematically lumped under this category. How do these practices variously relate to debt-bondage? Is *peshgi* always in the form of cash? Do all forms of cash flow from the employer to the labourers count as *peshgi*? How are the amounts and modes of payment related to setting up piece-rates, the productivity of the labourers, ability of the employer to extract labour and the market forces beyond the employers' control? What is at stake for the middlemen if the labourers default? Is there an implicit understanding on not returning the *peshgi* in full? In answering these questions, we are compelled to consider the difference in practices across a broad spectrum of economic activities in which bonded labour is prevalent, and revaluate our understanding of the link between advance credit and debt-bondage. And then ask ourselves more explicitly, if *peshgi* does not always lead to bonded labour, then what does? Secondly, we must revisit the figure of the owners or employers as monstrous, which is presented in most of the literature on bonded labour. Whilst strongly disagreeing with any attempt to elevate them to the status of benevolent lenders in times of extreme poverty, unemployment, and insecurity—what would be dubbed by some economists as 'imperfections' of the market and the state—we believe that the employers' own vulnerabilities in these circumstances, especially those operating in small industries, must form part of the picture we draw on bonded labour. We hope that this collection, which combines already published material with new findings from the field, serves to strike that balance and chart a new direction in the studies of bonded labour in Pakistan.

REFERENCES

Bales, K. (2000), 'Expendable People: Slavery in the Age of Globalization', Journal of International Affairs, 53(2): 461.
Bardhan, P. (1991), The Economic Theory of Agrarian Institutions. Oxford University Press.
Brass, T. (1994), 'Some Observations on Unfree Labour, Capitalist Restructuring, and Deproletarianization', International Review of Social History, 39(02): 255–275.
Breman, J. (2007), Labour Bondage in West India. From Past to Present, Oxford: Oxford University Press.
HRCP (2012), State of Human Rights in 2012, Human Rights Commission of Pakistan. http://hrcp-web.org/hrcpweb/wp-content/pdf/AR2012.pdf. (Accessed, 06 July 2015)
Kara, S. (2014), Bonded Labor: Tackling the System of Slavery in South Asia. Columbia University Press.
Lieven, A. (2011), Pakistan: A Hard Country. Public Affairs.
Lyon, S. M. (2004), An Anthropological Analysis of Local Politics and Patronage in a Pakistani Village (Vol. 12). Edwin Mellen Press.
Servet, J.-M. (2007), 'Entre protection et sur exploitation: l'ambiguïté de la rémunération par avance en Inde, Autrepart' (43): 103–119.
UNHR (2015), Slavery Convention 1926. United Nations Human Rights. Office of the High Commissioner for Human Rights. http://www.ohchr.org/EN/ProfessionalInterest/Pages/SlaveryConvention.aspx. (Accessed, 06 July 2015)
Wittenburg, V. (2008), The New Bonded Labour? The impact of proposed changes to the UK immigration system on migrant domestic workers. Kalayaan and Oxfam.

NOTE

1. Article 1(a) of the Supplementary Convention on Abolition of Slavery, the Slave Trade and Institutions and Practices Similar to Slavery of 1956. United Nations Office of the High Commissioner for Human Rights. http://www.ohchr.org/EN/ProfessionalInterest/Pages/SupplementaryConventionAbolitionOfSlavery.aspx (Accessed on 06 July 2015).

CHAPTER 1

Beyond Setting at Liberty: a Legal Study of Bonded Labour in Pakistan

ALI QAZILBASH

I n July 1988, the chief justice of Pakistan received a telegram from people working as bonded labour in a brick kiln, complaining of their miseries in captivity. Taking cognizance of the case under article 184 (3)[1] of the constitution, the chief justice turned the telegram into a petition before the Supreme Court and called it a case of public interest litigation. This was the famous *Darshan Masih and others v. The State* (PLD 1990 SC 513), which was the first case of its kind in the judicial history of Pakistan. During the proceedings of the case the Supreme Court identified a number of fundamental rights of bonded labourers which were being violated by the complainants' situation. Two years after this landmark judgment, Pakistan passed the Bonded Labour System (Abolition) Act, 1992.

The issue of bonded labour has mired labour relations in Pakistan for decades. Governments have tried to resolve this problem through legislative and executive means but the intent has failed to translate into action. The judicial system has applied the law merely to setting free of the *détenu*, stopping short of punishing the violation or holding the perpetrators to account. In other words, the courts have failed to punish the powerful people who benefit from the practice of bonded labour. Part of the reason for this failure is the continuation of strong ties between members of law enforcement agencies and the powerful rural aristocracy which is responsible for most of the bonded labour. This nexus between influential elements has hindered meaningful implementation of the existing laws on labour relations. Moreover, frequent military interventions in the political system have consigned issues like bonded labour to the margins of legislative and judicial activity. The passage of the Bonded

Labour Abolition Act (1992) was a significant breakthrough, yet this law has remained ineffective.

The Act envisaged establishment of a system of district vigilance to report the practice of bonded labour to authorities and facilitate action against such practices, but it hasn't managed to uproot this inhuman practice. Despite the designation of bonded labour as a crime under the Pakistan Penal Code and despite the framing of rules for the enforcement of the Abolition Act, violators are often not punished and bonded labour continues unabated. Despite the existing legislation and detailed judgments of the higher judiciary, when deciding on cases of bonded labour, the lower courts often merely hold that the labourers were recovered and 'set at liberty'. This chapter, as the title indicates, embraces the sombre reality that for labourers held in bondage, the struggle for liberty is not over with court decisions of setting them 'at liberty'.

LEGISLATION ON BONDED LABOUR

During the hearings of the Darshan Masih case, the Supreme Court criticized the system of advance payments or *peshgi* and appointed a committee from the bar to assist in the cases that involved violation of the fundamental constitutional rights of the labourer affected by this system. The court instructed the legislature to define bonded labour and enact laws to eradicate this deplorable practice. It laid down restrictions on the practice of giving advance loans to labourers and abolished past *peshgis,* turning them into credit and binding the creditors from using any illegal means for its return. Moreover, according to the judgment, the wages of the labourers could not be settled against past credit and women and children could not be forced by men in their families to join them into work in order to pay back the debt. The court ordered that *habeas corpus* petitions could be filed for the recovery of the bonded labour and that police must send a copy of the FIRs (First Information Report) to the Advocate General of Pakistan within 24 hours of the complaints, who must then present these with his own report before the Supreme Court within the next 24 hours.

The verdict on the Darshan Masih case proved to be an important milestone in the judicial history of Pakistan. It has been acclaimed as the first case of public interest litigation and widely quoted in judicial proceedings over past decades. It was in this case that the Pakistani judiciary, for the first time, took cognizance of the widespread bonded labour in brick kilns, agricultural fields and coal mines. For decades this modern form of slavery has existed side by side with Article 11 of the constitution, which claims that slavery is non-existent in Pakistan.[2] The detailed judgment on the case commented on the legal loopholes as well as the economic conditions and financial practices that were responsible for the pervasiveness of this inhuman system. It was because of this judgment that the legislation on anti-bonded labour laws was initiated in the early 1990s.

BONDED LABOUR SYSTEM (ABOLITION) ACT, 1992

'Bonded Labour System' has been defined in Section 2 of the Bonded Labour System (Abolition) Act, 1992 as below:

(e) 'bonded labour system' means the system of forced, or partly forced, labour under which a debtor enters, or has, or is presumed to have, entered into an agreement with the creditor to the effect that

(i) in consideration of an advance (*peshgi*) obtained by him or by any of the members of his family [whether or not such advance (*peshgi*) is evidenced by any document] and in consideration of the interest, if any, due on such advance (*peshgi*), or

(ii) in pursuance of any customary or social obligation, or

(iii) for any economic consideration received by him or by any of the members of his family;

he would-

(1) render, by himself or through any member of his family, or any person dependent on him, labour or service to the creditor or for the benefit of the creditor, for a specified period or for an unspecified period either without wages or for nominal wages or;

(2) forfeit the freedom of employment or adopting other means of livelihood for a specified period or for an unspecified period, or

(3) forfeit the right to move freely from place to place, or

(4) forfeit the right to appropriate or sell at market value any of his property or product of his labour or the labour of a member of his family or any person dependent on him; and includes the system of forced, or partly forced, labour under which a surety for a debtor enters, or has or is presumed to have, entered, into an agreement with the creditor to the

effect that, in the event of the failure of the debtor to repay the debt, he would render the bonded labour on behalf of the debtor.

This Act was introduced to prevent the exploitation of the labourer, to ensure their constitutional rights and to punish those who operate this exploitative system. It set free all bonded labourers and discharged them from paying back the *peshgis* with their labour. It ordained strict punishments for extracting bonded labour and restricted the advancement of *peshgis* by the brick kiln owners, landlords or other employers. It provided for punishment through imprisonment and a fine on the violators of the law in this regard.

Section 21 of the Act allows for the drafting of the rules for its implementation. These rules were drafted in 1995. Under Section 4 of the rules, the provincial government shall confer powers upon district magistrates to enforce the Act. He shall be authorized to inspect any premises or work sites where he suspects that bonded labour is being extracted. Under Section 4 (2) of the rules the magistrate has the power to move government and non-government agencies for the rehabilitation and help of the bonded labour. Under Section 5 of the rules, the magistrate can also delegate these powers to various classes of government officials. Moreover, since the offences in the Bonded Labour System (Abolition) Act 1992 are cognizable, the police can register cases against the people forcing others into bonded labour.

Section 6 and 7 provides for the creation of vigilance committees in districts and specifies the requirements for the membership of these committees and that the committees should set up their complaint cells in the offices of the district commissioners. The mandate of these committees is to report any cases of bonded labour in the district. Section 9 provides for the creation of a rehabilitation fund for the freed bonded labour, for their legal and financial aid, vocational training and help with seeking employment. The funds must come from federal and provincial governments as well as private sources. The Act recognized that if the freed bonded labour is not provided with alternate skills and resources for employment, they will again fall into the trap of advance payments and hence end up as bonded labour again.

After the devolution of power to districts in 2002, the powers of the district magistrate were delegated to the district nazim (elected mayors). Initially, there was no recognition of such power to the mayors. However, after some time the office of the district nazim was recognized by the government as the bearer of such powers. However, since the lapse of the

2002 local government system, the government has been unable to assign responsibility upon a specific government official to carry out these responsibilities.

Although the Act has been in place since 1992, the lower judiciary has not punished the perpetrators of this crime in accordance with its provisions. Instead, the lower courts have chosen to take cognizance of such cases only under the *habeas corpus* petition under Section 491 of Criminal Procedure Code of 1898.[3] Cases filed under this section only result in the freeing of the *detenue*, leaving the accused unpunished. The legal precedent set in the Darshan Masih case is also ignored by the judiciary when giving punishments in cases of bonded labour.

In an intriguing development in 2006, a group of brick kiln owners brought a case before the Federal Shariat Court on the pretext that certain provisions of the Bonded Labour System (Abolition) Act were unIslamic. They argued that the ban on *peshgi* and the *jamadari* system was unIslamic because it was not in accordance with the teaching of the Quran and Hadith. They also argued the Act was not in accordance with the directions of the Supreme Court in the Darshan Masih case. Upon hearing the case, the Shariat Court concluded that such arguments were unfounded. It concluded that the system of *peshgi* was exploitative and violated the Islamic principle of social justice. This was a major setback to interests vested in the brick kiln industry who wanted to find legal loopholes in order to continue the exploitative practice of bonded labour unabashedly.

PLANS AND POLICIES

The passage of this legislation has not improved the condition of bonded labourers. The federal government adopted a National Policy and Plan of Action for the Abolition of Bonded Labour and Rehabilitation of Freed Bonded Labourers in 2001 under the Ministry of Labour. This national policy went beyond legislative efforts as it aimed to create social awareness in the media and society against bonded labour. It aimed to register all brick kilns and to bring them under the ambit of the law. Non-governmental bodies were included in creating awareness against the practice of bonded labour as well as their inclusion in the fight against it. Further, this policy also aimed to study the plight of bonded labour in the field by collecting quantitative data and performing statistical analyses.

Going by the judicial and legislative intent and the existing laws of the country, bonded labour should not exist in Pakistan. Anyone responsible for the breach of law is also in contempt of court and should be duly prosecuted. However, as things stand, this is not the case. The practice of bonded labour continues to operate in an institutional framework where the socio-political power of the landed elite has allowed them a degree of impunity. The lack of formal education and access to resources among the labourers along with their powerlessness, the corruption of state officials, a general sense of apathy in society towards their predicament, and an attitude of acceptance of the status quo make it extremely difficult to eliminate bonded labour. The police are a key link in the prevalence of this practice. In most cases, they either flatly refuse to register a case against the accused or do so only if bribed heavily.

The lower courts are also notorious for their inefficiency and corruption. Their decisions are heavily influenced by political and religious parties and the proceedings are extremely slow. Cases that should take months to resolve span out over several years. As a result, there is a serious backlog. According to the National Judicial Policy the number of court cases pending with the superior and subordinate judiciary in 2009 was close to 1.6 million.[4] Some sources gave an estimate of over 3 million pending cases by the year 2013.[5]

Pakistan is a signatory to various human rights and labour conventions. Successive governments have failed to fully implement these conventions. For example, even though legislation is in place to enforce C29 (Convention Concerning Forced or Compulsory Labour) and C105 (Convention Concerning the Abolition of Forced Labour), it has not been implemented effectively. These international conventions require vigilance committees to be set up to monitor the progress of the elimination process. Such committees are yet to be set up across Pakistan. Of the few that exist, they have either not been fully operative or have proved to be complete failures. Pakistan has been criticized continuously for its inaction to implement the laws on forced and bonded labour and on a number of occasions, the country has been on the brink of facing international sanctions due to its inability to implement the ratified conventions.

COURT CASES

This section will examine cases relating to bonded labour registered in the Lahore High Court from 2006 to 2010 and an important judgment of the Supreme Court in a case initiated by the Human Rights Commission of Pakistan against the Government of Pakistan. Most of the cases were filed through *habeas corpus* petitions under Section 491 of the Code of

Criminal Procedure and Article 199 (4) of the Constitution of Pakistan.[6] What is significant in reporting these cases in some detail here is that while deliberating upon them the judges of the Lahore High Court ignored the Bonded Labour System (Abolition) Act of 1992. Even though some of the court decisions clearly mention torture and unlawful detention, the culprits were allowed to walk out freely, with no punishment awarded, while victims were merely 'set at liberty' with no recourse to compensation for their injury/loss or rehabilitation. This is against the spirit of the precedent set the Supreme Court in Darshan Masih case and a violation of the of the 1992 Act.

Farooq Masih v. Qamar Crl. Misc No. 1028-H-06
Brick Kiln, Thikriwala Faisalabad
Date of Hearing: 07-09-2006
Justice Syed Sakhi Hussain Bukhari

> Court decision: According to report of bailiff, detainees have been recovered from the residential quarter of brick kiln of respondents. The adult detainees state that respondents have not paid their wages and tortured them, therefore, they do not want to work with them. In this view of the matter, the detainees are set at liberty. Disposed of.

The petitioner in this case was 'set at liberty' and the accused employer was not given any punishment. Even though the provision for this is clearly given in Section 11 of the Bonded Labour System (Abolition) Act of 1992, which states that: 'Whoever, after the commencement of this Act compels any person to render any bonded labour shall be punishable with imprisonment for a term which shall not be less than two years nor more than five years, or with fine which shall not be less than fifty thousand rupees, or with both.'

Muhammad Akram v. S.H.O etc., Crl. Misc. No.1195-H-06
Brick Kiln, Saddar Tehsil, Gujrat,
Date of Hearing: 17-10-2006
Justice Muhammad Akhtar Shabbir

> Court decision: In compliance with the order of this Court dated 16.10.2006, the Bailiff, with the police assistance has raided at the *dera* of respondents No. 2 to 5 and found the detainees mentioned in the head note of the petition sitting on the cots[7] freely.

a. From the report of the Bailiff, it reveals that the alleged detainees were not detained illegally or improperly, they were sitting on cots freely. There is no reason to disbelieve the report of the Bailiff.

b. Be that as it may, if the detainees do not want to work with respondents No. 2 to 5, then no one can force them to serve against their will as they have the right to move freely and the Bonded labour is prohibited in view of the law laid down by the Honourable Supreme Court in case of Darshan Masih. The State (P.L.D. 1990 S.C. 513).

Therefore, the detainees are set at liberty to go wherever they like. Disposed of.

In the above court decision, the detainees are first declared as 'not detained illegally or improperly' and then 'set at liberty' by the court. The decision mentions the Darshan Masih case but the accused are not punished in accordance with the precedent set by this case or the provisions of the Bonded Labour System (Abolition) Act of 1992, which clearly prohibits under Section 12 any practice that might amount to bonded labour and lays down exact punishments for the violators. It states that 'whoever enforces, after the commencement of this Act, any custom, tradition, practice, contract, agreement or other instrument, by virtue of which any person or any member of his family is required to render any service under the bonded labour system, shall be punishable with imprisonment for a term which shall not be less than two years nor more than five years or with fine which shall not be less than fifty thousand rupees, or with both; and out of the fine, if recovered, payment shall be made to the bonded labour at the rate of not less than fifty rupees for each day for which bonded labour was extracted from him.'

Ghafoor Masih v. SHO etc., Crl. Misc. No.1307-H-07
Plastic Factory, Sheikhpura
Date of Hearing: 12-12-2007
Justice Syed Hamid Ali Shah

Court decision: Neither the petitioner has entered appearance nor the terms of preceding orders have been complied with. Dismissed for non-prosecution.

Kalvin v. Rana Bashir Crl. Misc. No.1357-H-2007
Brick Kiln, Qilla Kalar, District Sialkot
Date of Hearing: 27-12-2007
Justice Sh. Najamul Hasan

Court decision: Learned Counsel for the petitioner states that the detainees were kept by respondent no. 2 to 5, they went there for a job but later on they were detained and they want to go to their own homes.

On the other hand, learned counsel for respondent no. 2 to 5 states that in fact the detainees have received Rs. 660,000/-; they were free at the spot and nobody has detained them. Earlier petition was filed before the Session Judge, Gujranwala where the detainees stated that they were not kept by anybody and are working with their own free will and consent and that now this malafide petition has been filed.

In compliance of order dated 19-12-2007 passed by this Court Khawar Mahmood Bailiff has recovered the alleged detainees namely Mst. Bibi, Feroze Masih and Nasreen who are present in the Court. According to the report of the bailiff, the alleged detainees were not in the custody of the respondents and they were present at their own, without any restriction. No case for illegal confinement is made out and this petition is dismissed.

As in previous years, in 2008 most of the labourers were either 'set free' by the courts or the petitions taken back by the complainants. It must be emphasized that 'setting free' by the court in itself is not the solution to the problem of bonded labour. They are—according to the law—to be provided with assistance for their rehabilitation and alternate employment if this vicious cycle of exploitation has to end.

Jonge Masih v. State Crl. Misc. No.144-H-2008
Brick Kiln, Pasrur, Gujranwala
Date of Hearing: 29-02-2008
Justice Zubda-tul-Hussain

Court decision: The learned counsel wishes to withdraw this petition. Dismissed as withdrawn.

Abid Masih v. SHO Crt. Misc No.1106-H-2008
Brick Kiln, BhaiPhero
Date of Hearing: 03-04-2008
Justice Khurshid Anwar Bhinder

Court decision: Pursuant to the preceding orders, SHO Police Station Phoolnagar has entered appearance and has produced the alleged detainee Khalid Masih before this Court today. Learned counsel for the petitioner submits that since grievance of the petitioner stands redressed therefore, he wishes to withdraw this petition. Dismissed and withdrawn.

The petitions in the above two cases were withdrawn by the complainants or their counsels, possibly after reaching out-of-court settlement with the respondents. It may be that kiln owners themselves set the victims at liberty before the court could do it or that the petitioner was coerced by the powerful respondents to withdraw the petition or face the consequences. In either case, the courts do not appear to extend their role beyond proclaiming perfunctory judgment to making sure that justice was dispensed to the aggrieved.

Pervaiz Masih v. M. Saleem Kamboh etc., Crl. Misc. No.415-H-2009
Date of Hearing: 06-04-2008
Justice Muhammad Ashen Boon

> Court decision: Muhammad Shaq has entered appearance on behalf of respondent No. 2. Learned counsel for respondent No. 1 states that in fact the alleged detainee was previously working for respondent No. 1 as his servant. He has taken as advance, an amount Rs. 125,000/- and thereafter a statement took place between them on 21.03.2009. He has produced a copy of agreement which is placed on record as mark 'A'. He states that now just to blackmail respondent No. 1, present petition has been filed and respondent No. 1 does not know the whereabouts of detainee.
>
> On the other hand learned counsel for the petition contends that in fact agreements produced by respondent No. 1 were not executed with his free will and consent, and that is a result of coercion and the alleged detainee Ihsan Masih has been concealed by respondent No. 1, and the petitioner would be satisfied if Police Officer present in court be direct to inquire into the matter of recovery of alleged detainee.
>
> Be that as it may, the said agreement between the parties is not subject matter of the present proceedings as for that purpose the petitioner has remedy before the Civil Court. However, the custody of detainee by respondent No. 1 has been defined. The Police Officer present in the Court is directed to hear both the parties and shall ensure the recovery of alleged detainee and submit his report through Deputy Register (Judicial) within two week. Disposed of accordingly.

In this case the police was directed to recover the detainee and set him at liberty. However, no mention was made of protecting his economic interest and giving him a chance at rehabilitation, so that he may not have a reason to engage any further in bonded labour. This clearly does not abide by the provision of the Section 10 of Bonded Labour System (Abolition) Act of 1992, which states that, 'The District Magistrate authorized by the Provincial Government under section 9, and the officer designated by the District Magistrate under that section, shall as far as practicable, try to promote the welfare of the freed bonded labourer by securing and protecting the economic interests of such bonded labourer so that he may not have any occasion or reason to contract any further bonded debt.'

Sajjad Masih v. SHO and others, Crl. Misc. No.489-H-2008
Brick Kiln, Pattoki, Tehsil Pattoki, Kasur
Date of Hearing: 05-05-2008
Justice Muhammad Ahsan Bhoon

Court decision: The detainees, in compliance with the order dated 28-05-2008 passed by this court have been produced. They are set at liberty accordingly.

Muhammad Arshad v. Muhammad Iqbal, W.p, 6765-2008
Tehsil Malikwal, District Mandi Baha-ud-Din
Date of Hearing: 11-06-2008
Justice Muhammad Ahsan Bhoon

Court decision: In compliance with the order passed by this Court dated 10.06.2008, bailiff raided the premises of Police Station Gojra District, Mandi Baha-ud-Din and recovered the alleged detainee Zair Ahmed, who has been produced before this court. The police officer present in the court stated that neither he is enquired by the police nor he was detained by any one rather he on his own sat in a room to maneuver the proceedings of this petition, particularly when there were more than hundreds people present in the police station in connection with the investigation of another case bearing No.259/2008 offence under Section 489 of PPC, and taking advantage of the detainee entered the room of the police station.

Be that as it may, Zair Ahmad is set at liberty. However, the learned counsel for the petitioner states that alleged detainee is required to be examined medically and action is called for against the delinquent police officer. The alleged detainee shall be examined by the M.S. D.H.Q. hospital, Mandi Baha-ud-Din and Medico Legal Report will be issued accordingly, thereafter he may avail the proper remedy for the proceedings in accordance with law.

Manzoor Masih v. S.H. O etc., Cri. Misc. 1 106-H-08
Brick Kiln, District Faisalabad
Date of Hearing: 06-10-2008
Justice Khurshid Anwer Bhinder

Court decision: In compliance with order dated 29.09.2008, the bailiff has produced the detainees before this court today. All the detainees except for four, who had run away from the brick kiln are present in the court and have categorically stated that they were kept at the brick kiln illegally and were forced into bonded labour. When confronted with the question, as to whether they owe anything to the respondents, all of them had stated that they did not owe anything to the respondents; rather they were kept illegally and were being subjected to physical torture as well by the respondents.

In this view of the situation, all the detainees are set at liberty and respondents No. 2, 3 and 4 can have recourse to the civil court to file suit for recovery of money, but there is absolutely no reason on their part to unnecessarily confine the detainees. With these observations this petition stands disposed of.

The court set the labourer free without any mention of providing them with rehabilitation facilities. This is emphasized in Section 15 that 'vigilance committees shall be set up at the district level in the prescribed manner, consisting of claimed representatives of the area, representatives of the district administration, bar associations, press, recognized social services and labour departments of the federal and provincial government', and that the functions of these committees shall be '(a) to advise the district administration on matters relating to the effective implementation of the law and to ensure its implementation in proper manner, (b) to help in the rehabilitation of the freed bonded labourer, (c) to keep an eye on the working of the law; and (d) to provide the bonded labourers such assistance as may be necessary to achieve the objectives of the law'.

Muhammad Iqbal v. S.H.O. etc., Crl. Misc 1317-H-2006
Brick Kiln, District Sialkot
Date of Hearing: 17-11-2008
Justice Hafiz Tariq Nasim

Court decision: This *habeas corpus* petition is filed contending that respondents No. 2 to 4 have detained the alleged detainees and they are not allowed to move. In pursuance of the order dated 14.11.2008, the bailiff has recovered the alleged detainees and produced all of them before the court. Learned council for the respondents submits that the alleged detainees are not detained by the respondents rather they have filed this *habeas corpus* petition just to justify a sum of Rs. 300,000 which was received by them as an advance of their labour.

Be that as it may, the alleged detainees, present in court, are set at liberty and they can go whenever they want. This petition is disposed of accordingly.

The detainees were set at liberty, yet again ignoring Section 12 of the Bonded Labour System (Abolition) Act of 1992, referred to earlier. Similar decisions were given by the courts in year 2009 and 2010 as well.

Zameer Hussain v. SHO etc., Crl. Misc No.1692-H-2009
Brick Kiln, Tehsil Pasroor, District Sialkot
Date of Hearing: 24-11-2009
Justice Iqbal Hameed-ur-Rehman

> Court decision: The bailiff of this court has recovered the detainees from the custody of respondents No. 2 to 5 and produced them before the court. They are set at liberty and allowed to accompany the petitioner. If the respondents have any grievance in respect of any amount they may file a suit for recovery of the same before competent court of law. This writ petition has borne fruit and is accordingly disposed of.

Akbar Masih v. SHO etc., Crl. Misc. No.1721-H-2009
Brick Kiln, Kot Fazal Din Tehsil, Pattoki, District Kasur
Date of Hearing: 26-11-2009
Chief Justice Khawaja Muhammad Sharif

> Court decision: According to the report submitted by the bailiff, three detainees have been recovered. They are present in court and they are set at liberty. As this petition has borne fruit, the same is disposed of accordingly. If the petitioner has deposited the security amount, then the same should be returned to him.

The petitioner was set at liberty without any sanctions being imposed on the employer. Section 11 of the Act of 1992 clearly states that, 'Whoever, after the commencement of this Act compels any person to render any bonded labour shall be punishable with imprisonment for a term which shall not be less than two years nor more than five years, or with fine which shall not be less than fifty thousand rupees, or with both.'

Muhammad Ashraf v. SHO etc. Crl. Misc. No. 2-H-2010
Ghakar District, Gujranwala
Date of Hearing: 04-01-2010

> Court decision: As the detainees are present in court and state that they want to go to their own houses, in these circumstances they cannot be detained. They are set at liberty. They can go wherever they want. Regarding the money

matter, both the parties are at liberty to take legal recourse in respect of the same. With this observation this petition stands disposed of.

Liaqat Nadeem v. Cheema Brick Kiln etc., Crl. Misc. No.19/H/2012

Brick Kiln, Thatha Khokhran/ Ramgarh Tehsil, District Hafizabad.
Date of Hearing: 06-01-2012
Justice Sh. Ahmad Farooq

Court decision: The petition was filed under s. 491 Cr. P.C. for recovery and production of *detenues*. The counsels for the respondents submitted that the labourers were not in illegal custody. The SHO was directed to submit a report regarding the whereabouts of the alleged detainees. The report of the SHO mentioned that the alleged *detenues*, after receiving loans from the brick-kiln owner, have since disappeared. In view of this, the petition is misconceived under s. 491 Cr. P.C and accordingly dismissed. The petitioner is directed to have his statement recorded regarding the disappearance of the alleged *detenues* with the concerned SHO.

Pervez Vicky v. Naveed Bricks Co etc., Crl. Misc. No.1348/H/2012

Brick Kiln, Kingra Karyal, Raiwind Road, Lahore.
Date of Hearing: 12-07-2012
Justice Amin-ud-Din Khan

Court decision: The petition was filed in order to invoke the constitutional jurisdiction of the High Court to recover the *detenue*, Pervez. The *detenue* was working at the brick kiln of the respondent for the past one year, where the fixed rate by the Government in Punjab is set to Rs. 617/ thousand bricks, when this wage was demanded the respondent refused to pay due to which the *detenue* refused to work any further. The respondent forcibly detained him and forced him to work on gun point and took away his personal possessions. Since, the *detenue* has been in illegal confinement.

The *detenue* was presented to the court and set free. However, the bailiff is directed to file a complaint against those responsible for his illegal detention. The bailiff has stated the FIR has been lodged against the respondent and the petition is thus disposed.

Zafar v. SHO Katchi Kothi, Teh Pattoki, Dist Kasur etc., Crl. Misc. No. 1187/H/2012

Brick Kiln, BhaiPheero, Tehsil Pattoki, District Kasur
Date of Hearing: 27-06-2012
Justice Anwar ulHaq

Court decision: The report of the bailiff reflects that three alleged *detenues* namely Allah Ditta, Azhar Iqbal and Riaz themselves came to him from the connected fields when he was searching them by going towards a *dera* near the brick kiln. The bailiff was informed by these three alleged *detenues* that the other alleged *detenues* were removed by respondents No. 2 and 3 to some unknown place 10 minutes prior to his arrival.

The petitioner still insists that the other alleged *detenues* are in illegal confinement of respondents No. 2 and 3 but is unable to point out the exact place of their confinement. Therefore without commenting upon the report of the bailiff or the assertion made on behalf of the petitioner, this petition is disposed of. However, the petitioner is still at liberty to move a fresh petition after furnishing full particulars of the other alleged *detenues*, if so advised.

The court cases listed above were adjudicated under Section 491 Code of Criminal Procedure (*habeas corpus*) and article 199 (4) of the Constitution of Pakistan and not under the Bonded Labour System (Abolition) Act, 1992 and Article 11 of the Constitution of Pakistan. Therefore it may be concluded that the said precedents are not amenable towards the implementation of the real codified law. Releasing the detainee from bonded labour, from the clutches of the proprietors, is not the ultimate solution. The courts must dispense justice as per the law applicable thereto, which ultimately amounts to good administration of justice. However, the reading of the judgments given above leads one to say that the codified law is being flouted. This flagrant violation of law amounts to giving sanctity to the persons responsible for bonded labour. If the outcome of the court cases continues to be the way it has been, as documented here, then it will be impossible to abolish the system of bonded labour.

Human Rights Commission Pakistan v. Government of Pakistan etc. Crl. Misc. No.1721-H-2009
Supreme Court of Pakistan
Date of Hearing: 18-11-2008
Justice Sabihuddin Ahmad
    The Supreme Court granted appeals directed against the judgment of the High Court of Sindh, Circuit Bench, Hyderabad, C.P.D no. 35 of 2000. In the impugned judgment, the High Court did not to look at the facts of the case and did not heed the question of the appellant in light of the provisions of the Bonded Labour System (Abolition) Act 1992. Instead it said that the mechanisms for redress had been provided for in the Sindh Tenancy Act.

The judgment given in this case reiterated the principles laid down in the Darshan Masih case to alleviate the suffering of those shackled by bonded labour. The appellants challenged the ruling given by a division bench of the Sindh High Court, whereby it held that the cases of bonded *haris* (peasants) fell under the Sindh Tenancy Act of 1950 and that the summoning of Article 199 of the Constitution of Pakistan and/or section 491 of the Code of Criminal Procedure was invalid in this regard. The Supreme Court allowed the appeal and in the proceedings alluded to the Darshan Masih case, determined the scope of the Bonded Labour System (Abolition) Act 1992 and its prevalence over the Sindh Tenancy Act of 1950 due to its status as a federal statute, and deliberated on the inconsistencies between the two acts.

The respondents in this case alleged that a large number of people who were bound by the Sindh Tenancy Act 1950 had got loans from *zamindars* (landlords) and that, in order to avoid the repayment of these loans, they were misusing the legal system by invoking the *habeas corpus* writ in the jurisdiction of the High Court. However the appellants posited that by virtue of Section 5 and Section 6 of the Bonded Labour System (Abolition) Act 1992, both the contract between the landlords and the peasants and the obligation of payment stood extinguished. The Supreme Court observed with surprise that during the High Court proceedings the Bonded Labour System (Abolition) Act 1992 was not discussed in earnest. Subsequently the Supreme Court made reference to the Darshan Masih case and observed that the case not only directed the release of the persons detained in violation of Article 11 of the constitution but also appointed a committee whose recommendations were to underpin legislative measures for the inhibition of the practice of bonded labour. On a perusal of the sections of the Act defining Bonded Labour, the Court remarked:

> *'It is therefore, evident that all contracts whereby a person agrees to render services without wages or for nominal wages, forfeits the freedom of employment or movement or forfeits the right to appropriate or sell, at market value, any of his property or product of his labour must be held to be void. To this extent the statute basically gives effect to the mandate of Article 11 of the constitution (prohibiting forced labour), Article 15 (guaranteeing freedom of movement) and Article 23 (guaranteeing the right to hold and dispose of property).'*

The Court elaborated on the argument regarding the overriding effect of the Bonded Labour System (Abolition) Act (under section 3), declaring that by virtue of Article 143[8] of the Constitution of Pakistan, the act enacted by the parliament prevailed over an existing law made by the provincial legislature. Further the Court affirmed that the impugned judgment did not ponder upon the inconsistency between the two acts and subsequently undertook a detailed analysis of the provisions of the Sindh Tenancy Act. In doing so it held that it appears that the High Court deduced from Section 25 (4) of the Sindh Tenancy Act that if a tenant is indebted to his landlord, he could not leave before the settlement of the outstanding liabilities and can be forced to render services. However, under article 11 of the constitution all forms of forced labour have been prohibited with the exception of compulsory service by a person serving punishment for an offence or required by any law for a public service is permissible. As a result the Court overruled the High Court's earlier inference and regarding the Sindh Tenancy Act, posited:

> 'The Sindh Tenancy Act does not, strictly speaking, create a pure employer-employees relationship … On the contrary it creates a quasi-partnership whereby the tenant acquires certain interests in the land and does not receive wages but only a share in the produce in so far as his obligations as a tenant are concerned. This nevertheless does not lead to the conclusion that a tenant could be forced to perform his obligations under the Act … person may forfeit his legal rights … upon failure to perform his obligations but there could be no justification for forcing him to work against his will in flagrant violation of his fundamental rights guaranteed by the Constitution.'

The Supreme Court granted leave to appeal to look into the 'exact scope of Bonded Labour System (Abolition) Act, 1992 and its effects on the provisions of the Sindh Tenancy Act, 1950 and other laws'. The Supreme Court also held that 'a law requiring compulsory service for liquidation of individual debts would inevitably be ultra-vires of Article 11 of the Constitution'. With regards to this the Court postulated:

> 'The only effect of tenancy under the Sindh Tenancy Act is that a tenant incurring a debt during the subsistence of tenancy in his favour continues to remain liable for the payment whereas a bonded debt in terms of the Bonded Labour System (Abolition) Act, 1992 is not recoverable at all. In either case, however, any obligation to work cannot be enforced.'

It may be of interest to mention that the Habeas Corpus Act of 1679 required penalization of a Judge refusing to issue a writ without proper grounds. R. J. Sharp in his book *The Law of Habeas Corpus* (Second Edition, 1989) summarized the English law in the following words:

'In principle Habeas Corpus is not a discretionary remedy, it issues ex debito justitiae on proper grounds being shown ... Since Habeas Corpus is not a discretionary remedy the existence of alternate remedy does not afford grounds for refusing relief of habeas corpus.'

In addition to this the Court probed into the matter of whether or not the High Court could dismiss *habeas corpus* petitions on the ground that alternate remedies exist instead of directing the production of *detenues*. The Court held that *'the approach of the High Court was entirely erroneous'* and alternate remedies suggested by the High Court were neither adequate nor efficacious. Thus the petitions could not be dismissed on the grounds that alternate remedies were available to those unlawfully detained. It should also be asserted that in matters of fundamental human rights, the jurisdiction of the High Court is wider as clause (c) of Article 199 of the Constitution not only enables the court to declare an action of a state functionary inconsistent with fundamental rights to be unlawful, but also enables the court to enforce such rights by issuing a directive as is appropriate, and this power of superior courts is also exercisable against private individuals. The appeals are thus allowed and the impugned order set aside.

The Supreme Court summarized its lengthy discussion in the judgment as follows:

(i)   *the provisions of the Bonded Labour System (Abolition) Act, 1992 are also applicable to all persons employed in agriculture other than those enjoying rights as tenants under the Sindh Tenancy Act;*

(ii)   *the above however does not mean that no credit could be advanced by and employed to his employee but only that a condition making the employee subject to the Bonded Labour System cannot be imposed. In cases of debts not accompanied by any condition which makes an employee a bonded worker under the Act, may be enforceable through ordinary legal channels;*

(iii)   *that even the Sindh Tenancy Act does not empower a landlord to require a tenant to work on his lands against the latter's will. The only consequence provided for a refusal on the part of the tenant is forfeiture of his tenancy rights on the grounds of abandonment etc. and through mechanism provided for in section 23 of the Act;*

(iv)   *that even an undertaking by a tenant to work without remuneration or for remuneration less than the amount stipulated in section 22 (2) would be unenforceable;*

(v)   *section 25 of the Sindh Tenancy Act stipulates a mechanism for appropriation of a debt from a tenant to his landlord. Subsection (4) only stipulates that upon termination of a tenancy the entire outstanding amount of the debt would be recoverable notwithstanding the provisions relating to appropriations through the normal legal channels;*

(vi) *that in cases where wrongful detention or forced labour is complained of the onus to prove that the person detained was a tenant would lie on the landlord. The person detained would nevertheless invariably be entitled to restoration of his liberty and the freedom of his movement and the only difference would be that in the event of proof of his tenancy, the landlord would be entitled to recover the debt through normal legal channels;*

(vii) *that there is no requirement of law that stricter scrutiny of a petition regarding detention in private custody is to be made before issuing appropriate directions. Nevertheless in cases where the right to keep a person in private custody is claimed on the basis of some authority in law, the court may require that such right be adjudicated upon in properly held proceedings before the appropriate forum before issuing directions under section 491, Cr.P.C.*

A copy of this judgment may be transmitted to Honorable Chief Justice of the High Court of Sindh so as to enable him to circulate amongst his colleagues and to the learned Sessions Judges in the Province (who are now empowered to exercise jurisdiction under section 491, Cr.P.C.) for appropriate guidance in matters of like nature arising in future.

CONCLUSION: BEYOND SETTING AT LIBERTY

The Bonded Labour System Act, 1992 was passed as a result of the famous Darshan Masih case in the Supreme Court of Pakistan. The judgment of the apex court was hailed as giving voice to the bonded labourers. Since then, several cases have been brought to various courts and decided upon, yet a large number labourers remain oppressed and the system of bonded labour is far from abolished. This is partly due to the fact that the definition of 'bonded labour system' given under Section 2(e) of the act is vague and imprecise as it does not take into account an array of customary and non-customary practices which amount to bonded labour.

Failure of the police and lower judiciary is a major factor in the persistence of bonded labour in Pakistan. At times the police are complicit in protecting the perpetrators of this crime and the judges in courts do not go beyond setting the bonded labour at liberty. Both the police and the judiciary conveniently ignore the physical restraint and abuse of bonded labourers. In many cases police assist employers to recover and hand over runaway labour to the agents of the employers or even implicate the labourers in false cases. Police must be bound to treat bonded labour as a crime. Penalties must be put in place to punish those police officials who fail to take into account the instances of physical and sexual abuse in cases of bonded labour.

One of the ways to counter bonded labour would perhaps be to give powers of raid and search to the vigilance committees at the district level. Likewise, the district magistrates should be given powers to try this offence. There is also a need for better coordination between various laws enforcement authorities, district officials and the representatives of labourers.

The print and electronic media can play a vital role in highlighting the issue of human rights violation with regard to the practice of bonded labour and Pakistan's international obligations as signatory to various conventions on human rights. NGOs have a very important role in raising this awareness among common people and acting as pressure groups for the enforcement of existing labour laws. NGOs, human rights activists and trade unions have already played a significant role in the release of many bonded labourers. The government must step in to ensure the rehabilitation of the released bonded labourers by providing them employment opportunities and reintegration into society as productive workers and equal citizens. If the government fails in this, many of the labourers will fall back into the vicious cycle of taking *peshgis* to meet their needs and end up as bonded labour again.

All workplaces, including brick kilns and agricultural farms, must be registered with the government and monitored for any violations of labour laws. Labourers should have access to complaint cells at district level to report violation of their rights. The punishment and fine set in Section 13 of the Bonded Labour (Abolition) Act 1992 must be enhanced to reflect the seriousness of the offence. It should be made a non-bailable offence. The government must set minimum wage standards for all industries and all forms of labour. The minimum wage paid to daily labourers must be in line with the standard wages. Strict measures must be put in place to enforce the minimum age for employment so that no child is forced into labour. Pay-slips should also be made mandatory, which would not only reflect the pay that labourers receive but also help them keep track of their debts (if any).

Drafting and passing the Bonded Labour System (Abolition) Act, 1992 was a major breakthrough. The policies and action plans against bonded labour were also major achievements. However, there has hardly been any commitment by the government to implement its own laws and action plans. The reality is that bonded labour has not been abolished. If we look at the intent of the legislature, it is to free bonded labourers from the vicious cycle of work, debt, and bondage. However, this intent has remained only a theoretical victory. There are hardly any convictions of the landlords and brick kiln owners despite the fact that the police have recovered thousands of bonded labourers from brick factories, agricultural fields, and private jails of influential people.

NOTES

1. Article 184 (3), Constitution of Pakistan: *Original jurisdiction of Supreme Court;*
   (3) Without prejudice to the provisions of Article 199, the Supreme Court shall, if it considers that a question of public importance with reference to the enforcement of any of the Fundamental Rights conferred by Chapter 1 of Part II is involved, have the power to make an order of the nature mentioned in the said Article.
2. Article 11, Constitution of Pakistan, *Slavery, forced labour, etc., prohibited*
   (1) Slavery is non-existent and forbidden and no law shall permit or facilitate its introduction into Pakistan in any form.
   (2) All forms of forced labour and traffic in human beings are prohibited.
   (3) No child below the age of Fourteen years shall be engaged in any factory or mine or any other hazardous employment.
   (4) Nothing in this Article shall be deemed to affect compulsory service-
   (a) By any person undergoing punishment for an offence against any law; or
   (b) required by any law for public purpose:
   Provided that no compulsory service shall be of a cruel nature or incompatible with human dignity.
3. Section 491 of Code of Criminal Procedure, 1898 as amended by Act 2 of 1997;
   491. Power to issue directions of the nature of a Habeas Corpus. Any High Court may, whenever it thinks fit, direct:
   (a) that a person within the limits of its appellate criminal jurisdiction be brought up before the Court to be dealt with according to law:
   (b) that a person illegally or improperly detained in public or private custody within such limits be set at liberty;
   (c) that a prisoner detained in any jail situate within such limits be brought before Court to be there examined as a witness in any matter pending or to be inquired into in such Court;
   (d) that a prisoner detained as aforesaid be brought before a Court-martial or any Commissioners for trial or to be examined touching any matter pending before such Court-martial or Commissioners respectively.
   (e) that a prisoner within such limits be removed from one custody to another for the purpose of trial; and
   (f) that the body of defendant within such limits be brought in on the Sheriff's return of *cepi corpus* to a writ of attachment.
   (2) The High Court may, from time to time, frame rules to regulate the procedure in the cases under this section.

(3) Nothing in this section applies to persons detained under [any other law providing for preventive detention.].

4. National Judicial Policy 2009. Law and justice commission of Pakistan. Supreme Court Islamabad http://www.supremecourt.gov.pk/njp2009/njp2009.pdf (Accessed date 7 July 2015).

5. 'Over 3 million cases pending before country's judiciary'. *Pakistan Today*. February 8, 2013. http://www.pakistantoday.com.pk/2013/02/08/national/over-3m-cases-pending-before-countrys-judiciary/(Accessed 7 July 2015).

6. Article 199 (4), Constitution of Pakistan, *Jurisdiction of High Court.*

   4. Where-

      a. an application is made to a High Court for an order under paragraph (a) or paragraph (c) of clause (1), and

      b. the making of an interim order would have the effect of prejudicing or interfering with the carrying out of a public work or of otherwise being harmful to public interest or State property or of impeding the assessment or collection of public revenues, the Court shall not make an interim order unless the prescribed law officer has been given notice of the application and he or any person authorised by him in that behalf has had an opportunity of being heard and the Court, for reasons to be recorded in writing, is satisfied that the interim order-

      i. would not have such effect as aforesaid; or

      ii. would have the effect of suspending an order or proceeding which on the face of the record is without jurisdiction.

   4A. An interim order made by a High Court on an application made to it to question the validity or legal effect of any order made, proceeding taken or act done by any authority or person, which has been made, taken or done or purports to have been made, taken or done under any law which is specified in Part I of the First Schedule or relates to, or is connected with, State property or assessment or collection of public revenues shall cease to have effect on the expiration of a period of six months following the day on which it is made:

   Provided that the matter shall be finally decided by the High Court within six months from the date on which the interim order is made.

7. Cots refers to *charpais* or traditional woven beds consisting of a wooden frame criss-crossed by a set of knotted ropes. It is often used for sitting on as well as sleeping.

8. Article 143, Constitution of Pakistan, *Inconsistency between Federal and Provincial laws.*

   143. If any provision of an Act of a Provincial Assembly is repugnant to any provision of an Act of Majlis-e-Shoora (Parliament) which Majlis-e-Shoora (Parliament) is competent to enact, then the Act of Majlis-e-Shoora (Parliament), whether passed before or after the Act of the Provincial Assembly, shall prevail and the Act of the Provincial Assembly shall, to the extent of the repugnancy, be void.].

CHAPTER 2

Debt Bondage at Brick Kilns in Pakistan

A. ERCELAWN AND M. NAUMAN

This chapter intends to provoke reflection and action as well as to underscore how some things have changed so little in Pakistan's brick kiln sector over several decades.[1] Based on a rapid assessment, the findings have obvious limitations.[2] A picture has been pieced together from various sites and judgements should therefore be cautious and generalizations should be avoided.

Operators of kilns are generally not local landowners themselves but lease the land from a local landowner. According to kiln owners, or their *munshis*, leases span a number of years but rarely exceed 10 years (in some fertile agricultural areas of the KPK, leases are as short as a couple of years). Small and moderate kilns producing 400,000–600,000 bricks in a monthly *chakkar* were abundant. Large kilns with an output of 800,000 or more were found mainly in and around Lahore. These kilns' daily output, i.e. *nikasi*, ranged between 20,000 and 30,000 baked bricks. Some of the stock was stored, and with an allowance for damage, the production of unbaked bricks ranged between 25,000 to 50,000 bricks.

Kilns function for many years at each site. For some, owners changed over time, but for others, the owners were experienced in the area, operating different kilns over the years. A few had accumulated enough capital to own more than one.

We were unable to collect much information on the social capital of owners. However, we did find cases of ownership or of 'connections' with active or retired police and army officers. In more than one case, the owners of multiple kilns were from a powerful political family and therefore had stronger influence than usual upon the local and provincial administration.

Generally, owners run kilns under close personal supervision. Like their labour, kiln owners can be migrants too. In fact, many of those we met were migrants though often from a shorter distance than their labour. We heard of Mianwali Pathans in south Punjab but also found other Pathans in Sindh. Entrepreneurs from central Punjab were found in the (northern) Potohar area of Punjab.

Until the Federal Bureau of Statistics completes its national economic census, only rough estimates are possible for the current number and distribution of brick kilns. Using the wide range of tax rates per kiln, sales tax revenues indicate between 4,500 and 28,000 kilns in 1998–99. Field interviews suggested 6,000 working kilns, with the vast majority in Punjab. Hence, as many as a million children, women, and men workers are employed in this industry, most of them under conditions of debt bondage. Of these, the most numerous are the makers of unbaked bricks, *patheras*, followed by those who stack and unload the kilns, the *bharaiwalas* and *nikasiwalas*, and finally, those who bake the bricks, the *jalaiwalas*.

The next section presents an overview of the production process. The section after that will discuss findings on forced labour, debt and bondage. The chapter concludes with a brief discussion on apparent directions for relief and remedy.

LABOUR AND EARNINGS

A description of the main components of the production process is a good start to understanding the lives of the men, women, and children who work at brick kilns (or 'brickfields'). From early morning to late evening, Saturday through Wednesday, mud bricks are prepared and sun-dried by a hundred or more site-based or local *patheras* or *thaperas*, in a large area spread out in the vicinity of the kiln. One, and sometimes two, senior adult males among the *Patheras* will be the *jamadar* who organizes the labour, distributes advances, distributes earnings after debt servicing (deductions of debt), guarantees repayment of debts, and supervises the work. On Thursday the work stops at midday and then resumes late on Friday.

Patheras or *thaperas* work on the first part of the brick making process. Dried bricks created by the *patheras* are loaded from the brickfields and transported to the kiln—throughout the afternoon—by half a dozen or more local *kharkars* with donkeys. These bricks are then handed over inside the kiln to *bharaiwalas* for stacking. The *bharaiwalas* work under the supervision of a *mistri*. Normally, *kharkars* and *bharaiwalas* belong to a common piecework labour team, though sometimes *bharaiwalas* working inside the kiln can be separate employees. When a stock is to be built up to ensure uninterrupted kiln operation, additional bricks are also stacked up on the site. These stocks allow kilns to operate for a fortnight or more without concurrent output from *patheras*, for example, during the monsoons. The extra stock is also handy for especially large sales orders.

Inside the kiln, the bricks are covered by a mixture of mud and baked brick dust by one or two site-based employees called *keriwalas*, and then the bricks are baked for several days. The kiln is usually fired by coal brought mainly from Quetta and Hyderabad, but also from a few places in Punjab. To reduce the cost of fuel, kilns may use wood and waste (e.g., from sugar extraction and cotton ginning). At times, kilns also mix environmentally hazardous rubber and plastic, supposedly to improve quality of the baked brick.

Baking is done by a team of 4–5 site-based, salaried *jalaiwalas*, working in six-hour shifts of two persons throughout the week. This team is headed by a skilled *mistri* who usually recruits other team members. Among kiln tasks, *jalai* is the most obviously hazardous because it involves working with open fires. Kiln openings have to be examined frequently to determine whether additional fuel is necessary to keep a proper baking temperature. The heat is so intense that it seeps through ordinary shoes.

Six days a week, baked bricks are removed from the kiln by half a dozen or so *nikasiwalas*, sorted for quality and then stacked nearby. Customers cart away the bricks by bullock cart, tractor trolley or trucks. Usually transporters have their own labour, but *patheras* and others can join in for extra income. *Nikasiwalas* finish work quite early in the day so as to allow transport of bricks to nearby markets.

At most times, a kiln will have a week's sale ready to be unloaded. A kiln will close when the weather does not permit preparation of unbaked bricks and the stock of unbaked brick is inadequate. In some areas, kilns close for a fortnight or more after every 3–4 months, apparently to ensure a stable sale price, but closing down can also serve to offset pressures for higher piece rates by labour, as well as for prices of other input suppliers.

CHILD LABOUR

Children are conservatively defined here to be between the ages of 10–14 years. Attention has been drawn to the rare cases where children younger than ten years were found to be working. In the brick kiln industry, children work as *patheras*, *bharaiwalas*, and *nikasiwalas*. Both male and female children are found to be working as *patheras*, but only male children are seen amongst *bharai* and *nikasiwalas*. They will sometimes help load or unload bricks but more often will only be involved in the carriage. No children were found working as *jalaiwalas*, which requires skilled labour and constant alertness and is more hazardous and tiring work. Juvenile males frequently work as *jalaiwalas*, most likely because they are not considered (by owners and officials) to be protected by legislation.

FOOTLOOSE LABOUR

A broad definition of migrant labour includes those who reside on the kiln sites. This covers both seasonal and permanent migrants, as well as situations of migration within and between *tehsils* rather than across districts or provinces. All (self-declared) Afghans are taken to be migrants. The typical kiln description is one where almost all labour are from migrant families. Most kiln sites in this study, even in the Punjab, employ a combination of migrants and locals—both family and single male migrants.

Virtually everywhere, *bharai* and *nikasi* are done by locals. At most kilns, migrants dominate as *patheras* and *jalaiwalas*. Among migrant *pathera* families, the most common are 'classic' brickmakers—both Muslim and Christians—from central and southern Punjab. An entire family can spend many years at one kiln and then move to another kiln, sometimes hundreds of miles away. Family migration is not common among the 'new' brick labour, and generally not so in KPK. In these cases, only adult and juvenile males migrate, often just for a few months, though not necessarily across short distances. Afghan labour remains widespread in KPK; it is also found in Punjab, although less so in places close to Islamabad, and hardly any is to be found in Sindh. Afghan Pathans who work in the kilns are almost always male adults and juveniles, coming to work from a nearby Afghan settlement (official or informal).

Over time, locals have become a larger source of *pathera* labour for different reasons in various areas. The most common reasons seem to be increasing unemployment and stagnant or declining wages, which have made even brick kilns tolerable, especially for large families. It is likely that deteriorating conditions in agriculture are also pushing labour to seek additional or alternative work for some family members. Locals are also replacing Afghans.

FORCED LABOUR

We consider forced labour a broader category that includes some form of coercion or compulsion in situations both with and without debt. Among the dimensions that could be used to identify the incidence and intensity of forced labour, some are obvious.[3] First is violence, or the threat of violence to labour or to family, used to extract work in addition to what the worker is expected to do. It is obvious that we would not be allowed to observe any such case. However, on some occasions we were told of verbal and physical abuse of male workers by the *munshi* or owner when indebted labour was considered 'lazy'. We have the impression that withholding or reducing periodic advances, or demanding more rapid repayment are generally considered an adequate mechanism for 'disciplining' labour. Second, is any labour or family member regularly required to do additional tasks with no, or nominal, compensation? We neither observed nor were told of any such case even amongst the heavily indebted families (discounting the petty chores of bringing drinks for guests and the like). So, clearly such situations do not occur with the regularity that they apparently do for agricultural labour. One caveat is that we did not stay at kilns late enough to see what happens after the day's work was done.

There are also fewer opportunities for extracting *begaar* since the owner or *munshi* do not generally reside on the kiln premises. In addition, the kiln manufacturing process, which includes leased land, high fuel costs, continuous inputs and outputs, creates incentives for workers to do better in contracted tasks rather than forcing diversions from them. The splitting of various tasks between different labour groups also permits more opportunities for tailored exploitation of labour.

Could the criterion of no or nominal compensation be held to apply to women and children working as family labour on piece rates? More generally, does labour get compensated below prevailing labour rates in the area, taking into account working hours? Or is it below the minimum wage? Or below the poverty line income? Or below incomes that necessitate child labour for subsistence? To all of these, the answer is yes. Labour is forced when one refuses to equate outcomes of economic or political markets with truly 'voluntary' contracts. By tradition, adult men deal with all formal matters of earnings and debts. Hence, in one sense, forced labour is imposed upon women and children regularly engaged in making bricks. Once we consider the fact that earnings are usually shared in the household, however unequally, evaluations become more difficult.

Nevertheless, meagre and indirect compensation for kiln work is symptomatic of the broader inequity in economic opportunities.

DEBT

All categories of kiln labour can and do take advances when joining a kiln and subsequently as well. Those taking advances include both salaried workers, such as *jalaiwalas,* and piece rate labour. Since repayment is through labour, advances are based largely upon the size and quality of labour being offered by a household. After the initial advance, owners prefer to term subsequent advances as 'friendly loans', probably to avoid being held in violation of bonded labour law (with higher penalties than usual civil law), and to retain the right of recovery, in the infrequent case of being taken to court by rebellious labour. It is as likely that owners want to reduce the risk of losing funds in the event that the government or courts give a general public proclamation of cancellation of *'peshgis',* as they did in the late 1980s (see Qazilbash, this volume). But labour, too, differentiates between subsequent, small subsistence advances and *peshgi* as the large sum that can be demanded at the beginning of every season if past debts have been cleared (cf. Khan, Bushra, and Sultan, this volume).

Typically, advances go from the owner to labour through a *jamadar* or *mistri.* Since the owner holds the *jamadar* or *mistri* responsible for repayment, and labour repays debt through them, the debt could be said to be layered. But labourers always refer to their debt as due to the owner rather than the *jamadar* or *mistri.* The kiln *munshi* appears to be merely an accountant, but may also advise the owner on additional advances demanded by labour.

Usually the owner first hires a *jamadar,* who then recruits labour through the promise of large advances or better rates, and arranges for transportation. Recruitment is typically from persons well known to the *jamadar,* which can be through past work in the same kilns or area, or as a *gharain* (a neighbour or from the same village). At all times, advances go through the *jamadar,* who allocates a lump advance sum between himself and the workers, and remains responsible for repayment. It remained unclear if it was common practice for recruited workers to be responsible for the entire advance including the 'share' retained by the *jamadar.* When labour and the *jamadar* hail from different areas and have not worked together previously, the *jamadar* attempts to obtain additional guarantees for repayment of debt. Guarantors are not other kiln labour but usually residents in the area from which labour is recruited. Families that have been migrants for decades will, of course, find it difficult to offer any guarantors. If any indebted labour flees the kiln then it is the *jamadar* who must locate them as it was he who recruited them. However, further action is left to the owner.

As an average for kiln labour across the country, the size of *peshgi* and accumulated advances per family could be less than Rs. 5,000. The classic *pathera* family (large family and labour pool from central and southern Punjab) continues to have high and continuing debts of around Rs. 10,000 per adult worker, and hence totalling around Rs. 50,000 or more for the family. When a new kiln starts up, these families and even some of the new migrants will negotiate large advances to move to the new kiln. If labour migrates under pressure it may have to accept work from a creditor-owner who pays lower rates. Among the reasons often cited for large debts were 'lumpy' expenditures such as a major illness or marriage of children. Some labour suggested that the marriage of young unmarried daughters was a compelling demand of their *ghairat*—a matter of honour to provide protection (or respectability) to females—in a kiln environment where numerous young males work.

Afghans, in particular, and new labour, in general, are willing to work with smaller advances than the traditional migrant labour—they have lower debts of around Rs. 3,000 or less, which they feel can be repaid in a short time. One reason for accepting smaller advances would be greater poverty levels, including fewer alternative opportunities for work, especially for 'illegal' Afghans. But there were also indications that some needed smaller advances because of other sources of income, wealth or credit, e.g., rations and shelter in Afghan refugee camps, farm labour, and homesteads for locals.

Owners also feel a greater risk in lending to such labour: they may spend less time at a given site; debt redemption can be more difficult to enforce without the compulsion of shelter in the absence of women and children; and protection may be available to some runaways at their home locations. New labour offers less productive skills and hence a smaller return on advances. The hike in coal costs has also reduced the financial ability to make traditionally large advances to all labour. One of the views coming from the owners is worth mentioning. An office-bearer of the district Bhatta (brick kiln) Owners Association was quite candid. According to him, in this age of high cost living, labour is forced to take loans because of illness, festivals, death, etc. They have no collateral except their labour, but large debts continue because of extravagant consumption, which includes watching movies on rented VCRs during every holiday or gambling for high stakes (cf. Khan, Bushra, and Sultan, this volume, for similar claims by owners/employers).

DEBT BONDAGE

The most important question is whether labour *feels* bonded. Even if labour does not feel bonded—perhaps because they are 'fully aware' and 'voluntarily' accept the debt-for-labour contract—is there value in an external assessment of working conditions to determine if bondage exists? It is somewhat like asking whether a particular work is hazardous to one's health. It is not necessary that labour itself consider it so, and it is important that we are able to judge the nature and degree of the hazard. Labourers that were in debt (small or large) commonly agreed that the debt imposed a burden in terms of having to work at the kiln until the debt was paid off or to get an alternate creditor. Even when no incident or accident occurred at the kiln itself, labour was aware of violence at other kilns and hence conscious of the threat of violence against defaulters. Labour that lived on site often felt they were under surveillance. Only for nominal debts—of Rs. 1,000 or so—could they imagine a kind owner rescheduling or writing off the debts.

When debts are large, alternate creditors would usually be other kiln owners willing to buy off the debt in return for labour bondage. Labour pointed out that death or permanent disability transferred the obligations of debt and labour to family members—including young children—of the deceased or disabled labourer. Most labour did not think they or their children would, or could, ever be free of debt. At some of the kilns, labour and owners pointed out juveniles working off debts acquired by an incapacitated or dead father.

Government officials in Islamabad and its territories believe kiln work is to be regarded as a mutually advantageous contract of advances from the rich in return for labour from the poor.[4] When labour complains of debt bondage, some in the higher judiciary admonish them and ask them to honour their debts. This is a reflection of the growing reluctance of the judiciary to distinguish between good management (e.g., as shared prosperity within the prevailing social order) and ethical governance (e.g., as sharply reducing inequities). In such perspectives, these 'pillars of the state' echo widespread social values (and, increasingly, the values of domineering donors of Pakistan).

This perspective of labour-should-be-grateful is straightforward, if incomplete (and self-serving). Its arguments are as follows.

Objectively, however regretfully, poor households need credit and regular employment. Kiln owners need cheap labour and low turnover. Both are therefore better off by tying credit to labour, i.e., debt bondage. Given market and government 'imperfections', kiln owners are to be appreciated (rather than denigrated) as a lender of last resort to those whose only collateral are their bodies. Advances serve to ensure security of work, earnings and usually shelter. Agreeing to pledge family labour is then merely a premium for such insurance. Since the contract is voluntary, why the fuss?[5]

One may also frame the supply of advances as an incentive to induce a stable, disciplined, productive labour force to work under probably hazardous, certainly unpleasant conditions. Perhaps implicit, advances are also a response to the needs of labour for lumpy expenditures which cannot be delayed—treatment for unexpected illnesses for instance, or marriages (which, if delayed, may mean that young people will incur their own debt from other sources). Clearly, neither owners nor labour expect these lumpy expenditures to be financed by savings, not on the low earnings of brick-makers. Excessive debts—i.e., those that can never be repaid at the usual earnings from prevalent piece rates—result from greed or excessive consumption (including immodest lust that produces large families) of labour. Coercion occurs because indebted labour is lazy, i.e., does not produce the number of bricks that were agreed upon when the advance was given. Or labour is ungratefully scheming to run off without honouring its debt. Violence is rare, and claims of physical abuse, specially of women, are trumped up (since well-off owners can afford better services). What else can be done with such people except treat them like rebellious serfs, and swiftly bring them to justice that may be private if necessary (and more efficient)? Property has the right of state protection.

Since social constructs of labour issues are important for social action, obviously more needs to be said. If debt bondage of a family is defined simply as the obligation to continue the (adequate and uninterrupted) supply of labour until a debt is redeemed, then virtually all kiln labour is debt-bonded at some point or the other in their lives. For most, it is a persistent condition. Obligations rest upon the entire family, including children. If the owner considers labour as belonging to 'back home' or provides similar social collateral through the *jamadar*, then restrictions may be relaxed. If bondage is effective then the obligation of labour should be accompanied by the threat of (private) coercion, i.e., seen as enforceable. That is, in fact, the situation in brick kilns. The kiln owner can insist that some members of an indebted family stay behind as 'surety' when others take leave. In the extreme, we were told, the *chowkidar* and other hired toughs would keep a watch on suspect labour or even lock them up. Presumably the enforcer in the first instance, i.e., the *jamadar*, cannot or will not guarantee trustworthy conduct or repayment.

Debt bondage is effective when workers who flee can be tracked down and forced to return. *Jamadars* were confident, and labour agreed, that tracking down workers is not difficult. If labour is found working at another kiln, other owners usually cooperate in 'returning' them. The police also assist, sometimes by registering theft cases against labour. On some occasions a distant landowner may give refuge to labour who flees, and become a guarantor for loan repayment.

If bondage is substantive then labourers have no real option for debt redemption except to supply labour at the same kiln, or to transfer debt to another kiln—but only at the discretion of the owner. For labour with large debts, this is typically the case because their wealth is confined to the large pool of family labour. Some of the labour with small debts—particularly locals and non-family migrants—may have the option of redeeming their debt by allowing family members to work elsewhere. For these, alternative sources of credit (or at least a guarantor) such as a landowner or shopkeeper may also be more easily available; or perhaps they may sell livestock for debt repayment. When bondage is substantive then redemption of debt is excessive in comparison to usual earnings. Lifetime earnings, net earnings of families who maintain an even subsistence, could never pay back the debt. For smaller debts too, before previous debt can be repaid entirely, additional debt may be acquired for normal family needs. Some owners conceded that only half of indebted labour was able to redeem the advance; the remaining labour could not help but get into additional debt.

Debt bondage applies to the family, nevertheless, there are varying degrees of 'attachment' or 'tying'. Once any family member has worked as kiln labour for a while he or she cannot work elsewhere at his or her own discretion. Only *nikasi* and *bharai* labour can work elsewhere after the day's work is done; the vast majority of *pathera* labour cannot do so even if they have any energy left after meeting the day's target. Even when the kiln is closed, *pathera* labour cannot work elsewhere without the owner's permission. Migrants in particular are truly captive labour as their debt is used to convert them into unfree labour.

If a person has a separate *khata* (account), his or her exit option can be exercised if the debt is accepted by other family members and they appear capable of redeeming the debt through their own labour. In this regard, a probably atypical case was narrated by a mother who had to absorb the debt of a young son who ran away ('because of a clever wife') and where the father was incapacitated. We do not know if owners continue to pressure indebted labour to replace a married daughter with a daughter-in-law, i.e., engage in the practice of *watta-satta* (exchange marriage). Debts are generally not forgiven upon incapacitation or death. A father or brother must accept the debt of a son or brother; a woman must assume the debt of a husband; and a male child must accept the debt of a father. We did not inquire about the obligations of female children towards debts acquired by their fathers or brothers.

Locals with low debts may, on the other hand, even get permission to leave for harvest labour in their home areas (which can be quite distant). Kilns can close for short periods 'after a season' or for other reasons. One aspect of bondage is permission or refusal to work elsewhere temporarily. Discretion rests entirely with the kiln owner, and is available to 'safe' labour. Other indebted labour must not only stay on site, but also have to subsist on further advances by the owner.

Measured through the intensity and frequency of violence towards labourers, explicit severity of bondage was clearly observed to be low. One can only speculate why. Perhaps the risk of court action in a high profile sector is a deterrent. It is more likely that violence is seen by owners as counterproductive when labour is easily available in times of widespread unemployment. Owners may also realize that the costs of slacking by demoralized labour can be very high. No doubt, even a few well-advertised cases of violence do suffice to keep most labour in line.

Of grave concern should be the continuing cases of kiln labour selling a kidney to redeem large debts. These cases were encountered in northern Punjab (but news reports indicate that they also occur in other places in Punjab). In one family it was a middle-aged man (as the single male adult labour); in another, it was a juvenile daughter-in-law (orphaned, but married into a large family) who had used a local hospital for the same reason. In a third family, a juvenile daughter (from a family that had adult brothers in kiln labour) had gone to Lahore for arranging the sale of her kidney. Regretfully, we remain ignorant of the details of desperation that leads labour to commit such extreme violence upon themselves. Clearly, debt bondage can impose immense psychological burdens that remain veiled in the easier focus on physical violence.

Reports of sexual abuse were very rare in our sites. But it must be pointed out that women were reluctant to speak out on such sensitive subjects. Perhaps their reticence came from fear of retaliation by *munshis* or owners since strangers obviously cannot be trusted at a first (and last) meeting to keep names and information confidential. Many workers were aware that large advances had been declared illegal in the past (see Qazilbash, this volume). The older ones expressed knowledge of debts having being cancelled by courts, and referred fondly to the 'days of Benazir'. Most of them admitted that the bondage system had returned albeit with smaller advances. Some talked of having to pay back debts (as required by the earlier Supreme Court judgment) in order to continue working at kilns.

Among kiln labour themselves, none appeared to be aware of the general legislation that applies to bondage. In fact, few were aware of formal legislation against bonded labour, with the exception of limited areas where specific labour organizations are active. On a single occasion we were told of a 'strike' for higher rates in accordance with the higher sale price of bricks but this too was carried out by Afghani migrant labour (in Haripur). It was successful in raising rates by Rs. 10 per 1,000 bricks and did apply to all *patheras*—Afghan and non-Afghan—in that and neighbouring areas.

To reduce debt, labour frequently expressed the hope that owners could be obligated to bear at least the direct cost of work-related injury even if he would not provide some compensation for work days lost to injury. When kilns were near factories, some would even specifically talk of social security coverage for health and education. There was no widespread awareness of the national minimum wage, though *patheras* often did know of the minimum piece rate in Punjab. Even the more aware labour refer to general unemployment as an obstacle to mobilizing for collective action in defence of rights.

There is growing and mass poverty in Pakistan afflicting less than a fifth of the population in the 1980s but well over a third of the population now. Since advances provide a sense of security in earnings and shelter, it is no surprise that some labour consider bondage as a route to alleviate, if not escape, deprivation. Moreover, bondage offers an employment opportunity where more work is rewarded proportionately and hence debts, it is so perceived, can be repaid with less difficulty than otherwise. The *peshgi* system allows for additional loans over time to 'generously' respond to specific and unforeseen needs for large cash outflows. In these explanations—which centre on compelling needs but lack of alternatives—one must therefore also allude to the role of social structures in fostering seemingly private bondage.[6]

Certainly labour expressed its desire for higher wages and piece rates, compensation for injury and so on. But knowing that the owner can safely refuse these welfare measures and that only advances are available, labour make the most of available *peshgis*. A good owner is frequently seen as one who responds to 'genuine' need by giving an adequate advance. This may be thought of as indicating an absence of 'real' bondage. But it seems to us to be little justification for social inaction as would be the case in, say, child labour as a means to escape destitution. Most labourers consider it dishonourable to walk away from a 'fair' debt (an amazing but perhaps not atypical illustration of the effectiveness of internalization as social disciplining).[7] All do chafe at restrictions upon employment when kilns close down for extended periods, especially when it means adding to debts. However, few currently feel that they can avail of a real opportunity to repay their debts by higher incomes elsewhere.

In order to attract and retain labour, why are large and continuing advances preferred by owners rather than giving a much higher piece rate or regular wage, and providing treatment and compensation for illness and injury, etc? Until such time as frank discussions are possible with owners, one may only speculate on the cause. The advantage of an advance is that it is directly recoverable, and an implicit return may be earned through speeding up production via piece rates. For labour, larger production gives higher labour income, and allows swifter repayment of debt that enables future additional debt or an earlier release from bondage. Debt accounts can be fiddled with. Furthermore, advances give more flexibility of 'rewarding' particular workers through the size and frequency of *peshgi*.

Labour must complete enough daily work to attain subsistence earnings. The lower the piece–rate the more bricks must be regularly produced by a household. Furthermore, higher rates can lead to larger labour incomes, at which level the choice for lower working hours, and hence lower output, may become feasible. To owners, the disadvantage of higher rates is that once given they cannot be taken back, and rate discrimination is infeasible between workers. The rate strategy can lead to a 'price war' that goes out of control, endangering employer relations with other rural employers, in particular with landlords who remain part of the local social and state alliances. Perhaps more risk and supervision expense of additional profits is seen to follow when higher rates rather than larger advances are used to spur higher productivity. Above all, there may be system inertia in that advances are part of the accepted method for competing for labour—why fix what ain't broken?

Agriculture previously employed many kiln workers; it remains an obvious employment alternative and the sector is itself saturated by forced labour and debt bondage. These factors indicate a comparison between brick kilns and agriculture. Our rapid assessment suggests that conditions of forced labour and debt bondage in brick kilns are much less severe as compared to the oppression of landless farm labour and small sharecroppers. Factors explaining the differing conditions would include the following. Oppression and resistance both need social support. As compared to kiln owners who are mostly non-local land leasers, agricultural landlords are much more of a 'community' and hence more prone to collude in oppression. Landlords are also able to call upon the 'assistance' of local administration more easily. Whereas, some labour may be able to call upon a countervailing (and competitive) source of power through a landowner to dilute the power of the kiln owner. In some kilns—in and around large cities such as Lahore and Peshawar but also in Haripur—general trade unions and specific bonded labour associations provide a degree of countervailing power against the worst abuses: mediating with the owner, or assisting in court cases and providing refuge to runaway labour.

TRENDS

Some judgements may be made with regard to trends in bonded labour, but quite tentatively as official data does not exist or is unreliable (such as from provincial labour departments). The magnitude of nominal bondage is likely to have increased over the last two decades. Reflecting construction sector trends, the number of brick kilns appears to have increased across most of the country, and the average size of a kiln has also apparently grown. Field work did not suggest that the average number of workers per kiln has declined. We do not think that the large numbers of Afghan workers with low or no debts would have actually offset the number of other Pakistani new and old labour in continuing or fresh debt.

What has been happening to effective bondage? While a sizable proportion—especially of the traditional *patheras*—continue with much higher debts, the average would be smaller than reported in past studies, even for Punjab province as a whole. The decline in debt is due to a number of reasons. Most studies point to large advances and debts among the more numerous *patheras* as compared to the other, much smaller labour groups. However, the composition of *pathera* labour has changed more towards locals and Afghans, fewer migrants, and more male-only migrants rather than families. The latter situation can reduce the 'firm' labour on offer and hence the production level expected on a regular basis from a labour unit. Since profitability of advances is tied to production, the average level of advances is correspondingly smaller. In addition, male-only migrants are rarely accompanied with previous debt, and can therefore be engaged with smaller advances. It is also likely that the increasing number of non-local kiln owners with leased land is less willing to risk advances of large sums that cannot be generally recovered in the five years or so of the lease. Incidents of excessive violence by owners are rarer, in part because owners remain aware of possible court action that would extinguish debts altogether. These factors could be said to cause a diminution in effective bondage.

Yet, effective bondage can be said to have increased in other ways. Labour is only too acutely aware of growing unemployment and stagnant or falling wages in alternative occupations, even for the skilled and educated. Moving into brick kilns from other labour gives higher earnings (and even less bondage as compared to agriculture), but moving out of brick kilns is not a real option.

Table 1. Official Sample Survey of Punjab Brick Kilns, 2002

- The vast majority of workers were Muslims. More than a quarter of the kiln workers were migrants across districts. Over three-fourths lived in shelter provided by the kiln owners. Most labour owns no land whatsoever, but a substantial proportion do own homesteads. Livestock and other assets are of low value.
- A third of the population is not working in kilns, perhaps because the sample has a large proportion of locals. Nearly half of the children of 10–14 years work in kilns, and surprisingly, so do a significant portion of smaller children.
- Arduous work was common at more than 10 hours a day.
- Two-thirds of labour households had annual incomes smaller than Rs. 10,000, and only slightly more than 10 per cent had an income above Rs. 30,000 (equal to the current minimum wage of one adult worker).
- Nearly 90 per cent of labour took advances/loans from the kiln owner because of the absence of alternate credit sources. More than 10 per cent have debt above Rs. 25,000. Most repay debt through deduction from regular earnings but almost a third also report repayment through additional labour.
- In reporting the loan repayment period to be indefinite, most workers indicated being tied to kiln labour. The vast majority had inherited debt.

- Almost a third felt that onerous work conditions were present, presumably because of advances. Three–fourths complained of restrictions on seeking other jobs. One-half felt that permission was needed for any movement out of the kiln.
- While not universal, violence and threat of violence was quite frequently reported.
- Virtually no worker received benefits from government schemes for social protection.

Source: Federal Bureau of Statistics

Labour is also aware that when the Supreme Court forgave debts or the new legislation outlawed advances many owners got their loans back in installments. A constant refrain from indebted labour was that leaving a kiln was not a real option since they had nowhere else to go. Other work would mean lower family earnings—women and children could not work as easily or as long; employment would be irregular; factory work was unavailable or paid too little and openings were few. And 'where would they then go to live?'

At prevailing piece rates and productivity, even small advances typically continue to exceed the legal maximum of a week's gross earnings. Hence there has been no reduction in legal bondage even under the Supreme Court judgment. Despite national legislation which forbids any advance tied to labour, more labour is in debt bondage than before.

RELIEF AND REMEDY

Our findings on debt bondage suggest obvious measures for relief and remedy. These are discussed briefly here.[8] Increasing income is the obvious route to at least preventing the growth of debt or reducing its occurrence, and hence, against the increasing severity of bondage. Piece rates in all provinces remain below the equivalent of the national minimum wage (Rs. 2,500 per month): shortfalls are more severe once we account for family labour or for the official poverty line income. In Sindh and KPK, even official piece rates are much lower than that required by the national minimum wage. Curiously, few activists (including lawyers) have mentioned collective action on minimum income. This may reflect the perceived distinction between poverty and bondage; and also that bondage is seen to deserve action only when accompanied by overtly extreme violence.

Low wages are linked to credit and shelter. Workers agree to low wages when owners provide credit and shelter. The threat of homelessness serves to reduce labour's threats of seeking higher wages with another employer, or simply even of quitting.[9] Hence the linkages between 'markets' need to be countered by government action.[10]

As long as incomes remain inadequate, alternative sources of credit are needed to complement increases in expenditure. Extension of microcredit schemes to support subsistence and health can be of obvious importance as investments in human capital. If 'own' shelter is assured then microcredit for direct income generation can be relevant to all labour rather than just the locals who already live off-site. Income generation requires adult labour, and would therefore be possible only when some adults can be freed from kiln work through higher piece rates and lower debt. The threat of women and children being rendered homeless is enormous, and hence bondage is most severe for families that must live on the kiln site because they have no alternative shelter and cannot afford any due to low incomes and high debts. Hence, if the government has to take even some limited action, it should make arrangements for alternative shelter.

The sluggish pace of implementation of the National Policy and Plan of Action provides no room for being optimistic about serious action by the government, generally, and by senior labour officials in particular. There are no obvious reasons why even simple steps remain apparently daunting for the government, who is complicit in the evasion of whatever little legislation is in existence. More than two decades ago, kilns were declared by the Punjab government to be factories and all labour was considered to be workers. Yet, kiln registration remains grossly incomplete even in Punjab. For the small number of kilns already registered, the government has yet to ensure coverage under social security for even the limited number of labourers that owners have declared to be industrial workers.

Education is frequently declared a priority in various official pronouncements, but the government is yet to mobilize resources for kiln workers through the Workers Welfare Fund. Perhaps most tragic is that the government has yet to provide relief and rehabilitation to bonded labour through the special fund of Rs. 100 million created by General Musharraf during his tenure as chief executive. The Bait-ul-Mal even asked the ministry of labour to return the fund, presumably reflecting incompetence of the ministry and the especially cavalier denial of the Sindh government vis-à-vis the masses of bonded *haris* in the province.

Child health and safety require special attention and action. But government and judiciary do not interpret the Employment of Children Act to include brick kilns within the 'building and construction industry' specified in the federal list of prohibited child labour. The government may even disagree with the obvious since the National List of Hazardous Forms of Child Labour (September 2002) does not explicitly include brick kilns. When children are not deemed to have rights independent of family, then exclusion of family enterprises remain another loophole for evading action.

Reducing deprivation and exclusion is the primary goal of development. Expanding opportunities for decent work follows as a priority objective of social policy. This, in turn, requires strategies to implement labour standards as a focus on realizing core labour rights. Such concerns escape the attention of national (such as the ministry of agriculture and SMEDA) and international (e g, ADB) policy makers in formulating strategies for accelerating employment growth through agriculture and small industrial enterprises. Their focus on capital—ignoring that both labour and capital form an enterprise—leads to unacceptable analysis. This includes completely ignoring the widespread and increasing use of child and bonded labour. Their emphasis upon expansion evades recognition that larger enterprises do not necessarily provide better working conditions, as illustrated by brick kilns. Irresponsible recommendations follow, such as lax application of or exemption from primary labour legislation even concerning working hours and minimum wages, rather than verifiable compliance with labour standards, in return for financial assistance to accelerate enterprise growth.

Whether sector- or economy-wide, growth with equity has to remain the goal of sustainable development. Much political action, therefore, remains necessary to move the state to act seriously against the oppressive exercise of unequal social power, and hence also to eliminate the immense inequity of wealth that underpins the power to amplify exploitation into oppression.[11] Collective bargaining by labour has become even more urgent as the government retreats from protection of labour. Yet legal action is even more difficult after the promulgation of the new Industrial Relations Ordinance—what one general (Yahya) giveth is for another general (Musharraf) to take back.

NOTES

1. Pioneering work was done decades ago by Yameema Mitha, Karamat Ali, Nighat Said Khan and others, published as *Patterns of Female Employment in Mining and Construction Industries*, Lahore, Systems Ltd, 1981 and *Women in the Brick Kiln Industry*, Lahore, SR, 1989. More recent assessments are by Zahoor Awan in *Bonded Brick Kiln Workers: 1989 Supreme Court Judgment and After*, Rawalpindi, APFOL, 1998, and by Kevin Bales in *Disposable People: New Slavery in the Global Economy*, London, ASI, 1999.

2. The full study on brick kilns, available from PILER, contains a discussion of the sample and assessment methods and provides site-specific observations.

3. Though unexplored explicitly, *qaum* and *biradari* could be important factors in the imposed severity of bondage; see e.g. Tom Brass, *Towards a Comparative Political Economy of Unfree Labour.* London, 1999. Since state protection and patronage is not a matter of anonymous citizenship or even class, cultural differentiation would remain important in relations between labour and owner. The fieldwork also did not explore cultural differentiation in labour perceptions of bondage which could be substantial. Of course, the social fact of oppression is not vitiated by individual or group perceptions of rights and obligations.

4. The 'double coincidence of wants' has been pointed out often in the literature on tied or attached labour. For e.g., by Pranab Bardhan in *The Economic Theory of Agrarian Institutions*, London, 1989. A trenchant critique is given in Tom Brass, op cit, especially chapter 7.

5. 'If we want to decide whether a particular market is free or not, we need to take a position on the legitimacy of the underlying rights-obligations structure for the participants in the relevant market (and, indeed, certain non-participants too),' as expressed by Ha-Joon Chang, 'Breaking the Mould: An Institutionalist Political Economy Alternative to the Neo-liberal Theory of the Market and the State', *Cambridge Journal of Economics* 26, 2002.

6. If we grant that an employer exercises no individual coercion in offering advances and shelter in return for labour to a worker seeking them, social coercion is evident in the fact of dismal alternatives available to the worker.

7. Brass draws attention to how debt provides a political/social legitimacy for tied labour and consequent exploitation: there is an 'ideological decommoditization of the wage from itself, a process whereby labour-power is separated from the value it produces ... a bonded labour works to pay off a debt rather than for a wage.' See Tom Brass, 'Unfree Labour and Capitalist Restrictions in the Agricultural Sector', *Journal of Peasant Studies* 14(1), 1986. The social construction of bondage may even lead to a 'cultural preference' for the debt-labour relationship over an explicit employer-employee relationship, especially since women and children are part of the family labour; see Vinay Gidwani in 'The Cultural Logic of Work: Explaining Labour Deployment and Piece-Rate Contracts, *Journal of Development Studies* 38(2), 2001.

8. A more detailed review is given in the full study, and in two previous PILER studies: *Mitigation and Abolition of Bonded Labour: Policy, Law and Economy in Pakistan*, Karachi, 2001; *Bonded Labour in Pakistan: An Overview*, Geneva, 2001.

9. Low wages are with reference to a social wage since prevailing wage rates in alternative employment are usually themselves depressed by the availability of large numbers of unfree labour.

10. Some would point to efficiency losses, especially in the all-or-nothing monopsony scenarios, where debt for labour at low wages or piece rates is the labour market

counterpart of two-part tariffs in monopolistic commodity markets. We consider such efficiency losses to be irrelevant in a framework of citizen's rights to be free of oppression. One just cannot ignore the macro distribution of power and wealth that keeps wages, productivity, and opportunities so low as to engender the so-called efficiency gains of bondage. For a broad critique, see Tom Brass op cit.

11. 'Any attempt to problematise the connection between unfreedom, the law, and the state must begin by addressing the issue of class power;' Brass op cit. Work by Mark Granovetter is an earlier, renowned exposition of the thesis that behavior and institutions cannot be understood without reference to social relations; see 'Economic Action and Social Structure: The Problem of Embeddedness', *American Journal of Sociology* 91, 1985, 2242. *Economic and Political Weekly* May 29 2004.

CHAPTER 3

Peshgis in the Mining Sector

AHMED SALEEM

Pakistan is endowed with significant mineral resources and holds considerable potential in the exploration of mineral deposits. It has the world's second largest reservoirs of salt in Khewra (Punjab) and significant reservoirs of coal and other industrial and construction minerals in various other places. More than fifty valuable minerals, including marble, chromites, magnetite, fluorite, sulphur and basalt, are under exploitation albeit on a small scale. The current contribution of the mineral sector to the GDP is approximately 0.5%, with a potential to increase considerably after the discovery of deposits of copper, zinc, lead and most notably coal (over 175 billion tonnes of reserves in the deserts of Tharparkar in Sindh) (GOP 2010). Geologists have also indicated the presence of precious and semi-precious stones and minerals including gold and silver in areas of southern Pakistan (FBS 2006). Despite this potential, Pakistan's mining sector has remained underdeveloped. Mine owners have continued to depend on primitive techniques involving low technology and non-capital intensive methods. Consequently, the mining labour force works in very harsh, sometimes appalling conditions.

This chapter is based on a study of miners, their conditions of work and organization of labour in 2002.[1] The fieldwork for this study was conducted over a period of 35 days during which a team of trained researchers visited 50 mines across Pakistan and conducted informal interviews with more than 100 miners, labour recruitment agents and mine-owners. In some cases, the researchers also held informal discussions with family members of the miners to elicit their perspective on the situation. Insights from my previous work in the mining sector and labour relations in Pakistan and discussions with members of civil society, government officials, labour activists, and representatives of trade unions are also included in the analysis. In the following, I will first trace the historical roots of the mining sector in Pakistan for its bearing on the current situation. I will then explore the nature of existing labour arrangements and their implications for the miners. A particular focus of analysis will be the practice of *peshgi* or advance payments to the labourers. The chapter concludes with a comment on how this system of advance payment is sustained to work for further entrenchment of the mine workers into exploitative labour relations.

THE HISTORICAL DEVELOPMENT OF MINING IN PAKISTAN

According to the Royal Commission on Labour in India 1931, the average annual production from coal mining between 1896–1900 was around four million tons. Coal-mining during this period employed more than 60 thousand workers which accounted for two-thirds of all employees in the mining sector. By 1929, the figures for coalminers were 165 thousand out of a total of 22 million miners across British India (Whitley 1931). Pakistan's largest salt reservoir at Khewra, which according to a local legend was first discovered accidently by the dehydrated horses[2] of Alexander the Great's army in 327 BCE, was developed for mining along scientific lines between 1853 and 1856, after the British conquered Punjab in 1849 and took control of its mines. The existing tunnels of the mine were renovated, additional openings were added, and a system of ventilation was introduced. The older method of cutting salt rock was replaced by mechanized techniques. A five mile long road from Khewra to Pind Daden Khan in district Jhelum was built to link the mine with the neighbouring town. By 1887, the government of India built the Victoria Bridge (Chak Nizam) over the river Jhelum which connected Khewra with the main railway lines of India, thus making Khewra salt accessible to a wider domestic market.

During this period, a number of other mining sites were developed across areas that now constitute Pakistan. These included several sites in the Potohar area of Punjab, Mianwali, and the tribal belt of the North-West Frontier. However, most industrial development in pre-partition India was concentrated in the areas that came to constitute present day India. The mining industry was no exception. Pakistan inherited far fewer mines and even in these, the industry had not been fully developed. The absence of an established indigenous industrial class, and poorly developed industry at the time of independence greatly affected industrial development in all sectors. In the first few years after independence, mining was not even recognized as a separate entity. The first five-year plan mentioned policy on mines only cursorily under the general heading of 'industry'. Only in the second plan were 'Fuels and Minerals' discussed separately in terms of policy and planning.

This failure to promote the mining sector within the government led to the policy of leasing out sites to petty contractors, usually on a short-term basis. Most of the lessees lacked the resources, scientific knowledge or technical skill to develop this sector. The short duration of the lease also gave little incentive for long-term development of the mines. The focus was on short-term profit maximization. Mines were operated by hundreds of small and medium-scale mining groups. As a result, little investment in modern equipment and machinery was made and methods of extraction remained primitive. Furthermore, this myriad of small mining and processing units had no proper legal, financial, commercial, technological, and social support from the government. In fact, recommendations made by a nine-member panel on mines and oil fields in 1948 stated strongly that the policy of leasing small areas of coal-bearing land to petty contractors should be discontinued and the industry be nationalized. The report also noted the continued use of primitive methods and the need to enforce the use of modern machinery and equipment (Salim 2004). Neither of these recommendations was heeded.

The unsystematic development of mines, the lack of investment in adequate physical infrastructure including elementary mining machinery such as haulages, fans, and pumps, and the unsatisfactory conditions for labour became major stumbling blocks in the way of expanding mining in Pakistan. In the 1960s, in the face of demand for energy sources to support industrialization, some industrialists, who had been involved in the mining industry before partition, established a limited number of large, well administered mines. Rather than handing the mines over to contractors, the owners themselves became involved in the day-to-day operation of the mines. However, these mines remained exceptions and, on the whole, the mining sector was characterized by low investment and little development. This has contributed towards the appalling living and working conditions found in the sector.

WORKING CONDITION AT MINES

Miners have to work in hazardous conditions which expose them not only to disease and disability but to the risk of losing their lives. Basic mining equipment such as electric lamps and mechanical ventilators were not provided at many of the mines visited during this fieldwork. Mechanical ventilators were introduced in coalmines of the Punjab province in the 1970s but other mines have continued to rely on natural means of ventilation. For example, the rock salt mines, despite their increasing depth, still rely on natural means of ventilation. Likewise, the use of electric safety lamps is mandatory for mines that have been declared gassy but there is rarely any equipment to detect the presence of poisonous gases. The use of flame lamps for underground illumination continues as an accepted practice. Workers are rarely provided even the most basic safety equipment, such as face-masks or goggles.

The statistics on occupational accidents in the mining sector in Pakistan are alarming. A high number of people lose their lives or are disabled every year while working in the mines. For example, in 1999 alone, out of an approximately 40,000-strong mining labour force in Punjab, 32 people were killed and 20 were seriously injured. In Sindh, the corresponding figures from a labour force of 10,000 were 25 killed and 10 seriously injured. In Balochistan, 61 were killed and 16 seriously injured out of a labour force of 32,000. In KPK, 19 were killed and four seriously injured out of a labour force of 32,000 (Salim 2004).

The legal framework relating to mines empowers the federal and provincial governments to make regulations for providing for the safety of persons employed in mines, their means to enter and exit, the number of shaft outlets to be furnished, the fencing of shafts, pits, outlets and pathways, safety of roads and the workplace; the ventilation of mines and the action to be taken in respect of dust and gases; and the regulation of the use of all machinery. However, despite these legal provisions, the law is often flouted with impunity. The penalties for infringements are so low that mine owners prefer to pay them rather than invest in ensuring that their mines are in line with the safety regulations. For example, in case of loss of life, the prescribed penalty is imprisonment for up to one year and/ or a fine of four thousand rupees (US$70). In case of serious bodily injury, the penalty may be limited to imprisonment for up to six months and/or a fine of two thousand rupees (US$35).[3]

The vast majority of miners are uneducated, untrained and over-worked. They are paid very low piece-rate wages that lead to malnutrition and poor health, and necessitate long working hours, which further increases the chances of accidents at work. The prevalence of disease among miners is high. Many of them reported spending considerable sums of money on the treatment of occupational diseases. For individuals whose wage levels are already low, the additional shock of medical expenditure invariably leads to increased indebtedness.

The living environment outside the mines is hardly any better than the working conditions inside them. Miners live in dilapidated quarters which barely meet the basic needs of life. Only a few of the mines visited during the fieldwork provided *pukka* rooms or barracks with washrooms. On average, five to seven miners shared a room. However, this type of accommodation was found in no more than a quarter of the mines. Far more common were huts constructed from *katcha* material. These structures, measuring approximately 20 feet by 10 feet, had *charpais* (string beds) on either side with just enough room in between for individuals to pass single file. Two miners occupied a single *charpai*, meaning that as many as 20 workers lived in one hut. Miners were also frequently 'housed' in tents. In this case, miners slept on the floor and, on average, four to five individuals shared one tent. Water and electricity were rarely available in either the huts or the tent accommodation. Workers also pointed out that, while employers provided a minimal amount to construct the huts and put up the tents, the actual construction was left to the workers. Only occasionally do owners provide bedding for the miners (See also Salim 2001).

The hazardous nature of work in the mining sector and the working and living conditions are such that the sector tends to attract only the hardiest and most disadvantaged workers and one of the main ways in which they are attracted and retained is through a particular mode of recruitment and wages—the provision of advance payment or *peshgis*.

MIGRATORY LABOUR

The practice of *peshgi* in the mining sector is inextricably linked to the fact that the majority of the workers are migrants. It is this system of recruitment and wages which help to retain the migrant workers at the mines and ensure a continued supply of cheap labour. Two-thirds of the mine workers interviewed in Sindh, Punjab, and Balochistan were migrants from the province of Khyber-Pakhtunkhwa (KPK). Half of these came from the Swat and Shangla regions and a significant number hailed from the districts of Dir and Kohistan. Some had also migrated from different areas of Azad Kashmir. Among those working in mines in KPK, the majority had migrated from neighbouring districts within that province.

The channels of recruitment of the mine workers seem to have remained unchanged for almost a hundred years since the British controlled these mines. As the report of the Royal Commission on Labour in India 1931 observed:

... for the most part, perennial factories have now passed the stage at which it is necessary to go beyond the factory gate to secure labour. Conditions in the coalfields, however, are very different. Although, in respect of the demand of the labour, the position has become easier in recent years, many of the workers have still to be engaged away from the colliery. In consequence colliery proprietors still find it necessary to spend, directly or indirectly, substantial sums in recruiting. Most collieries recruit through a contractor. Some make a special contract for the supply of labour, which is then employed and paid by the mine management; but the more usual method is to employ a raising contractor to whom are assigned other important functions which we discuss later. Two other systems exist: under one, a miner Sardar brings a gang to the mine and is responsible to the manager for the work undertaken by the gang; under the other, the management sends out its own recruiters. Whichever the system adopted, the actual procedure of securing recruits is much the same. The recruiter or his agent visits the village—which is generally the one with which he has a steady connection—makes advances, pays railway fares and brings the workers to the coalfield. An increasing number of miners find their way to the coalfields from outside without the assistance of a recruiter. (Whitley 1931: 116)

According to Rahim and Viaro (2002), workers from the mountainous regions of the north traditionally migrated for work in the coalmines of Punjab, Balochistan, and Sindh on a seasonal basis. These northern areas have extreme climates and cultivation is undertaken in the summer months only. During the freezing winter, individuals search for opportunities in other areas. Some are able to find work in the closest urban centre and may even be able to commute on a daily basis. Others have to look further afield, leading them towards mining. Moreover, these areas are particularly poor regions where opportunities for employment remain limited. The high rate of population growth has also put further pressure on natural resources and has adversely affected agricultural output as land holdings are increasingly divided. Employment opportunities have diminished further because of the decreasing number and size of public sector projects, due to the paucity of development funds allocated to the provincial government. The consequence of these conditions is a strong economic push for labour migration. Mines, especially underground ones in Balochistan, Punjab, and Sindh have provided the main avenue for employment for poor labourers from the upper hill tracts of Swat and Shangla for generations and this 'tradition' has continued to the present day. As a trade union leader at one of the mines in Punjab said:

Anyone who cannot get some job goes for mines. In Swat and Azad Kashmir, no labour to be had during the months of winter, while in the mines here it is working season.

The importance of 'pull' factors for labourers from these areas cannot be understated. Mining is extremely physically demanding work. A common line of reasoning among labourers as well as their recruiters and mine-owners was that men from mountainous areas of the north are tough and hardy. Therefore, they are physically more capable of handling such arduous tasks as demanded of them in mining. The main pull factor for them to take up work in mining is the possibility of *peshgi* to support their families back home. One leader of a miner's association shared with the author:

Mining takes a heavy toll of health and physique, that is why hardened labour has to be imported from Swat and other mountainous places. Those people are very poor and have to take advance (peshgi) for their families to live on.

MIDDLEMEN AND PESHGIS

Workers who accept work in mines do so on the basis of securing an advance, or *peshgi,* from a labour agent or middleman. The middleman, known as a *mate* in Punjab and *jorisar* in Sindh and Balochistan, is dispatched by mine owners to recruit labour from selected villages. The middleman is armed with advances of money known as *peshgis,* as enticement for employment in mines. A *jorisar* interviewed during the fieldwork stated:

Shangla is a backward area. The majority of people are poor. Those that we recruit often owe about seven or eight thousand rupees to shopkeepers. This individual then seeks an advance from the jorisar *in order to arrange provisions for his family while he is absent from home.*

Recruitment, therefore, is done by the *mate* or *jorisar.* The mine owner has no direct dealing with the worker. By giving the advance to the middleman, the mine owner ensures that the middleman will be responsible for giving and reclaiming the advance, meaning that the latter, in turn, is likely to give advances only to those workers he trusts and/or is confident of 'controlling'. Labour agents are therefore most likely to recruit workers from their own localities since, in case the worker defaults,

it is the sub-contractor that has to compensate the company for the loss
of the advance. In order to protect his own interests, it is also common
practice for the middleman to receive the workers' wages and then
disburse them.

> As a jorisar, I bring labour from the villages. I go there at least once a year. Men
> also come by themselves in search of work but most are recruited by jorisars. The
> advance payment to a worker is through us. If a worker runs away we have to
> compensate the company for the loss of advance.

Advances vary between Rs. 5,000 and Rs. 50,000. For mines in Punjab,
the average *peshgi* ranges from Rs. 5,000 to Rs. 20,000. In Sindh, the
equivalent range is Rs. 10,000–Rs. 25,000. *Peshgis* are highest for mines
in Balochistan, ranging from Rs. 15,000 to Rs. 50,000 reflecting the
greater depth of the mines, the more difficult working conditions and the
need to retain an experienced labour force for work in mines where the
coal is of relatively high quality. The larger advances in Balochistan and
Sindh are also linked to the practice of withholding wages until coal is
sold. In Punjab, the tendency is to pay miners as soon as the coal is
excavated. Advances for mining activities in KPK are rare, possibly
reflecting the fact that workers are more local than migrant. Furthermore,
the quality of the coal in Punjab and KPK is lower than in Sindh and
Balochistan. As such, the market price is correspondingly lower and mine
owners have less cash to offer miners.

From the point of view of the employer, the *peshgi* (and the
indebtedness that follows) serves several purposes. Most importantly, it
secures a permanent, suitable and cheap labour force at a time when
demand is high. Much mine work is seasonal—winter being the busy
period. However, the 'fallow' period in summer means that a considerable
amount of effort is needed to make the mine operational again for the
winter season. As such, mine owners prefer to retain a work-force year-
round. *Peshgis* assure a labour supply for the busy winter season and also
keep this labour in place during summer. While workers may initially have
planned to migrate for only a season, their increasing indebtedness often
means that they are obliged to continue working year-round.

Once an advance is secured from a *jorisar* or *mate,* repayment usually
takes the shape of deductions from fortnightly or monthly wages.
Generally, the larger the advance the more money is deducted from wages.
There is little evidence of interest being charged. But, once *peshgi* is taken,
the worker cannot move from the current employer without repaying the

advance in full. This means that availing of better wages in another mine or in some other employment is forfeited, unless another advance is taken to pay off the original loan. According to one mine manager in Punjab;

> *Workers always want advances amounting to Rs. 10–15,000. If they want to go and join some other mine, this advance has to be returned. We give the advance amount to the* mate, *not directly to the worker.*

The importance of the *peshgi* for the employer, therefore, lies in retaining labour. *Peshgis* are rarely fully reclaimed by owners nor is interest earned. Rather, *peshgi* gives the employer considerable leverage over his middlemen and, through the middlemen, his labour. Moreover, not only are mine owners assured of a labour supply, they are also provided with a compliant labour force. The fact that migrant workers are keen for advances makes them even more attractive to potential employers. It was revealed by a number of workers that local labourers were far less likely to ask for or receive advances and that they were not the ideal workers for mine owners. Local workers tend to have stronger links within the community and are, therefore, more likely to take collective action or join trade unions. As a social activist and the producer of *Sang Zad*, a TV serial revolving around the poor state of miners, stated:

> *Being poor and lonely and far from home, and away from the labour movement, the migrant worker is far more likely to become bonded. On the other hand, the local worker is close to home, is organized and in contact with the labour movement and is not obliged to get bonded. He is less in need of advance and does not get entrapped in this relationship.*

Thus, apart from surrendering the right to freedom of employment, migrant miners are under pressure not to join trade unions. At several sites, informants mentioned instances of mine owners insisting on *peshgis* being returned or refusing further advances in the event of trade union activity. The result is that trade union activity in the mining industry is minimal and where it does exist is so feeble as to have no noticeable impact. The few mines where there was 'trade union' activity' the union was actually being run by labour-contractors or even mine owners!

However, the initial *peshgi* is only the first step in a cycle of indebtedness that continues to grow over time. It is the combination of *peshgi* and low wages that together make this a long-term, substantive phenomenon.

PIECE-RATE WAGES

In almost all mines in Pakistan the system of piece-rate work is prevalent. At hiring, piece-rates are set by the labour agent and the agent's own commission is settled. During the digging of the mine, payment is made on a per square foot basis. When mineral excavation begins, wages are given on a per ton basis. The older and larger mines, mainly located in Sindh and Balochistan, tend to offer better wages. These mines are amongst the small numbers that were taken on by industrialists before partition. The smaller and newer mines are almost entirely controlled by short-term leaseholders or petty contractors who invest as little as possible in their operations. This obviously affects wage rates. A comparative observation of coalmines in the early 2000s reveals that the highest wages per ton excavated were Rs. 400–500 while the lowest were Rs. 100–120. The higher rates were found in the mines of Balochistan, reflecting the higher quality of the coal excavated and the more difficult working conditions (deeper mines). The lowest rates were found in KPK where coal quality is low and the need to attract migrant workers less important. In the mines of Punjab, wages were around Rs. 200–250 per ton. Similarly, in Sindh, wages were around Rs. 200 per ton up to Rs. 300, in rare instances. In terms of earnings per month, the range was between Rs. 3000–4000 in Balochistan, Rs. 2500–3000 in Sindh and Punjab and Rs. 2000 in KPK.

Despite the relatively high wages in the coalmines of Balochistan, the most exploitative wage system encountered is found there, in the onyx mines of Chaghi. This belt of mines runs along the Afghan border and enters Iran after passing through Pakistan. Somewhat surprisingly, the miners are mostly local, explained by the fact that excavation work is relatively easy. In the past, miners here worked on a daily wage basis, but this system is being replaced by a 'more work, more income' system. More disturbing is the practice of not paying wages to miners if the excavated material is not of a certain quality. In coalmines, the size and shape of the coal excavated is immaterial. But in onyx mining, the size of the block has to be of prescribed dimensions. It takes three people a whole day to dig out a 3x3 foot block and if the output is not acceptable to the owner, the entire effort of three workers is wasted. This is known as the *Gulla* system.

In addition to the problem of low wages further reduced by *peshgi* deductions, there is also the problem of late payment. This is connected to a continued recourse to advances. Labour leaders and workers interviewed during the course of this research stated that it was common practice for wages to be paid only when material was sold. This delay appears to be more common in the mines of Sindh and Balochistan. Some informants stated that payment tended to be regular in those mines where business was regular. But as one worker stated:

In many mines, wages are paid after loading the coal, i.e., after its sale. But loading itself has many hazards: much of the coal dust is blown away by wind, or rain washes it away. The loss is ultimately that of the worker. Moreover, the coal is weighed in the factory which buys it where the miner, who is most concerned with its weight, is not present. Here, too, the worker sometimes suffers as some of the coal is rejected for allegedly low quality.

In contrast the system devised for the payment of wages by one of the older, established (and, therefore, better run) private mines involve no direct contact between worker and mine administration. According to the chief engineer of the mine:

We have a regular system for all kinds of payment. The owner hands over the money to the jorisar, *while the workers jointly nominate a clerk to look after their accounts. The wage rate is announced on the notice board; therefore, the* jorisar *cannot do any underhand business. Also the* jorisar *is paid per ton separately. If there are 20 workers their total wage is divided into 21 parts and he is paid that as commission.*

Delays in distributing wages mean that workers are forced into a situation where, in order to meet daily expenses, they must accept more *peshgis* from the labour agents. This additional amount is added to their previous balance. The importance of the provision of timely wages is summed up in the words of a Kashmiri miner working in Sindh:

One sure way of bringing about improvement is through enforcing timely payment of wages. The consensus is that if wages are paid punctually and regularly there will be no need for advances. In most of the mines in Pakistan, wages are paid after the sale of the coal. The fortnightly compensation gets deposited with the mate and is given to the worker only when he goes back home. In both the cases, the worker has to rely on advances for his immediate needs.

One of the other issues associated with taking *peshgis* and one of the reasons for the persisting cycle of debt is the vast potential for fraud. An advance is always part of an unwritten agreement in itself leaving ample scope for the 'fiddling' of accounts, particularly as miners are

overwhelmingly illiterate. Workers often complained that their original
peshgi amount had been inflated by the *jorisar* or *mate*. A labour leader in
a mine in Punjab related the following incident:

> *A worker from Poonch in Azad Kashmir had borrowed Rs. 20,000 as advance
> from a mate in order to buy a donkey for use in the mine. For several months he
> managed to repay the* peshgi *from his wages, despite the hardship that this caused.
> When he had paid back all but Rs. 4,000 of the original Rs. 20,000 he asked the*
> mate *whether he could look for work offering better wages. The* mate, *though, had
> invested all his capital in the mine and did not have enough money to hire another
> donkey-owner. So, to ensure that the worker would not leave, he falsely claimed
> that the worker owed him Rs. 40,000 and not just Rs. 4,000. The* mate *was a
> man of influence and I saw this donkey-owner being brought to the mine in chains.
> He was made to work in the mine in this fashion, while the* mate's *son kept watch
> outside armed with a revolver. After working for hours he was escorted to his room
> and kept imprisoned in chains. After about twelve days, the man somehow
> managed to escape, only for the* mate *to arrange a search party of jeeps and armed
> men. Two days later, the unfortunate worker was apprehended, severely beaten and
> put to work again. When this came to the knowledge of some good people of the
> locality, they arranged a settlement by paying the* mate *some money and begging
> him to let the prisoner go.*

Such cases in the mining sector reflect the degree to which labour is forced
to forfeit the freedom of employment due to *peshgi* and the cycle of debt.

More common than blatant use of force and deception, though, are
more surreptitious ways of inflating the outstanding debt. One of the
most common ways is through the common kitchen or *langar* system
practiced in most of the mines of Sindh, Punjab and Balochistan. An
agent of the mine administration (not himself a mine worker) brings in
monthly rations and the amount is divided amongst the mineworkers and
added to their advance accordingly. As there are no written accounts, the
amount added to the existing *peshgi* is easily fiddled. In KPK, the *langar*
expenses are simply deducted from the wages, given that far fewer miners
take advances.

In some cases, the miner arranges rations for his family in his village
of domicile with the shopkeeper through the *jorisar*. Occasionally, the
jorisar himself is responsible for providing rations to the miner's family.
But a number of workers stated that the collusion of shopkeeper and
jorisar often means that the full value of rations do not reach their families
and the amount added on to the initial *peshgi* is arbitrarily increased.
These complaints and the fact that the *jorisar* is often seen as responsible
for the worker's increasing indebtedness say much about the relationship

between recruiter and labour. Despite the fact that the agent is usually from the same locality, caste and, occasionally, the same extended kinship group as the labour he recruits, the labour agent does not appear to favour his labourers beyond offering them employment. Workers hold the *jorisar* responsible for exploiting them and cheating them out of their meagre wages. It is worth remembering that wages are given to the labour agent and not directly to the worker.

EVIDENCE OF FORCED LABOUR

The International Labour Organization (ILO) defines forced labour as: *The term forced or compulsory labour shall mean all work or service which is extracted from any person under the menace of any penalty and for which the said person has not offered himself voluntarily* (ILO Convention 29, 1930).[4] Within this definition debt bondage refers to a specific form of forced labour in which a worker renders service under conditions of bondage arising from economic considerations, notably indebtedness incurred through the provision of a loan.

Unlike the agriculture sector, the mining sector does not appear to have a system whereby workers are expected to contribute free labour as part of their 'contract' with the employer. Mines tend to be located in remote areas where there is little other work available and where mine owners are rarely based. Forced labour in the mining sector takes on a more flagrant form. Indebted miners are pressured to continue to work for low wages for the same employer without complaint about working or living conditions. Those who try to escape are tracked down by the *jorisar* or *mate* and forced to continue to work at the mine. Miners interviewed during the research gave accounts of fellow workers being severely beaten and chained following attempted escapes. Here, the linkage between the labour agent and the worker proves crucial, as most labour agents are from the same region as the miners and, therefore, usually personally know the 'errant' miner and his family. As one *jorisar* remarked when asked what would happen if one of his workers decamped with the advance, 'Where will he hide from us? We know him and his family. He will have to move to a different province.' Furthermore, *jorisars* have taken to giving *peshgis* to more than one member of a family.

For workers, the incentive in this strategy is that it allows a much larger total advance to be received. For the *jorisar*, it means that in the event of one family member escaping, the others are held as collateral. This phenomenon is, in fact, common in the mining sector. Miners who wish

to go on leave to visit their home village normally do so by ensuring that
a family member remains in the mine during their absence. More
common than physical chaining of workers is the collusion of the mine
owner or middleman with local police officials when workers attempt to
leave a particular employer. Workers may be threatened with jail and, in
some cases, be locked up. But it is not only the worker who risks
intimidation at the hands of the local police and mine owners. Better-off
jorisars occasionally offer advances to workers from their own funds and
then reclaim this advance from mine owners. However, as a labour leader
stated, mine administration and the police may plot in conjunction
against both workers and middlemen.

> *Sometimes the worker decamps with the advanced amount. Only five per cent of*
> *the blame in such cases falls on the worker. The owners are at fault in 95 per cent*
> *of cases. This is because they try to withhold the dues, not only of the worker but*
> *also of the* mate. *Often the owner owes more than a lakh of rupees (Rs. 100,000)*
> *to the* mate, *but tries to avoid payment through various excuses. If the* mate *presses*
> *too much, the owner seeks the help of the police. He bribes the police and gets the*
> mate *arrested. The usual ruse of the police is to accuse the* mate *of possessing* charas.
> *Not knowing who is responsible for the police action, the worker or the* mate
> *appeals to the owner or contractor for assistance. The owner/contractor 'recommends'*
> *lenience, and the police promise to let him off if he leaves the area. The* mate
> *accepts the conditions and, forfeiting his money, he leaves the area. There have been*
> *dozens of cases of this nature. In Choa Saidan Shah and Chakwal, the owner's*
> *hand is always behind police victimization.*

The collusion with police and district government officials further
strengthens the hand of the already dominant party in this unwritten
contract, initiated through the advance of pay.

Miners are not 'born' into this profession but once they take it up due
to poverty and lack of alternative opportunities—often in pursuit of
peshgis—there is clear evidence that the *peshgi* works to ensure that they
remain bound. Moreover, their entrapment is strengthened through
strategies like the withholding and non-payment of wages; through the
threat or actual use of physical violence against a worker or family or those
close to them; through imprisonment or other physical confinement;
through collusion between employers and the police and through the
deprivation of food, shelter or other necessities.

PESHGI AND CHILD LABOUR

The increasing burden of *peshgis* coupled with low, piece-rate wages leads to another phenomenon—the use of child labour in mines. To lighten the burden of *peshgis,* some mine workers have taken to involving their children in mining. These boys can be as young as 10 but the majority are closer to 15. They either migrate with their father or are sent to join their father or elder brothers.

In Punjab and KPK, boys are usually assigned the job of taking donkeys underground and bringing them out laden with coal. They are known as *tapali* and, on average, make Rs. 80–100 per day. Apart from working as *tapalis,* the boys are also found working in the *langar,* or common kitchen. Additionally, they may be assigned tasks such as carrying goods to and from the mine.

In Sindh and Balochistan, children were not seen working as *tapalis,* although there were children going in and out of the underground mines. More children were found working in the common kitchen. A chief engineer at one mine stated:

> *Boys work with us as support staff. No one below 18 years of age is allowed to go down into the mine. Actually, we are opposed to having juvenile labour. But sometimes we are obliged to engage a boy when we are told that he is the only breadwinner in the family. In Punjab, boys are employed to drive the donkeys because the mines are smaller and it is not feasible for an adult to drive a donkey in them.*

Apart from children working as part of a family group, a subset of children has no relatives in the mines. Often these children are the eldest able male child and the *de facto* breadwinners—usually as a result of death or incapacity of fathers and/or elder brothers. These children represent the most vulnerable subset of workers. Children have to face the added menace of sexual abuse, as well. The appalling living and working conditions, in conjunction with the complete absence of a family life, sustain the incidences of child sexual abuse by miners, *jorisars* and other workers such as donkey-owners and cooks. This abuse is compounded by the relatively recent but increasing prevalence of drug-use amongst miners. Miners stated that drug-peddling is a profitable profession and peddlers often sell opium, heroin, and *charas* to miners.

CONCLUSION

In the mining sector, bonded labour as a system of recruitment clearly exists, but it does not conform to the common stereotype of debt bondage (cf. Ercelawn and Nauman in this volume). Other social mechanisms that might lead to bondage are not clearly in evidence, such as social linkages involving mutual obligations between groups. Social linkages play a role in the initial recruitment through middlemen, but there is no traditional bond between employer and employee as is the case between landlord and tenant in agriculture (see Martin in this volume). The relationship is only established once a *peshgi* is offered and accepted—therefore the key role of the *peshgi* in this sector. Neither is there evidence of extra work being extracted without remuneration, as opposed to that observed in the agricultural sector across Punjab and Sindh (see Ahmed in this volume). This is largely a reflection of the fact that family labour is not involved in mining and that other work opportunities at the mining site are severely restricted. Forced labour in the mining sector is characterized by physical force, the threat of violence and a relationship between unequals. There is no question of equal bargaining power between the 'partners' in this unwritten contract. Furthermore, the active collusion of powerful mine owners with state machinery further unbalances this relationship in favour of the employers. Conditions are exacerbated by the remoteness of mines and the fact that the majority of workers are migrants. It is these conditions—rather than the typical ones—that give the sector its particular bonded characteristic.

REFERENCES

FBS (2006), Census of Mining and Quarrying industries (2005–2006). Federal Bureau of Statistics, Government of Pakistan: Islamabad.

GOP (1955), The First Five Year Plan 1955–60. National Planning Board, Government of Pakistan: Karachi.

GOP (1960),The Second Five Year Plan 1960–65. Planning Commission, Government of Pakistan: Karachi.

GOP (2013), National Mineral Policy 2013. Ministry of Petroleum and Natural Resources, Government of Pakistan: Islamabad. http://www.mpnr.gov.pk/gop/index.php?q=aHR 0cDovLzE5Mi4xNjguNzAuMTM2L21wbnIvZnJtJtRGV0YWlscy5hc3 B4P2lkPTEyJmFtcDtvcHQ9cG9saWNpZXM%3D. (Accessed, 13 January 2015)

GOP (2010), Annual Plan 2010–11. Planning Commission, Government of Pakistan: Islamabad. http://www.pc.gov.pk/annual%20plans/2010-11/Manufacturing%20 and%20Minerals.pdf

Rahim, I., & Viaro, A. (2002), 'Swat: An Afghan Society in Pakistan – Urbanization and Changes in a Tribal Environment', Geneva: Institute of Development Studies and Karachi: Karachi City Press.

Salim, A. (2001), 'Mine Workers: Working and Living Conditions'. Working paper Series 62. Islamabad: Sustainable Development Policy Institute. http://www.sdpi.org/ publications/files/W62-Mine%20Workers.pdf. (Accessed, 13 January 2015)

Salim, A. (2004), 'Rapid Assessment of Bonded Labour in Pakistan's Mining Sector'. Sustainable Development Policy Institute, Islamabad. http://www.ilo.org/wcmsp5/ groups/public/@ed_norm/@declaration/documents/publication/wcms_082032.pdf. (Accessed , 13 January 2015)

Whitley, J. H. (1931), Report of the Royal Commission on Labour in India: Presented to parliament by command of His Majesty, June 1931. London : Majesty's Stationery Office.

NOTES

1. 'A Rapid Assessment of Bonded Labour in Pakistan's Mining Sector' (2004), Sustainable Development Policy Institute (SDPI) and International Labour Organization.
2. Legend has it that the dehydrated horses made a dramatic recovery when they licked the walls of the salt mines leading to replenishment of lost salt.
3. *Mines Act 1923*. http://www.ilo.org/dyn/travail/docs/1007/Mines%20Act%201923. pdf accessed on 13/1/2015.
4. ILO (1930). Forced Labour Convention No. 29. Adopted and proclaimed by the General Conference of the International Labour Organization. June 28, 1930.http:// www.ilo.org/dyn/normlex/en/f?p=1000:12100:0::NO::P12100_ILO_CODE:C029. Accessed on 13/1/2015.

CHAPTER 4

Recruitment and Wage Systems in Selected Sectors

ALI KHAN

B onded labour in Pakistan and India accounts for the largest number of forced labour in the world today. The government of Pakistan adopted a National Policy and Plan of Action for the Abolition of Bonded Labour and the Rehabilitation of Freed Bonded Labourers in September 2001 which provides for an integrated range of measures to combat the problem. It also identifies the inadequacy of existing statistical and qualitative information on the extent and nature of bonded labour as one of the major constraints to effective action against it. The 1992 Bonded Labour System (Abolition) Act (BLSA) casts a rather broad definition of bonded labour, embracing situations in which a debtor who has received an advance (or *peshgi*) in cash or in kind has to work for the creditor for no or nominal wages; one who does not do so forfeits freedom of employment, movement, or the right to sell labour at the market rate.

In an attempt to address the limited economic or social research on the issue and to provide a balanced, holistic picture of the ground realities, the ILO and the government of Pakistan instituted a number of research studies in the early 2000s. Surveys were undertaken on bonded labour in brick kilns in Punjab and among *haris* (sharecroppers) in Sindh.[1] In contrast to such reports, this chapter draws on material from a range of qualitative studies that have been undertaken since 2003. The purpose is to set aside preconceived notions and perspectives, an issue that has been prone to widely differing accounts in the past, and approach the topic with a clean slate. This allows us to move beyond the stereotype of bonded labour and highlight a range of labour arrangements, thereby shedding a fresh perspective on the issue. The primary focus of the chapter is the systems of recruitment and wages in sectors which are commonly associated with bonded labour. As the chapter shows, these two areas are key to understanding how an individual falls into a bonded labour relationship (recruitment) and how she or he may remain bonded (wage systems). The older forms of coercion and bonded labour are mutating into new ones. Although bonded labour continues to exist in agriculture, often rooted in traditional agrarian systems, the problem has spread to other economic sectors where intermediaries recruit workers through wage advances that lead to significant indebtedness and, ultimately, debt bondage.

The first section of the chapter describes the methodology of the research. The second section discusses recruitment mechanisms in various segments of the agricultural sector as well as in selected industries. The third section discusses wage systems, causes and consequences of wage advances and how they lead to bonded labour. The final section is the conclusion.   .

METHODOLOGY

The research process, at the outset, was overseen and guided by a Bonded Labour Research Forum that comprised representatives of the Pakistan government and researchers with an interest and expertise relevant to the issue of bonded labour. The role of the forum was to assure the quality of the research process and its outputs, such that the results would be credible and useful in terms of guiding practical and effective action. I was part of the forum as the research coordinator. My role was to assist the researchers on questions of research design and methodology for fieldwork, to facilitate contact and exchange of information and lessons learned between the researchers, and to assure the quality and uniformity of the final output. The research coordinator also undertook fieldwork with the separate researchers.

SECTOR AND SITE SELECTION

The Research Forum selected agriculture, brick making, marine fisheries, mining, carpet-weaving, hazardous industries (tanneries, construction, and glass bangle manufacturing), begging, and domestic service for fieldwork and investigation. These sectors or economic activities were suspected of highest incidence of bonded labour in Pakistan. In the case of agriculture, brick making, mining, and carpet-weaving, the widespread nature of these sectors and the potentially significant regional variations meant that the assessments would have to be undertaken in all four provinces.[2] The countrywide coverage would also assist in confirming or refuting assumptions that in certain sectors problems were limited only to particular provinces. This was particularly the case for agriculture, where it is often assumed that Sindh is the only province in which bonded labour is widespread. This is not the case, and some of the worst abuses that researchers encountered were found in the areas of northern Punjab. The inclusion of hazardous sectors was driven by the hypothesis that the nature of working conditions was such that coercive recruitment and wage systems could explain why workers continued to remain in employment in these sectors, particularly considering the low wages on offer.

In the case of the hazardous industries, two of the three subsectors are largely concentrated in a few main locations.[3] Therefore, it was decided that these major concentrations be geographically targeted and focused on rather than spreading the survey to locations where the sector is too small for meaningful information to be gathered. In contrast, the construction, begging, and domestic work sectors are so widely spread out that it was decided that research would be best served by concentrating on three types of population centres: large cities, small cities/towns, and rural areas. The fieldwork on marine fisheries was confined to Sindh and Balochistan, as those are the only two provinces with a coastline.

Overall, it was decided that the assessments should be undertaken on a sectoral rather than provincial basis. Researchers felt more comfortable working on their sector of expertise rather than being assigned a particular province and multiple sectors. Moreover, as most had experience of working throughout Pakistan, provincial differences were not seen as an obstacle. In addition, the fieldwork was undertaken by teams that often utilized the services of local researchers. This was particularly advantageous where key local information or expertise was required or where informants were reluctant to speak openly to outsiders. Where a sector was particularly large and conditions were likely to vary considerably between regions, the research was undertaken by two separate researchers—as in the case of agriculture.

The choice of sites within each sector was made on the basis of detailed interviews with key resource persons as well as the past experience of the researchers. Furthermore, rather than concentrate on selecting random sites from a wider list of sites where the incidence of bonded labour was suspected, it was felt that the quality of the information would benefit from selecting sites with which researchers were familiar and in which they had personal contacts. The final selection of sites in the different sectors nevertheless represented a balanced provincial cross-section.

FIELDWORK

The fieldwork for the study was conducted over a period of 12 weeks. The appointed researchers worked with and supervised field teams. The use of teams allowed covering a greater number of locations and informants. In light of the specific characteristics of each sector, the different field teams adopted slightly different techniques to best suit conditions on the ground. Nevertheless, there were certain common themes that were built upon and used to form the basis of investigation. These included (1) an analysis of existing secondary information including national surveys and censuses, NGO and international organization reports, demographic and labour force surveys, and newspaper and magazine reports, and (2) the use of ethnographic methods to generate qualitative information.

Flexibility and adaptability of the rapid assessment tools used in this study make them well suited for research on bonded labour due to the sensitivity attached to it. Bonded labour is an illegal activity and workers are hesitant to speak openly about their experiences from fear of repercussions from their employers. The fieldwork focused on qualitative methods of data collection such as informal interviews, focus group discussions, building on existing contacts, case studies, key informant interviews, community and workplace profiles, and observation. The studies covered interviews with employers (mine owners, landowners, small-scale industrialists), intermediaries (contractors, subcontractors), and workers and their families. Meetings were also held with concerned government officials at the federal, provincial, and district levels and with trade union leaders.

Certain sectors proved to be particularly challenging. Research on domestic workers is among the most difficult to gain entry into because it is confined to the private sphere of the home. The begging sector is often associated with criminal elements and drug use. Mining involves exposure to hazardous conditions. A more general difficulty is that employers are often influential people with links to government and police officials. This means that government and police officials are also often unwilling to divulge information on a system in which they may be implicated.

Although employers did not show an inclination toward threatening researchers in the field, there were some attempts to disrupt interviews with workers. On one occasion an interview with a mine worker was interrupted by the mine owner's repeatedly revving the engine of a truck while the interview was ongoing. On another occasion, carpet weavers in a workshop were warned against speaking to researchers. Despite the cooperation of the federal government, some district government officials also tried to dissuade researchers from visiting certain sites. Informants were reluctant to speak to researchers in the presence of government officials or employers. Thus, wherever possible, interviews with the different groups were undertaken separately and often away from the place of work and after 'work hours'. This went some way to decreasing the threat felt by some of the informants.

The fieldwork for this study used qualitative methods of data collection—pioneered in anthropology—to enable the researchers to gather in-depth information on a sensitive topic. However, it must be pointed out the researchers did not engage in the intensive, long-term participant observation that characterizes anthropological fieldwork. Therefore this chapter does not provide the level of intricate detail that ethnography does. Nevertheless, the analysis of the recruitment and wage systems presented here is based on the strength of in-depth information from various sectors collected by qualitative methods.

RECRUITMENT SYSTEMS

The starting point for an arrangement that may lead to bonded labour is the recruitment system. How do individuals fall into relations of bonded labour, and, more important, why do they? A holistic response to these questions requires an understanding of the socio-cultural factors that underpin the institution of bonded labour. Such an analysis will also address the more subtle, noneconomic factors that are sometimes overlooked when examining bonded labour. Recruitment mechanisms differ broadly between the agricultural and industrial sectors, although there is an increasing amount of overlap between the sectors. The two sectors will be analyzed separately, as this will allow both differences and similarities between recruitment in agriculture and industry to be highlighted.

The agricultural sector should not be seen as an undifferentiated mass, however. The sector displays what I shall refer to as 'traditional' as well as 'modern' forms of recruitment corresponding respectively to older forms of debt bondage based on traditional hierarchical relations and those of newer forms of bondage or what Kevin Bales (2000) has described as neobondage. This chapter will use the provinces of Sindh (traditional) and Punjab (newer) to highlight the two different kinds of bonded labour within agriculture.[4] There will also be examples that highlight the transition between the two forms. In examining these variants, it becomes clear that different modes of recruitment can lead to different forms of bonded labour.

AGRICULTURE: SHARECROPPING AREAS

The agricultural sector in Pakistan comprises 45.1 per cent of the workforce and accounts for some 21.5 per cent of the gross domestic product (GDP). It is therefore unsurprising that the majority of bonded labourers are to be found in this sector. But this is not solely because of the number of workers in the sector; it is also owing to factors intrinsic to the agricultural sector and in particular the influence of the caste system and the patron-client relations that underpin this system.

These patron-client arrangements can be viewed as an institution whereby wealthy individuals commit themselves to guaranteeing the subsistence of their labourers in exchange for the latter's ready availability (Platteau 1995: 637). Theoretically the patron-client relationship can be a mutually beneficial and reciprocal one, such that this particular kind of system ensures poor people against the risk of starvation. For poor people, it is essentially an effort to maximize security in an uncertain environment. The patron secures access to a readily available, trustworthy, and compliant labour force, not only for productive tasks but also for ritual, social, and political activities or duties. Keeping this in mind, it is unsurprising that large landlords will often emphasize that their 'contract' with their sharecroppers is to the benefit of both parties. The system is characterized by a simultaneous exchange of resources such as support and loyalty, long-term credit, and obligations.

Beginning in the nineteenth century, a series of legislative measures in the form of Tenancy Acts was instituted to 'legalize' these relations and provide the tenants some protection.[5] Therefore, labour arrangements and recruitment in agriculture were mediated not through middlemen or subcontractors but through traditional relations between landowners and tenants and through the relevant Tenancy Acts that addressed the issues of tenancy rights, duties of tenants and landlords, and the division of produce between them. The patron-client relationship is reinforced, however, through ritual ties and a set of duties and obligations known as the *jajmani* system in South Gujrat and the *sepidari* system in Punjab. Alavi argues that this system is best described as a form of master-subject relationship (Alavi 1987: 352). Essential to this relationship are ritually enacted acts that project the landlord as kindly and humane. Indebted, the recipient of this 'kindness' is persuaded to reciprocate with what he can offer, that is, his labour.

In the province of Sindh, such tenancy still remains the most common arrangement for agricultural production. Hence, it is traditional relations between landowners and cultivating castes as described above that determine recruitment patterns. Relations between the two groups are often hereditary and of long standing, sometimes stretching back generations. In such a situation, sharecroppers will often belong to traditional tenant castes such as Meghwars and Kohlis, whereas landowners will belong to traditional landowning castes such as Khosas and Talpurs. These traditional relations between landowning and non-landowning castes provide the link or channel through which recruitment will typically be undertaken in the traditional agricultural sector.

Within this framework, recruitment is sealed through the provision of credit or a *peshgi* to the tenant by the landowner. Most tenants will have little or no collateral and savings. As a result, the *peshgi* is essential for subsistence purposes, and many tenants borrow cash or grain from a landlord at the start of their contract. This lump sum amount could be interpreted as the 'start-up cost' of a tenant and does not relate directly to the agricultural process. So although recruitment will follow lines of relations between groups who have traditionally tilled the land for those who have owned it, it is the offer of the advance that clinches the deal. The *peshgi* therefore becomes the essential element of the recruitment process, and tenants will often decide on which landlord to work for on the basis of the initial credit amount that is offered. Moreover, tenants may also instigate a move from one landlord to another based on subsequent loans that landlords offer in order to secure a reliable workforce.

AGRICULTURE: SELF-CULTIVATED AREAS

Since 1960 there has been considerable change in land tenure patterns as many landowners have shifted from sharecropping to self-cultivation. From 1980 to 2000, the percentage of workers in sharecropping declined from 45 per cent of the total farmers (on 48 per cent of the entire cultivated land) to only 23 per cent of the total farming population (on 27 per cent of the land). Punjab is the main driver of change, with the tenant population declining from 58 per cent in 1972 to only 21 per cent of farmers in 2000. In Sindh this process is less advanced, but substantial changes have still occurred, with tenant ratios going down from 78 per cent of farmers to 34 per cent during the same period (Agricultural Census of Pakistan 1960, 1972, 1980, 1990). It would therefore be correct to state that the increasing trend toward self-cultivation has been at the expense of sharecroppers and small farmers.

In response to these changes, the recruitment system has also altered from one dependent on traditional relations to one based on a far less personalized, more market-driven relationship involving two types of workers: casual and permanent. Casual labour refers to labour employed occasionally on a daily-wage basis for specific agricultural work. Permanent labour means persons who work on the farm on a full-time basis, are employed for longer periods, and receive wages in cash or kind on a fixed-period basis. Casual labourers, in both Punjab and Sindh, are found most commonly in self-cultivated and large owner-tenant operated farms. These workers are mobile, tend to be used in the peak season, and usually negotiate wages according to the existing labour supply and demand situation. In both provinces this labour is recruited for the landowner through a labour agent or *jamadar*. These agents charge a finder's fee per labourer from the landlord. Mostly, agents charge the landlord in advance for the labour they provide. Some agents also charge landowners a specific share of their crop in lieu of labour.

The mode of payment is generally on a daily-wage or contract basis. Casual workers may take advances or *peshgis*, but this rarely leads to bonded labour, as the amount of the *peshgi* is low and is adjusted as soon as work is completed. The *peshgi* is taken from the labour agent rather than from the landlord. For example, sugarcane cutters in southern Punjab work in groups for about three months. They receive advances that are subsequently adjusted at the time of final payment. Recruitment is for a fixed duration, and casual workers are not bound for further work. This casual labour is used particularly for livestock feeding, application of fertilizer, sowing, and irrigation.

Permanent labour is found mainly on large farms—owner-operated as well as owner-tenant-operated. In Punjab, 51 per cent of owner-operated farms in the 100- to 150-acre size range reported the use of permanent labour in 2000. These labourers perform various farm activities and domestic work. They are paid either on a monthly or yearly basis

depending on the initial contract. Most permanent labourers are required
to stay at the employer's house and are provided with two meals a day.
Unlike sharecroppers, permanent agricultural labourers have no share in
produce but are given a monthly salary. They are known in central Punjab
as *seeris* and in southern Punjab as *rahaks*.

As in the case of sharecroppers, the initial advance or *peshgi* plays an
important role in recruiting this kind of labour. The difference between
the recruitment systems of sharecroppers and permanent labourers lies in
the fact that the traditional tie between the landowner and his prospective
worker has been weakened or severed. As such, the *peshgi* takes on an even
more important role, namely that of creating a new relationship of
dependence between employer and employee. With the patronage and
protection that characterized the sharecropper-landlord relation having
been replaced by a more market-oriented system of recruitment, workers
are left with a situation of open but less personalized 'contractual' bondage
(Breman 1999: 402).

In Punjab, all three kinds of permanent labourers were recruited on
the basis of the initial advance offered. Under the arrangements of the *seeri*
system, the *seeri* receives a loan from a landlord and in return works as a
servant. Landlords often offer large *peshgis* to unemployed workers in
return for their becoming their *seeris*. Some *seeris* were highly indebted to
their employers, to the level of 150,000 rupees (US$2,500). These
employees are then expected to work exclusively for their creditor. In
return they receive 40 *maunds* of grain each year[6]—equivalent to
approximately 1,000 rupees per month. But the quantity of the grain
reduces as the loan amount increases. *Peshgis* are also present in other
systems of permanent labour found in Punjab. Loans tend to be smaller
than is the case with *seeris*, however, and as a result the severity of bondage
is also less.

As a result of these systems, the most severely indebted agricultural
labourers in Punjab were not sharecroppers but permanent agricultural
workers who did not have a 'traditional sharecropping' relationship with
the landowners. Hence, it may be argued that in the transition to agrarian
capitalism, the bondage of farm labourers has certainly not changed into
a free labour system. 'Bondage of labour is not a static phenomenon.
While debt bondage has always existed, we may expect it to increase rather
than decline, given the increasingly desperate economic situation faced by
rural labour' (Patnaik 1983: 14). The labourers continue to be indebted
to the landowners and are therefore unable to hire out their labour power
to other employers, whether in or out of agriculture. Most of the time

landowners still continue to immobilize permanent workers through the payment of an advance.

RECRUITMENT SYSTEMS IN INDUSTRY

As more and more former tenants and small farmers are alienated from the land and from direct cultivation, they join the growing ranks of unemployed rural workers. Some are absorbed back into the modern sector of agriculture as permanent or casual farm labourers. Others search for work in possible alternatives such as brick kilns and mines or in the manufacturing and industrial sector. At the same time, the higher landowning castes with historically more wealth and resources have been able to move into industry and now continue to draw on their 'dependent' service castes to provide the workforce. Thus, even though the general patron-client relations that underpinned society through the influence of the caste system are more apparent in agriculture, their effects are also visible in the industrial sector, particularly where specific castes have dominated a particular occupation. For example, industries such as construction, tanneries, glass bangles, begging, and brick making are particularly susceptible to ethnic- and caste-based clustering. In these sectors, the patron-client bond is still important and operates against horizontal solidarity in the form of, for example, trade unions.

Apart from the influence of the caste system on industrial relations, the most significant aspect of recent industrialization in Pakistan has been its increasing decentralization and reliance on subcontracting. Initially the impulse for decentralization came in the 1970s, following the coming to power of Zulfiqar Ali Bhutto on the basis of an Islamic socialist manifesto. Bhutto's policies led to a tightening of labour laws, and stronger unions demanded increased representation, higher pay, and better working conditions in factories across Pakistan. As labour laws were not applicable to units employing fewer than 10 full-time workers, however, factory owners simply decentralized their operations, thereby pre-empting the possibility of further dissent. As a result, work was increasingly done at home. The result was a return to a distributed cottage industry relying not on a fixed labour force but on a casual and cheap pool of workers. This also allowed industrialists to avoid large capital outlays, overheads, and the provision of workers' benefits such as medical coverage, educational benefits, and old age pensions. A decentralized, often home-based labour force meant that trade unions were difficult to establish. Later, the trade union movement was also hampered in Pakistan because of the effects of decades of military rule, which has historically been hostile to any organized opposition to state policies.

The trend towards decentralization is not specific to Pakistan but has been a feature of industrialization in several developing countries that have increasingly seen a move toward dependence on a more flexible workforce (see Knorringa 1996, 1999; Kapadia 1999; Breman 1999; and De Neve 1999). Indeed, the path toward economic development for much of the developing world has seen the expansion of the formal sector outpaced by growth in the labour force. Hence, much of the work force has been absorbed by what Hart (1973) first termed the 'informal sector'. Although regular factory employees appear to be relatively well paid and enjoy a range of benefits and rights as guaranteed under the existing labour laws, the much larger number of workers who are not part of the 'formal' workforce are subcontracted and are not covered by labour laws.

To separate the economy into tight informal and formal segments would be inaccurate, however, as these two sectors are rarely independent of one another and in fact usually interact closely. For example, the tanneries and glass bangle manufacturing industries clearly have some processes completed in a formal factory environment, but a much larger number of tasks are dependent on a vast informal network. Other sectors such as mining and brick making may have an outwardly formal organization but again depend on a largely informal work force.

The most important factor for labour relations and critically for recruitment, the decentralization of industry, has led to the re-emergence of the subcontractor or labour agent—re-emergence because these middlemen also played a role in the early industrialization of Pakistan. Then, subcontractors acted to provide workers from rural areas to industry. But as the industrial sector became increasing formalized in the 1960s and rural-urban migration increased, the role of the subcontractor declined. In their new role, subcontractors have emerged less as leaders of gangs of workers and more as foremen recruiting workers and implementing orders from above and from factory owners to avoid the conditions set by labour laws such as the Factory Act.

Typically, recruitment now starts in the industrial sectors when owners provide a middleman with a sum of money to be offered as advance payment for workers. This, as in the agricultural sectors, is known as a *peshgi*. This middleman then begins the process of recruitment. By giving the lump sum to be used as an advance to the middleman, the employer effectively removes himself from any direct dealings with workers. Once the owner provides the labour agent with a sum of money for a particular 'job', the subcontractor becomes responsible for labour arrangements. For a commission, it is the subcontractor who arranges recruitment of a group of workers, supervises their work, mediates on disputed accounts, negotiates and distributes advances, and is responsible for the recovery of debts. This additional pressure on the labour agent means that he, in turn, is likely to give *peshgi*s only to those workers he trusts or is confident of 'controlling'. This normally means workers from his extended kinship network or from his own village.

But even though these middlemen are frequently from the same locality and caste and occasionally from the same extended kinship group as the labour they recruit, these ties do not appear to make the subcontractor favour his labourers past offering them employment and in moderating the worst cases of abuse and gross fiddling of accounts. In fact, in order to protect his interests, the subcontractor needs to be able to reduce the chances of non-accountability of labour, and ensuring compliance is easier when the subcontractor has some previous links with those he recruits. It is also common practice for the middleman to receive the workers' wages from employers and then disburse them at his own convenience. Thus, labour and recruitment arrangements are entirely handled by the subcontractor. The subcontractor may be a co-worker, but his primary role is to enforce the work contract, and he should not be expected to defend workers. In other cases, some subcontractors further contract orders out to smaller subcontractors so that another link is added to the chain and the process is further decentralized.

The tendency to rely on a particular caste or kin groups for recruitment often leads to a clustering of workers around ethnicity, caste, and kinship. This is even more pronounced in those sectors where industrial production is broken down into discrete tasks. Decentralization, then, occurs not only at the level of geographic locations but also at the level of tasks and skills. As a result, in those sectors where production consists of a series of related processes, a number of different subcontractors may be involved. For example, in brick making there are often different labour agents for each of the separate processes of moulding unbaked bricks, stacking unbaked bricks, baking, and finally removing finished bricks.

Moreover, not only are there multiple subcontractors, but there exist also different levels of autonomy among middlemen—from those with very little autonomy to those who are budding employers themselves. In cases where the subcontractors have established greater autonomy from their owners, they may actually have their own capital at their disposal. In such cases, instead of employers placing orders for items and then

providing the raw material and advance for wages to the contractor, it is
the contractor himself who is responsible for the entire production
process, including the provision of raw material. Once a product is
completed, he then sells it to exporters. These contractors provide their
own advances to their labour rather than acting as a conduit for the
advance. Where the subcontractor has less autonomy, it is the owners who
finance the production of goods through providing advances and raw
material, but labour arrangements are the responsibility of subcontractors.

All these subcontractors make use of an informal workforce—usually
working at home (carpet-weaving, glass bangles) or in small workshops
(carpet-weaving) and occasionally even in factories—but as the labour
agent's subcontracted labour force rather than as employees of the factory
(tanneries, mines, and brick kilns). Thus, the role of the subcontractor is
to act as the link between capital and workers. Factory owners have little
or nothing to do with the recruitment of labour, apart from the few
regular employees that make up the formal workforce. Labour and
recruitment arrangements are entirely handled by the labour agent rather
than the factory owner or manager. In all these arrangements, the wage
advance or *peshgi* plays a crucial role, acting as the seal in the recruitment
process and enticing workers to accept the conditions of employment
offered by the subcontractor along with the advance. As in agriculture,
the manipulation of this *peshgi* can become an instrument to ensure that
labour remains attached.

HIGH DEBTS, LOW WAGES, AND BONDED LABOUR

We now move to the question of how labour—once recruited—is kept in
place or immobilized. So this section progresses from recruitment to wage
systems, but the common mechanism remains that of the *peshgi* or the
advance on wages. Present in both recruitment and wage systems, it acts
as the initial hook for recruitment and also the key element of the wage
system. *Peshgi*s or advances, as already discussed, are an essential element
in the recruitment process. It was the *peshgi* that acted as the initial hook
in recruiting labour in all the sectors in the urban areas. In the case of
agriculture, the *peshgi* is used to 'strengthen' a pre-existing, often
hereditary, linkage; where these bonds have been severed, it creates a new
link. The *peshgi* initiates and completes the recruitment process. But along
with the initial advance, subsequent advances form the dominant element
in the wage system—and have important implications for those who
become increasingly indebted. Indeed, it is through the increasing

indebtedness that the *peshgi* becomes an instrument that ensures that once recruited, labour remains in place.

AGRICULTURE

In the sharecropping agricultural sector, there are, broadly speaking, two types of credit arrangements that are extended by landlords to tenants. First, many of the tenants borrow cash or grain from a landlord at the start of their contract. This lump sum amount may be considered the 'start-up cost' of a tenant and is unrelated to the agricultural process. Second, tenants receive agricultural inputs on credit from landlords throughout the crop cycle, against the notional expectation that the amount will be settled at the time of harvest. Debts outstanding at the end of the crop cycle are added by the landlord to the tenant's account. This amount is maintained on the books and would have to be repaid in full if the tenant stopped working for the landlord and sought tenure with a different landlord. The new landlord would then clear the tenant's debt with the old landlord and open a credit account of his own.

In principle, the credit extended by landlords to tenants is supposed to be interest free. In effect, however, landlords charge interest on credit by overvaluing inputs and undervaluing outputs (Gazdar, Khan, and Khan 2002: 35). Moreover, nearly all landowners, in turn, borrow from trader-moneylenders. Thus the *seth* (or moneylender) maintains credit transactions with the landowner, and the landowner, in turn, maintains credit transactions with tenants. Any interest that is charged on the loan to the landowner is usually passed on to the loan given by the landowner to his tenant. Thus, even in those areas where sharecropper families work on a 'half-share' tenancy basis, they rarely receive half-shares from the production owing to the deduction of input costs and debts. In some cases, landlords were able to recover the entire harvest as repayment of the sharecroppers' share of the input costs or as repayment of earlier loans. The end result is that, at the end of the season, the share of the agricultural produce taken by the landlord invariably exceeds the value of the credit he has provided.

For example, in the province of Sindh, the persistent drought, water shortages, and crop failure have meant, as Gazdar, Khan, and Khan (2002) report, that on average, a tenant's credit built up to around 4,000 rupees per acre for just one crop. This was the value of the tenant's share of inputs such as plowing costs, seed fertilizer, and pesticides. The tenant's share of the cost of running the tube well was also added to the total credit extended by the landlord. Once the tenant's share had been accounted for, the final crop shares in the *Rabi* 2000–2001 wheat crop bore little resemblance to the notional 50–50 division of the crop. The average size of the crop per tenant was 95 *maunds*, and the average amount handed over to the landlord by each tenant was 82 *maunds* (i.e., more than 85 per cent). Only around 10 per cent of *haris* managed to retain half the crop or more. A large number of tenants reported that they were left with no grain from the harvest at all. These tenants immediately re-entered a credit arrangement in which they received a lump sum advance (Gazdar, Khan, and Khan 2002).

NON-AGRICULTURAL SECTORS

In a sector related to agriculture, that of domestic work, the wage and recruitment system is similar. Recruitment follows traditional caste divisions, with the majority of domestic workers coming from castes that have historically been associated with this line of work. For example, the Muslim Sheikhs who represent those groups that were part of the Hindu untouchable castes but converted to Islam are still associated with tasks that they undertook as part of their traditional caste obligations, and these include domestic work.

In rural and town settings, a dominant feature of labour arrangements for domestic service is the use of in-kind payment, usually by way of wheat, as a means of compensation. In some villages, there is a tradition of certain families working for the Makhdoom (a landlord caste). Servants who work for them receive 40 *maunds* of wheat for a year's work. Some family members may also earn an additional 200 rupees and a sack of wheat each for additional work done around the house. This extra income is often used to meet loan repayments. A modified version of in-kind payment is also in evidence in the cities. Domestic servants who work for landlords in their urban homes receive wheat in their villages by way of payment. Men and women, domestic servants with other, nonlanded employers, also say they receive occasional food and clothing. This is not in lieu of their salaries, however, but in addition to their monthly remuneration.

In non-agricultural sectors, advances are offered at the start of the 'contract' and may be offered subsequently as well. These *peshgis* are taken against the understanding that the worker-borrower will clear his or her account by deducting the advance from the remuneration for his or her labour. Generally, the larger the advance, the more money is deducted from wages. Except for the carpet-weaving sector, there was little evidence of interest being charged on advances. And even in the carpet sector, interest was only charged on large loans. Wages are typically given on a weekly basis.

Workers who were indebted were rarely penalized through a lower wage rate. They may receive lower wages, but that is the result of a fair amount being cut for debt repayment. As such, the wage systems do not appear to have a hidden profitability. It could be argued, however, that the provision of *peshgi* does mean that overall wages are kept low, thereby increasing the employer's profits. Employers as patrons offer workers the 'service' of a loan but in return will demand 'compensation' through the provision of lower wages across the sector. But to understand fully how the *peshgi* can be manipulated to ensure that labour remains bonded, it is important to examine, briefly, why *peshgi*s are taken and what the implications are of taking them.

REASONS FOR RECOURSE TO *PESHGIS*

*Peshgi*s are taken for a number of reasons; the most basic one is the inability of the worker to support his needs through returns in the sector, and it is this chronic and growing debt that the worker incurs while working that is largely responsible for debt bondage. In other words, wages are often below subsistence level, and the ensuing shortfall that the family faces is met by recourse to loans. With a lack of other forms of collateral, the only recourse is to take *peshgi*s and effectively replace collateral with labour (Ray 1998). Furthermore, work in some sectors, namely glass bangle manufacturing, mining, brick making, fisheries, and agriculture, is characterized by a seasonal demand for labour. In the slack season the worker's income dries up, particularly in areas where options for alternative work are severely limited. For example, our research found that fishermen and agricultural workers found it extremely difficult to find any alternative work off-season. For some, *peshgi*s may instigate migration over large distances for employment in other provinces, as in the case of agricultural workers in certain parts of the Khyber Pakhtunkhwa province who took up mining in Sindh, Balochistan, and Punjab in between cropping seasons at home.

A further reason for taking *peshgi*s and subsequent loans was to try to cover expenditure 'spikes' that invariably occur. Even those families that are able to subsist on the meagre income of their individual members cannot cope with the costs related to a sudden illness or death. It is important to remember that the majority of employment in the sectors where our studies were undertaken takes place in the unorganized sector of the economy where there are no unemployment benefits, no health allowances, and no social benefits. In the absence of this social security and lack of savings for the segment involved, *peshgis* are often the only way to make ends meet at times of high expenditure. Life events such as weddings and funerals similarly demand considerable expenditure. The failure to arrange an 'appropriate' wedding leads to an immediate loss of face (*izzat*) for the family in the larger community. It may also result in an unsuitable match for daughters. The expenditure associated with weddings can easily exceed the annual earnings of a family. Some observers have reported this spending to be on average more than 80 per cent of the annual income.

THE DEGREE OF INDEBTEDNESS AND EFFECTIVE BONDAGE

The different reasons for taking *peshgis* influence the amount of the advance taken. Small subsistence loans, usually less than 1,000 rupees (US$15), are taken by workers in all sectors. These small loans are taken and returned on a fairly regular basis, although sometimes these small loans do accumulate to larger debts. Those taking (and returning) small loans face far fewer restrictions, however, than those accepting larger loans. Therefore, if we consider all those who at some point in their working lives have taken loans to be bonded labourers, then the incidence of bondage expands to cover almost all labour. But generally small loans do not appear to have the serious implications associated with long-term indebtedness.

Far more problematic are the large *peshgis* that are characteristic of loans taken for marriages or sudden illnesses. Large advances tend to be less common than the smaller loans but were found in all the surveyed sectors. It was these large *peshgis* that typically led to substantive bondage—a condition leading to long-term indebtedness with no real option for debt redemption except to supply labour to the same employer or to transfer the debt to another employer but only at the discretion of the owner. It is here that the *peshgi* becomes an economic instrument of coercion that increases the leverage that the employer has over the indebted worker. In contrast, *peshgi* loses its utility to the creditor when it is returned on a regular basis, as is more common with smaller loans. Repayment decreases the leverage that a creditor has over labour.

Workers take advances ranging from a few hundred rupees to several thousand rupees from their employers. Taking *peshgis* immediately imposes certain conditions on the worker, however, beyond the obligation to return the original amount. At the most basic level, once *peshgi* is taken the worker cannot move from the current employer without repaying the advance in full. This means that better opportunities are forfeited unless another advance is taken from an alternate creditor to pay off the original loan. Again, those with smaller loans will find it far easier either to pay back and move onto better paid employment or to have their (small) loan refinanced by another employer.

But if bondage is to be effective along with being substantive (long-term indebtedness), then the obligation of labour should be accompanied by the threat of non-economic coercion, that is, it should be seen as enforceable. Non-economic coercion comes in the form of surveillance, physical confinement of labour, and the threat of violence as well as the actual use of violence. These methods ensure the effectiveness of bondage. They also show that accepting an advance on wages opens up the possibility of severe implications, including being subjected to physical and verbal abuse, the threat of or actual use of violence, the provision of wages below the market level, and the inability to exercise freedom of employment.

In agriculture these implications appear to be more extreme than those evidenced in other sectors. They also impinge on almost every aspect of the indebted individual or family's life as well as denying the freedom to control the produce of one's labour. The decision on the crops to be sown is made by the landlord, who also handles the sale of the crop and afterwards 'settles accounts' with the tenant. Tenants are usually oblivious of production costs and output prices, and the decision on how much is received as a share is largely at the owner's discretion. The severity of bondage varies, usually according to the size of the loan (compared to the earning power of the worker) as well as through regional variations. In Sindh, a household survey[7] specifically asked people whether they could discontinue working for the *zamindar* (landlord) while their debt remained unreturned: in Umerkot and Mirpurkhas, 79 and 76 per cent of sharecroppers (*haris*) respectively stated that they could not discontinue work without repayment, whereas only 10 per cent in Badin reported the same.

In our fieldwork, there was also clear evidence of substantive and effective bondage in the brick making, mining, carpet-weaving, agricultural, and domestic work sectors. For mining and brick making, the owners could insist that some members of an indebted family stay behind as 'surety' when others took leave. In more extreme cases guards were hired in order to keep watch over or even lock up 'suspect' labour. In one case, the researcher came across a worker who had been kept in chains to prevent his escape. Violence, though rare, was reported in the agriculture, mining, and domestic work sectors.

The increasing burden of *peshgi*s coupled with low, piecemeal wages also encourages the inclusion of children and women in the production process. Although child labour is common in all the surveyed sectors, the situation appears most acute in those industries where children are often separated from their families as a result of their being pledged. This occurs in domestic work where a pledged child can be sent to another employer's home or in carpet-weaving where, in some cases reported in the rapid assessment, children work and live in carpet workshops. The fact that children are paid considerably less than adults simply means that despite the pledging of their labour these unfortunate families are unlikely to ever emerge from their indebtedness. Mention should also be made of the mining sector, where, in order to lessen the burden of debt, parents resort to taking their young sons (usually between 12 and 15) with them to work in the mines.

THE NEVER-ENDING DEBT

The initial *peshgi* as a mode of recruitment can be an entrance into what may become a cycle of increasing indebtedness. How that advance and initial debt subsequently grow to unmanageable proportions is linked to the wage system in place. In fact, the most fundamental factor as to why the advance can lead to a continuous cycle of debt is the low level of wages. *Peshgi*s on their own reveal only half the story. It is the combination of *peshgi* and low wages that together makes for long-term, substantive bondage.

In industry, payment is often made on a piece-rate basis. The piece-rate system is particularly advantageous for the employer when it is used in conjunction with *peshgi* or advances. If advances are combined with wages not based on a piece rate, workers have less incentive to ensure that their output remains high, particularly if they are unsupervised (as is likely in cottage industries and particularly in home-based production). This can lead to a slowdown in worker output once an advance is obtained. If workers are paid on a piece-rate basis, however, the ability to repay a *peshgi* is linked to the worker's output and thereby the production output. Therefore, incentives for workers to maintain a high output are ensured.

In the agricultural and mining sectors, there is also the problem of wages not being paid on time. Interviewed labourers stated that it was common practice for wages to be paid only when material or agricultural produce is sold. This is deeply connected with the continued recourse to advances, as the delay in distributing wages means that workers are forced to meet daily expenses through asking for more *peshgis* from the labour agents. This additional amount is added to their previous balance. In this way even small loans can surreptitiously build up to unmanageable levels.

It must also be remembered that an advance is always part of an unwritten agreement between two 'unequal' partners. One party to the contract is often illiterate and has little or no bargaining power and only limited recourse to official or informal enforcement mechanisms. The worker also has little say in maintaining accounts. It is almost without exception the case that the employer or subcontractor maintains the accounts of workers and makes adjustments according to the work performed. It was commonly agreed, however, that account registers did not maintain correct entries. In some cases workers also maintain their own accounts, but these often did not tally with the amounts supposedly owed to employers. Thus, it was not uncommon for workers to complain that their original *peshgi* amount had been inflated by the subcontractor or owner but that due to their illiteracy and powerlessness they could not challenge this. In the event of any disputes, the threat of violence or the use of the police was a strong deterrent for the workers. For example, in both Punjab and Sindh, it was a common complaint by tenants that landlords did not maintain accounts fairly, and payments to tenants were frequently delayed. This simply leads to an increase in the debt of the tenants.

The unequal nature of the relationship means that the negotiating power of the labourer is minimal. In some cases, particularly noted in the construction sector in Balochistan, workers take *peshgis* largely because they are aware of the fact that at the end of a job they may well not be able to enforce the payment of their remaining wages from an existing employer who in all likelihood is also an influential tribal chief and landowner. It is extremely difficult for the weaker partners in a bonded labour relationship to have their part of the deal enforced.

CONCLUSION

Indebtedness is widespread in rural Pakistan: the 1990 Census of Agriculture showed 2.2 million rural households being indebted, and the 1985 Rural Credit Survey set the figure at 2.9 million households. The great majority of rural credit is non-institutional, that is, the creditor is a landlord, commission agent, moneylender, or relative or friend. Rural indebtedness varies by region and farm size or tenure. The 1985 Rural Credit Survey, for example, showed that 68 per cent of tenant farmers in Sindh were indebted (as compared to 45–50 per cent of tenant farmers in other provinces). More detailed case studies show an even higher proportion of indebtedness among tenant farmers in parts of the country, with many casual labourers also reported indebted to their employers. There is less information on the indebtedness of workers in urban areas.

The exact scale of bonded labour in Pakistan remains unknown, however. Indeed, it is the subject of enormous debate and polarized views, from outright denial of the existence of bonded labour in various sectors to estimates in the range of 6.8 million people in families of debt-bonded sharecroppers alone (Ercelawn and Nauman 2001). Reporting on bonded labour has been prone to 'extremity'. Some of this is justifiable, as there have been well-documented cases that represent the worst examples of abuses of human rights. But the tendency to favour extremity at the expense of understanding has promoted a partial understanding of bonded labour, wherein its extreme forms, which are often highlighted in some journalistic and activist reports, have come to colour a range of experiences with the same brush. This overwhelmingly negative stereotype may well be part of the story, but it is not the entire story. Moreover, although activists have highlighted shocking incidents, there has been an equally strong denial of these reports by opposed lobbies—resulting in the widely differing accounts of bonded labour in Pakistan.

The present chapter is based on empirically grounded studies that produced substantial qualitative data on the nature and significance of bonded labour in selected sectors of the economy. The information gathered provided an in-depth perspective that had previously been lacking from studies on bonded labour in Pakistan and as such has produced a new understanding of many of the more intricate issues involved in the study of bonded labour. Wage advances (or *peshgi*) are a key component in both the agricultural and industrial recruitment systems. Larger *peshgis* have more serious implications than smaller advances. These implications include lower wages, increasing indebtedness, and the greater possibility of noneconomic coercion and physical abuse. Ultimately, the advance can lead to an increasing cycle of indebtedness and the immobilization of the worker. Whilst it is essential to obtain a better understanding of the magnitude of bonded labour in various provinces of Pakistan, the insights from this qualitative study must form part of any future policy interventions.

REFERENCES

Alavi, H. (1988), 'Introduction to Sociology of the Developing Societies'. In Teodor Shanin (ed) 'Peasant and Peasant Societies'. Penguin.

Agrodev/Asian Development Bank (2000), Sindh Rural Development Project – Final Draft – Social Assessment Report.

Arif, G. M. (2004), Bonded Labour in Agriculture: A Rapid Assessment in Punjab and North West Frontier Province, Pakistan. Islamabad: The International Labour Organization.

Breman, J. (1999), 'The Study of Industrial Labour in Post-Colonial India – The Formal Sector: An Introductory Review'. In Jonathan P. Parry, Jan Breman and Karin Kapadia (eds) The Worlds of Indian Industrial Labour. New Delhi: Sage Publications.

Breman, J. & Lieten, K. (2002), 'A Pro-Poor Development Project in Rural Pakistan: An Academic Analysis and a Non-Intervention', Journal of Agrarian Change (July 2002).

De Neve, G. (1999), 'Asking for and giving baki: Neo bondage or the interplay of bondage and resistance in the Tamilnadu power-loom industry'. In Jonathan P. Parry, Jan Breman and Karin Kapadia (eds) The Worlds of Indian Industrial Labour. New Delhi: Sage Publications.

Ercelawn, A. & M. Nauman (2001), Bonded Labour in Pakistan. Geneva: International Labour Organization.

Gazdar, H., Khan, A., Khan T. (2002), Land Tenure, Rural livelihoods and Institutional Innovation.

Gazdar, H. (1999), Review of Pakistan Poverty Data. Monograph Series #9. Islamabad: Sustainable Development Policy Institute.

Hart, K. (1973), 'Informal income opportunities and urban employment in Ghana', Journal of Modern African Studies. (Reprinted in several readers).

Hussein, M., Saleemi, A. R., Malik, S., & Hussain, S. (2004), 'Bonded Labour in Agriculture: a Rapid Assessment in Sindh and Balochistan, Pakistan'. Islamabad: International Labour Organization.

Knorringa, P. (1996), Economics of Collaboration: Indian Shoemakers between Market and Hierarchy. New Delhi: Sage Publications.

Knorringa, P. (1999), 'Artisan labour in the Agra footwear industry: Continued informality and changing threats'. In Jonathan P. Parry, Jan Breman and Karin Kapadia (eds) The Worlds of Indian Industrial Labour. New Delhi: Sage Publications.

Patnaik, U. (1983), 'On the Evolution of the Class of Agricultural Labourers in India', Social Scientist, Vol. 11, No. 7 (July 1983).

Ray, Debraj (1998), Development Economics. Princeton University Press.

NOTES

1. The surveys have been conducted by the Federal Bureau of Statistics, with the support of the ILO's Social Finance Programme.
2. In fact the survey on brick kilns was confined to three provinces and was not undertaken in Balochistan. This was because the onset of the rainy season meant that kilns in Balochistan shut down for the duration of the survey.
3. Tanneries are concentrated in the district of Kasur (Punjab) and in Karachi (Sindh). Glass bangles are manufactured in Hyderabad (Sindh).
4. The incidence of debt bondage in agriculture in the provinces of the KPK and Balochistan was seen to be negligible and existed only in isolated cases. As a result, the discussion in this chapter is restricted to the provinces of Sindh and Punjab.
5. The First Rent Act of 1859 and the Tenancy Act of 1885 in East Bengal marked the beginning of this policy of protection in favour of the tenants. Some rights were conferred on tenants, and they were secured against arbitrary eviction. This was followed by a series of acts in India beginning in the 1920s aimed at securing the rights of tenants (Hussein et al. 2004).
6. 1 *maund* = 37.32 kilograms.
7. This was the Sindh Rural Development Project, Social Assessment Report, of the Asian Development Bank in March 2000.

CHAPTER 5

The Political Economy of Bonded Labour in the Pakistani Punjab

NICOLAS MARTIN

This article examines economic and social relations in order to understand political assertion and mobilization among rural bonded labourers in the Pakistan Punjab. Bonded labour, characterized by economic and extra-economic forms of compulsion together with vertical ties of patronage, remains widespread in the region. I propose that the perpetuation of these relations is largely explained by the capture of state institutions by a traditional landlord elite and its monopoly over the means of coercion coupled with a highly seasonal demand for labour. I examine how employment and indebtedness combine to restrict workers' physical and economic mobility. I argue that labourers have not been able to unite politically as a class and challenge their employers because years of authoritarian rule in Pakistan have entrenched a highly factional style of politics dominated by the landed elites. My article contributes to the literature on agrarian change, class formation and the state in South Asia.

I

INTRODUCTION

In its World Labour Report of 1993, the International Labour Organization (ILO) described the problem of bonded labour in Pakistan as among the worst in the world (ILO 1993). According to a 1994 estimate by the Human Rights Commission of Pakistan (HRCP), around twenty million people worked as bonded labourers in agriculture, brick kilns, fisheries, construction and domestic service (HRCP 1995: 120). Reports suggest that bonded labour is most widespread in agriculture and most coercive in areas of southern Punjab and interior

Sindh, where land distribution is particularly unequal. Landlords in these areas are known to have maintained private jails where labourers were kept locked up and guarded by armed men at night, and sent to labour in the fields by day. Female labourers were frequently assaulted by landlords and their strongmen as well as by the police who were complicit in the maintenance of these jails. In 1991, in a widely publicized case, the army raided the private jail of a major landlord in Sindh and released 295 labourers.[1]

In the central Punjab district of Sargodha, where I carried out my research, there were no private jails and I did not hear of anyone operating any in the recent past. Nevertheless debt-bondage, whereby labourers could spend an entire lifetime working under abusive conditions in order to repay a landlord's loan, was widespread. Furthermore, my data largely confirm reports that the practice was often characterized by the threat and the use of physical and other forms of coercion by landlords. Although debt-bondage was formally banned under Pakistani law, it operated with the tacit as well as active cooperation of the police and other authorities. Since the practice largely took place outside formal state law and was based on informal agreements between employers and labourers, this article deals with the issue from a sociological rather than a legal perspective. In addition to exploring the element of coercion involved in debt-bondage, an aspect generally emphasized by the ILO and human rights groups, I stress that debt-bondage also relies on an element of patronage. However, contrary to what is argued in some of the literature on the topic, I show that patronage does not usually mitigate the exploitative aspects of debt-bondage, even though it allows for acts of benevolence by landlords. In this article, I show that the landlords' role as patrons in a village in the central Punjab stemmed from their monopoly over local state institutions, economic resources and the means of physical coercion. This monopoly worked to make the rest of the village population dependent upon landlords for their basic welfare and security as well as their livelihoods. Furthermore, landlords' exclusive control over resources enabled them to extend assistance strategically, deploying it in the idiom of generosity and patronage in order to obtain votes and labour and, in the process, further strengthen their stranglehold over villagers. Thus, I argue that, despite the paternalistic ideology of generous care and protection invoked by the landlords, the extension of patronage to labourers was frequently used as a means to secure cheap and permanent labour. Having said this I do not claim that the particularly harsh situation described in this article was necessarily representative of the entire Punjab or even of the entire central Punjab. There were villages in the central Punjab where both power and land were somewhat more equally distributed than in the village of study. This was, for example, the case in some canal colony settlements (*chaks*) of the Sargodha district, as well as in much of the more industrial northern Punjab where landholdings and political power were more fragmented. The evidence presented in this article suggests similarities with southern and western Punjab where political power and landownership were more concentrated.[2]

The widespread existence of debt-bondage in certain areas of the Pakistani Punjab where labour relations are characterized by economic and *extra-economic* forms of compulsion together with vertical ties of patronage raises a question which is conceptual as well as political. In this context, is it meaningful to talk about the emergence of a proletarian class, a social group characterized by two kinds of freedom—freedom from the ownership of private property and freedom to sell its labour power in exchange for wages? In the literature on debt-bondage, the question of class formation assumes political significance because, by virtue of being free from personalized ties of dependence, proletarians are supposed to be able to develop horizontal ties of allegiance and unite in order to overthrow their oppressors.

In this article, I show that while the decline of sharecropping consequent upon the introduction of citrus orchards in the 1970s and the demise of traditional village occupations due to the availability of industrially manufactured goods have brought about partial economic proletarianization, attempts at political resistance by labourers remain isolated and fragmented.[3] Labourers in Pakistani Punjab are still largely the de facto political subjects of landlords who frequently occupy high ranking government positions and have personal ties of allegiance reaching up to the highest levels of the state. This means that labourers often cannot freely dispose of their own labour power and are in a weak position to combat their own oppression. I therefore argue that the process of proletarianization is complicated by political factors such that class formation is not the inevitable outcome of changes in economic relations. I conclude by arguing that class formation in the Pakistani Punjab has largely failed to take place and political mobilization retains a vertical factional character which cuts across both caste and class. The result is that labourers remain the political subjects of their local landlords and that vertical patron–client ties persist at the expense of horizontal ties of class.

Before analysing debt-bondage in rural Pakistani Punjab, it would be useful to briefly examine the political situation of rural labourers in India. A comparison of the labour situations in rural India and rural Pakistan sheds light on the larger issues of unfree labour and worker assertiveness and their relation to broader political and state processes. I take the literature from South Asia, and India in particular, as my main reference point given that the rural social structure of Pakistani Punjab shares many of the characteristic features of the fertile plains of north India. Both areas are marked by high population densities, sharp inequalities in wealth and landownership and stark inequalities in status associated with caste. I argue that, in spite of these broad similarities, the present-day labour situations in India and Pakistan differ significantly and that the explanation for these differences lies in the nature of the respective political processes that have characterized the two countries.

In India, the deepening of competitive electoral politics and reservations for Other Backward Classes (OBCs) as well as for Scheduled Castes (SCs) have posed a serious challenge to traditional structures of authority and have curtailed the power of traditional landed elites to enforce debt-bondage and to coerce their labourers. Although as Tom Brass' work (1999) shows, the eradication of bonded labour may not have been evenly achieved throughout India and that it persists in parts of north India, such as pockets of Haryana, evidence from the neighbouring state of Uttar Pradesh suggests that competitive electoral politics have curtailed the power of landed elites to enforce debt-bondage. Thus, for example, Jeffrey and Lerche (2000) show how, in Uttar Pradesh, the rise to power of the Dalit political leader Mayawati in 1995 and 1997 resulted in greater assertiveness on the part of the SC labourers. The authors show that Mayawati's ascendance forced the landed middle and upper castes to stop some of the more abusive and exploitative practices towards SC labourers. Thus, in one instance, a Chamar woman from Mayawati's Bahujan Samaj Party managed to indict some Thakurs for paying agricultural labourers below the stipulated minimum wage. Similarly, the molestation of the SC women by the Jat landlords came to an end in certain villages. Although it may be overhasty to assume that these developments are evenly distributed throughout Uttar Pradesh, they are nevertheless significant and contrast sharply with the situation in the Pakistani Punjab where the stranglehold of the traditional landed elite remains largely unchallenged. Finally, even in Bihar, India's 'lawless' and caste ridden state, the dominance of the upper caste Brahmins and Rajputs has been challenged by the rise to power of the OBCs and leaders such as Laloo Prasad Yadav. Also, as Corbridge et al. show, years of Naxalite agitation in Bhojpur district, Bihar, meant that SC groups were actively pressing for their rights and had reached an 'uneasy truce over agricultural pay and conditions' (2005: 105). Moreover, they claim that slights to the honour of the SCs could quickly escalate into public confrontations. Thus, although agricultural labourers from the SCs were still afflicted by chronic poverty and were largely excluded from governance, they were pressing for rights and empowerment in a way that their Pakistani counterparts were not.

II

LANDLORDS AND SERVANTS: ECONOMIC AND POLITICAL POWER IN BEK SAGRANA

As was generally the case throughout the rest of the Pakistani Punjab, the principal social distinction among people living in the village of Bek Sagrana and its surrounding area was the one between the *zamindars* (landowners) and the landless menial and artisan castes referred to as *kammis*.[4] Among the *zamindars* in the area of Bek Sagrana, the Gondal *biradari* (patrilineal clan) of Jats was dominant in terms of status, political influence and wealth, the last owned principally in the form of land dedicated to citrus orchards. They made up fourteen out of the 120 households in the village and shared a common apical ancestor four generations back. They owned most of the land surrounding the village.[5] Their status was reflected in the terms of address and reference: they were usually referred to with the honorific Chowdri (chieftain), but could also be called Mian Ji or Sufi Sahib if they had a reputation for piety and saintliness. One very wealthy Gondal landlord in the village even established himself as a *pir* (saint). It was in fact not uncommon for major *zamindars* in the Punjab to be hereditary *pirs*, thereby giving them particularly high social status.

On the other hand, the *kammis*, who constituted the majority of the population in the area of Bek Sagrana, largely owned no land and had low social status.[6] The *kammis* included carpenters (Tarkhan), potters (Kumhar), blacksmiths (Lohar), cobblers (Mochi), breadmakers (Machi), weavers (Julaha), barbers (Nai/Hajaam), bards (Mirasi) and sweepers (Musalli) among others. Members of these castes (*zat/qaum*)[7] traditionally carried out a variety of tasks for several village patrons who paid them in kind, giving grain from the yearly wheat harvest. Among them the

Musallis were the poorest and had the lowest status and were also generally the ones who, along with the bards (Mirasi), were historically the most closely associated with the Gondal Chowdris as domestic and farm servants. Part of the reason for this lay in the fact that unlike some other *kammis* who were skilled artisans, the Musallis were associated with performing low-skilled manual labour. Among other things, these included agricultural labour, construction, cleaning and domestic service for the landlords. They were traditionally assigned the tasks of covering the chaff and the straw collected during the wheat harvest with mud, preparing the mud to place on the roofs of traditional dwellings and making the rope that others then wove onto *charpais* (wood-framed string beds).[8] Like other *kammis*, they also fulfilled specific roles during life cycle ceremonies such as weddings and funerals during which they were in charge of the cooking fires as well as of preparing the hookahs.

Another reason for the particularly low status of the Musallis was related to the fact that prior to their conversion to Islam, they had belonged to a Hindu sweeper caste known as *Chuhras*; both Hindus and Muslims refused to eat with the *Chuhras* because they removed night soil and ate the flesh of impure animals such as the pig (*khanzir*). Reports suggest that many of them converted to Islam and Christianity in the 18th and 19th centuries in order to raise their social status. In modern-day Pakistan, those who had converted to Christianity (of which there were none in Bek Sagrana), retained their low status and, in addition, faced various discriminatory laws and social attitudes. Those who converted to Islam fared only marginally better and Chowdris and other *kammis* frequently commented that they were largely nominal converts to Islam (*sirf naam ke Mussulman*). They were considered to be dirty and thieving and were morally condemned for their frequent association with bootlegging.

In contemporary Pakistani Punjab, however, the differences in status between Musallis and other *kammis* were not always reflected in the occupations that they pursued. The availability of competitive, industrially-manufactured goods meant that many traditional artisanal occupations had become obsolete. Moreover, the advent of agricultural mechanization meant that locally-produced farm implements had largely been replaced by machinery. As a result, those artisans who had been unable to turn their traditional occupations into successful businesses were increasingly resorting to selling their labour in order to survive.[9] Many former artisans thus became wage labourers as well as bonded labourers. Similarly, many former tenants from landowning (*zamindar*) *biradaris* were displaced by mechanization and by the introduction of citrus orchards in the 1970s and were forced to turn to wage labour and even debt-bondage. Therefore, although Musallis continued being the people most commonly associated with wage labour and debt-bondage, they were no longer the only ones.

The picture at the other end of the social spectrum stood in sharp contrast to the gradual pauperization of the *kammis*. Although the Gondals of Bek Sagrana already had influence as village headmen during British colonial times, their local influence and wealth increased dramatically after members of the lineage first entered provincial-level politics during the time of the populist leader Zulfiqar Ali Bhutto. Subsequently, members of the Bek Sagrana Gondal lineage became members of provincial assemblies on several occasions and developed close personal ties with national leaders such as Benazir Bhutto and Nawaz Sharif. They were widely known to have used their increased political influence to enrich themselves and to further expand their power base. Several Gondals were also able to get involved in lucrative criminal activities in the 1980s when cheap weapons and heroin flooded Pakistan as a result of the Afghan Jihad supported by the military government of General Zia ul-Haq. Competition over political and economic resources coincided with the influx of cheap weapons from the tribal areas of the North West Frontier Province, leading to increasingly violent conflict. As a result, influential Gondal Chowdris came to require well-armed retainers that they often recruited from among the village *kammis*. Some recruits came from the ranks of wanted criminals who were offered political patronage and protection from the police and courts in exchange for their services. Armed retainers were used to fight, harass, and intimidate opponents, unruly villagers, and voters during election times. Their privileged relationship with the Chowdris meant that some of these armed men harassed villagers for their own ends, for instance snatching chickens and goats from them.

Besides privatized control over the means of coercion through the use of private militias, the landowning Gondal Chowdris buttressed their economic power with political power by also controlling access to various state institutions. Their entry into provincial politics had allowed many Chowdris to secure an upwardly mobile path away from agriculture. The generation now between twenty and forty was more educated than its parents. Many members of this cohort had been brought up in cities such as Sargodha or Lahore and were fluent English speakers. Several had become lawyers, politicians and civil servants while others joined the police and the armed forces. As a result, the Gondals were becoming increasingly established within the highly personalized institutions of the Pakistani state thereby further enhancing their capacity to act as political patrons for the local population. Members of the *kammi* castes, on the other hand, were largely excluded from politics and the highest rank that they were likely to achieve within state institutions was as school or hospital guards (*chowkidars*). Furthermore, the only way they could obtain such positions was through the patronage and goodwill of a Chowdri.

Villagers relied almost exclusively on personal contacts with Gondal patrons for any matter involving state institutions such as the police, courts, hospitals, and even schools. If, for example, a person needed to file a complaint with the police in the form of a First Information Report (FIR), they needed to go through a Chowdri. The Chowdris could use their political contacts to influence the police or they could mobilize their kinship and friendship connections within the police force itself. It was also widely known that various Chowdris had more business-like connections with the police by virtue of their varied criminal activities that included buffalo theft, heroin trafficking and the smuggling of stolen cars, the proceeds of which had to be shared with the police.[10] *Kammis* and poor *zamindars* were unlikely to have such connections and for them to personally approach the police was, at best, futile and, at worst, costly and dangerous. The Punjabi police was, and remains, notorious for torture and extra-judicial killings.[11] Villagers also feared that the police would implicate them in fabricated cases in order to extract money from them.[12] Those who did muster the courage to approach the police to file a complaint could end up spending a month's wages in bribes and expenses for filing the FIR.[13] Additionally, it was taken for granted that it was impossible to win a court case without the support of an influential Chowdri with contacts in the judiciary. The patronage of Chowdris was also necessary for more mundane issues such as obtaining an identity card, a school certificate or in order to obtain treatment in a public hospital.

Since the *kammis* were entirely dependent on the Chowdris for access to state institutions, for the villagers, the Chowdris were the state for all practical purposes. Most villagers were keenly aware of the need to retain the favour of the Chowdris for their present and future needs. Thus, most villagers, and *kammis* in particular, paid at least lip service to the public norms of deference and obsequiousness required when dealing with the Chowdris.

Similarly, the Chowdris' privileged access to the state also meant that they could get away with a wide range of exploitative and coercive practices towards servants and *kammis*. *Kammis* and servants were often subjected to humiliating verbal and physical abuse. It was widely known that some of the more disreputable members of the Gondal caste sexually abused female servants, most commonly the low-caste Musalli women, and would boast about their sexual exploits. Although the more devout Gondal Chowdris were likely to be less abusive, they could still arbitrarily refrain from paying their daily wage labourers (*dihari*) or their attached servants (*naukar*). It was also common for the Chowdris to make random *kammis*, who happened to cross their path, and who were not their paid servants, perform all sorts of odd jobs and errands free of charge. Refusal would invite the anger of the Chowdri. Rather than provoke their anger and be subjected to various forms of humiliation, the *kammis* tried their best to avoid places where Chowdris might be sitting in assembly unless they needed something from them.

Chowdris had the power to forcefully evict labourers or servants from their houses, to confiscate livestock, or impose fines on the basis of perceived or real offences. Although Zulfiqar Ali Bhutto's reforms in the 1970s had granted villagers the right to legal ownership over their homesteads, landlords around the Punjab continued to arbitrarily evict house tenants.[14] In the village of Bek Lurka, for example, one Gondal Chowdri evicted the family of a servant who was from a landless *zamindar* family, and whose parents had once been agricultural tenants, after the servant decided to take up more profitable employment as a driver in the town of Sargodha. While the servant was away in Sargodha, the Chowdri cut off the servant's family's electricity supply and forced the family members to vacate the house. The family was allowed to return only after the servant returned to work for the Chowdri. Subsequently, the same servant again faced the threat of eviction for seeking patronage from the factional rival of his master in a case involving the police. The relation between Chowdris and their house tenants, agricultural tenants and servants contained a significant political element, and the tenants, and servants were expected to be loyal to their master's faction and to vote for the candidate supported by their master during elections.[15] Finally, house tenants were keenly aware that they faced the threat of eviction for not performing tasks free of charge for their masters. Thus, for example, a family of Tarkhans told me that they had to do electrical work worth Rs. 5,000 free of charge for their Chowdri who was organising an *urs* to commemorate the death of his *pir*.[16] They told me that if they had not done it he would probably have evicted them from their house.

Many Chowdris also imposed fines upon village *kammis* for both real and perceived offences. One elderly Gondal Chowdri was known to frequently impose fines of up to Rs. 500 if he saw a *kammi's* livestock (*mavaishi*) trampling or feeding upon his fields. The same Chowdri once imposed a fine of Rs. 30,000 on three young carpenters and humiliated them by beating them with his shoe for having stolen large amounts of citrus fruit to sell in the local market town.

From these instances, it is clear that in the Punjabi village of Bek Sagrana, the Gondal Chowdris retained significant powers of economic coercion as well as political patronage. Their virtual monopoly over access to state institutions meant that they continued to play an indispensable role as local patrons for the inhabitants of the area such that their relationship with labourers and tenants contained a strong political element. Additionally, the Chowdris could publicly justify their social prominence through a paternalistic ideology of protection and patronage that often made reference to their high moral and social status as Muslims. Although, as will be shown further, there had been an increase in free wage labour and an expansion in the job opportunities beyond the village, labourers still had to approach the Chowdris for credit and patronage during times of hardship. In the following sections, I will examine the reasons that led labourers to seek patronage and employment with the Gondal Chowdris as well as the reasons why the Gondal Chowdris actually extended patronage and credit to labourers. Finally, I will look at the ways in which labourers who had taken loans were coerced into repaying them.

III

WAGE LABOUR AND PATRONAGE

Becoming an attached farm or household servant with one of the Gondal Chowdris was not an attractive option to most people. Nonetheless the seasonal variations in the availability of daily wage labour as well as the need for credit to cover large expenses such as a wedding or illness meant that servitude was an option to which people frequently had to resort. Working for a Chowdri was both physically and mentally exhausting. Servants were poorly paid and had to constantly be at the beck and call of their masters who, as the servants often claimed, treated them like animals.

The increased seasonal variation in the demand for agricultural labour was largely the result of the turn to horticulture that began in the 1970s in Pakistani Punjab. The Chowdris started to grow tangerines and oranges because citrus fruit was both more profitable and less labour intensive than other forms of cultivation including sugarcane, wheat, cotton, maize, fodder, rice, and vegetables. This meant that they could afford to spend less time in the village overlooking agricultural tasks and village affairs and spend more time in the cities where their children were now being educated. Besides making agricultural work more scarce, the turn to citrus cultivation also increased the number of people looking for wage labour. As Chowdris resumed cultivation of land that was earlier let out to sharecroppers, many erstwhile sharecroppers were forced to turn to wage labour.[17]

The greatest demand for labour in the citrus orchards occurred during the three-month period of January to March when the fruit was ready for harvesting. A contractor, who estimated yields and purchased the fruit while it was still on the trees, was in charge of organizing the harvest. This included recruiting and organizing labourers as well as transporting and selling the fruit. Depending on the size of the orchard in question, and on the speed with which the contractor wanted to complete the harvest, teams could comprise as many as forty people. This included fruit pickers who climbed the trees, people to carry away the fruit in large wicker baskets and load the trucks, and sometimes a group of people to sort the fruit according to grades of quality and box them. At this time of year, it was common for various contractors and their teams of labourers to be working simultaneously in the orchards of different Chowdris.

The Chowdris had nothing to do with the process other than finding the contractor who offered them the best price. During this time, therefore, labourers dealt directly with the contractors rather than with the Chowdris. Fruit pickers earned between Rs. 100 and Rs. 120 per day, so if they worked for 25 days in a month they could earn Rs. 2,500 per month for the three months of the citrus harvest. This was significantly more than what attached farm or domestic servants earned in monthly wages. It was also more than what daily wage labourers could expect to earn during the rest of the year with the exception of the wheat harvesting season.

During the rest of the year, the demand for labour from the citrus orchard was relatively minor and the Chowdris, or their overseers (*munshis*) if they were wealthy enough to have one, directly organized and recruited labour for the few tasks at hand. The orchards had to be irrigated throughout the year and in particular during the flowering of the trees in the spring. This task was usually carried out by a single labourer, usually an attached farm servant. The orchards also had to be fertilized once a year and sprayed with pesticides about six times a year. These tasks were also frequently carried out by a farm servant and a couple of hired wage labourers who were paid a standard wage of Rs 80 per day. In addition, during the summer months, some labourers were hired to trim the trees and get rid of the dead branches not already removed by people for firewood.

The second greatest demand for agricultural labour occurred around the middle of April, shortly after the end of the citrus harvesting season, for the wheat harvest. Although citrus provided the bulk of the Gondal Chowdris' agricultural income, all of them dedicated some of their land to wheat and fodder cultivation.[18] Wheat in the form of unleavened bread (*roti*) was the basic staple of everyday life and all households stored wheat to last them for the entire year if they could afford to do so. The Chowdris also kept a significant quantity aside for the fixed payments in kind to their servants and the *kammis* that occasionally provided services to them.

During the wheat harvest, plots of land were allotted by the Chowdris to teams of labourers of up to five people who were frequently, but not necessarily, close kin belonging to a single household. The work was considered to be physically exhausting, and only the able-bodied took part in it, but it was also considered to be the most important and profitable work of the year. Teams of labourers were given three *maunds* (a *maund* = 40 kg) per acre harvested. Thus, at Rs. 400 per *maund* of wheat, a team of five labourers could make Rs. 250 per head if they harvested an acre in a day. Although wheat could be sold immediately, most people stored it for consumption through the year and only occasionally sold some whenever they needed cash.

Besides the wheat and citrus harvest, there was no other time when there was work for almost everyone in the fields. The rest of the year, people took up wage labour both in and out of agriculture and frequently found employment in construction and sometimes in factories in places like Sialkot and Faisalabad. However, most of the labourers that I interviewed only took up industrial employment for a few months at a time and at most for a year or two. Although wages in industrial jobs were higher than those in agriculture, living expenses in town were significantly higher than those in the village where accommodation was free and where food was cheaper. Additionally, as industrial labourers they were far from their families, whom they could not easily take with them because of the difficulty of finding cheap accommodation, and were often homesick. Finally, while young and unmarried men were free to go away, labourers who were the heads of independent households were reluctant to leave their wives and children to fend for themselves in the village.

Labourers from the various artisan castes as well as displaced agricultural tenants told me that the main advantage of free wage labour was that it allowed them to take advantage of the peaks in the agricultural cycle during the wheat and citrus harvests when daily wages were at their highest. Wage labour gave them a greater degree of freedom than the extra-economic forms of compulsion that they were subject to if they became attached servants with a Chowdri. Labourers could now find work with employers as far afield as Islamabad and their livelihoods no longer solely depended upon the Gondal Chowdris of Bek Sagrana who in any case spent more of their time living in cities. Both Chowdris and *kammis* told me that villagers were freer from the influence of the Gondal Chowdris than they had been in the past.

The disadvantage that labourers saw in free wage labour was that it could be difficult to find work on a daily basis outside the peak harvest period demand between December and May. Free wage labourers also faced a significant degree of uncertainty as to whether and when employers with whom they did not necessarily have longstanding relationships would actually pay them. In addition to this, free wage labourers faced greater difficulties than attached farm and domestic servants in obtaining patronage and loans, both small consumption loans as well as larger loans to cover wedding and medical expenses. Both the uncertainty of free wage labour and the need for patronage meant that many free wage labourers opted to become attached servants with the Chowdris, sometimes out of necessity and at other times simply for the sake of security, despite lower wages and work conditions that were known to be exploitative and abusive.

Labourers frequently took up employment with the Gondal Chowdris because it allowed them access to credit and was supposed to entitle them to other forms of patronage including support in case of a dispute, mediation with state institutions and even help in retrieving an eloped wife or daughter. On their part, the Chowdris extended such forms of patronage and gave labourers large loans in order to secure a cheap and stable supply of labour, a scarce commodity given the reluctance of many labourers to work for the Chowdris. Chowdris frequently complained that the *kammis* had inflated job expectations as a result of education, television, and easier access to urban centres. Extending loans meant that

Chowdris guaranteed themselves cheap labour that was at their constant beck and call until the time when the debt was fully repaid. Because of the Islamic prohibition on interest, these loans were interest free. Nevertheless, as will be shown further, landlords profited because loans allowed them to reduce their workers' wages. A loan could secure servitude for a few weeks or an entire generation depending upon the size of the loan and upon whether the debtor had able-bodied siblings that could help him repay the amount. For the Chowdris, having servants was also part of a display of status that demonstrated power and influence.[19] Having dependents in the Pakistani Punjab continued to play an important political function for the Chowdris because servants, and especially gunmen, were frequently used to settle disputes with enemies (*dushman*) and because dependents more generally were mobilized for their votes during election times.

IV

DEBT AND BONDAGE

The Chowdris generally extended loans and other forms of patronage to people from whom they could obtain some form of labour. They generally required farm servants, domestic servants and drivers as well as gunmen. Most attached servants ended up having to do a combination of domestic and farm work, despite being generally hired for either one or the other task. Only in instances where they were hired by village factional leaders involved in politics was it usual for them to become gunmen and only the wealthiest Chowdris were likely to hire drivers.[20] Farm work usually involved feeding and milking the livestock,[21] irrigating the orchards and the crops, as well as sowing crops and driving the tractor. The domestic tasks that farm servants were also made to do included serving food and tea to the Chowdris and their guests, cleaning and being sent on errands to fetch and buy things, often well into the night. Even though they might have their own house in the village, servants were frequently asked to stay the night in order to guard the livestock from roaming cattle thieves and in order for them to be at hand if the need for their services arose. Additionally, attached servants had to work throughout the year and if ever they wanted to take a day off it was generally the case that they had to personally provide a replacement who would carry out their work for them.

For all their labour, farm and domestic servants rarely earned more than Rs. 1,500 plus eight *maunds* of wheat per year, plus two meals and a cup of tea a day, and at least one *shalwar kameez* suit per year on Eid. In total, this amounted to roughly Rs. 18,000 per year or Rs. 70 per day which was less than the lowest wages of the agricultural cycle (usually around Rs 80. per day), and significantly less than peak daily agricultural wages earned during the citrus and the wheat harvest. However, if the servant happened to have a large debt, his wages were often significantly lower at around Rs. 10,000 per year. Even if the loan amount were factored in, the wages paid to the attached servants were far below the going rate. It therefore appears that the reason why the Chowdris extended loans to servants was because it allowed them to reduce their wages and thereby assure themselves a cheap and permanent supply of labour.

The cheapest source of labour available to the Chowdris was children as young as five years old. Poor households sometimes gave their children away to work with the Chowdris, either in their village homes or in their homes in Lahore or Sargodha. In exchange for their child, the parents obtained some form of patronage, which might include a loan, or payments of around Rs. 6,000 per year. This practice was justified by the Chowdris with the argument that they were doing the children and their families a great favour because they would be able to provide for, protect and educate them better than their parents. Thus, one Chowdri told me that the eleven-year-old girl who worked in his house in Lahore was there for the protection of her modesty (*hayaa*) because there were no adult males in her family to keep the young men of the village at bay. In most cases, the Chowdris told me that they took on such children for them to learn how to read the Holy Qur'an as well as how to read and write Urdu.

However, these children would not be sent to school and it was widely known that they largely spent their time washing dishes, carrying trays, sweeping floors and running errands. The mindless drudgery of their work was clearly illustrated by the case of one seven-year-old Musalli who worked for the wealthiest Chowdri in the village and who, since he constantly ran around communicating messages between his master and different labourers, was affectionately referred to by villagers as 'Nokia'— like a mobile phone. He also went back and forth from the Chowdri's house and his men's house with heavy trays laden with food and drinks for guests. By evening time, he was exhausted and I often saw him pass out at the men's house while the guests were eating. Like other children in his situation, he was generally tired and homesick. In their rare moments of free time, they often had no one to play with because, from an early age, the children of the Chowdris learnt to treat them as servants and frequently excluded them from their games. Thus, even if they learnt how to read and write, many of these children had a miserable time and several adults who had been child servants, and who sometimes were still servants, invoked God's mercy in the hope that their children would never have to work for a Chowdri. Some villagers even told me that such children frequently ended up with mental problems and illustrated this by pointing to specific cases. As a result of this, the parents who sent their children away were often somewhat ashamed of it and offered the same justification for their act as the Chowdris, claiming that it was in order for their children to learn how to read and write.

As a result of being overworked, poorly paid, and abused, servants— including children—were often resentful towards their employers and frequently vented their feelings towards them by badmouthing them, stealing from them, and by dragging their feet. On one occasion, I saw a servant throw angry punches and spit at the photograph of his master. One twelve-year-old child boasted to me about how he purposely ran up large phone bills on his master's phone by calling his friend in town. Servants often stole fruit from their masters' citrus orchards at night and sold it in the nearby market town. Finally, the greatest statement of discontent was when servants—and gunmen in particular—had no debts, deserted their masters and sought the patronage of their rivals to whom they revealed their former master's secrets. Servants with debts could not do this because the Chowdris had an agreement not to poach them from each other unless their debts were settled.

These acts were largely individual and isolated and never openly challenged the Chowdris. In public, servants and villagers generally continued to perform displays of subordination towards the Chowdris whom they greeted with a bow and with their right hand upon their hearts expressing thankfulness. When they sat in assembly with the Chowdris, it was still quite common for *kammis* to squat on the floor while the Chowdri sat above them on a *charpai*. The fact that they did not just walk out of their jobs but instead resorted to such 'weapons of the weak' illustrated the absence of any real bargaining power on their part. As will be shown below, this lack of bargaining power was particularly evident in the case of indebted labourers who were compelled through a variety of means to service their debts.

Various factors combined to ensure the servants repaid their debts towards the Chowdris. To begin with, the servants could not simply run away because they had nowhere to run to. If they went to nearby villages or even to the local town of Sargodha, the Chowdris were likely to find them through their political and friendship networks. In the rare instances when *kammis* did have friends or relatives in faraway cities like Rawalpindi, Faisalabad, Jhang, or Lahore who could help them find employment and accommodation, relatives that stayed behind in the village could be pressured to reveal that information to the Chowdri. It was also widely believed that the Chowdris could enlist the support of the police in order to retrieve and even jail escaped bonded labourers. Although this had not happened to any bonded labourers that I knew, this was confirmed by the investigations of Human Rights Watch (1995: 70).

In most cases, however, the Chowdris could rely on the kin of attached servants to ensure that they repaid their loans and did not run away. When a Chowdri made a loan to a labourer, he generally obtained a guarantor (*zaman*) from among the labourer's close kinsmen who was responsible for repaying the loan, in labour or in kind, were the labourer to default by running away, illness, or death. In cases where the house of an attached servant was located on the employer's land, it was taken for granted that other able-bodied household members would be made responsible in case of default. It was therefore in the interest of kinsmen to help their attached relatives to service their debts and to prevent them from running away. They could economically assist the debtor by covering his basic needs so that he did not need to take monthly wages from the Chowdri.

Thus, an indebted attached servant who was paid Rs. 10,000 per year could eliminate that amount from his debt if he refrained from claiming his wages by relying on his kinsmen.

The amount of time that an indebted servant took to repay a loan with his labour largely depended upon whether he had the financial support of close kinsmen, most commonly his siblings. One Musalli who took a loan of Rs. 60,000 to cover his father's medical treatment and his elder brother's wedding expenses, managed to repay the sum within a two-year period with help from his two siblings and by selling some livestock. He managed to reduce his debt by Rs. 10,000 in the first year by forgoing his wages, and by subsisting on Rs. 300 per month from his siblings to cover for basic necessities (food was provided by the Chowdri). In the second year, he shifted to another Chowdri who offered to pay him Rs. 15,000 per year and who purchased his remaining debt of Rs. 50,000 from the previous employer.[22] In that year, he further reduced his debt by Rs. 15,000 by not taking his wages. The remaining Rs. 45,000 was repaid by selling some goats and a buffalo. Another bonded labourer who belonged to a family of impoverished *zamindar* tenants, who did not belong to the dominant Gondal *biradari* in the village, also managed to pay off a debt incurred with a Chowdri thanks to the income and labour of three able-bodied siblings and the sale of some livestock. In this case too, the labourer had obtained a loan of Rs. 50,000 from the Chowdri because of his father's illness. The loan was repaid after two and a half years of hard labour.

When indebted servants had no able-bodied siblings or parents to help them out, repaying a loan could take an entire lifetime and, rather than see their debts diminish, they were likely to see them grow. Repayment was even more difficult if a household was afflicted by additional crises such as illness or drug addiction. In one instance, a Musalli who was a heroin addict had given his seven-year-old son Fazi over to a Gondal Chowdri in exchange for Rs. 6,000 per year and various small cash advances. The family had come to economically depend on the young boy because of the father's addiction and the absence of other able-bodied males in the household. By the time Fazi turned seventeen, the debt had risen to Rs. 20,000 as the household was continually short of money. The father had sold much of the furniture in the house in order to finance his heroin addiction. The debt further increased by Rs. 30,000 when Fazi and his sister got married. At the time of fieldwork, the outstanding amount had reached Rs. 50,000 and the Gondal Chowdri had decided to cut off any further flow of credit because it was becoming unlikely that the loan would ever be repaid.

The situation for Fazi had, however, become more hopeful as he now had a younger sibling of working age who was working in a vermicelli (*sevian*) factory in Sargodha and who was contributing to family finances. The father had also ceased to be a burden since he went to Islamabad where he managed to find work in a market carrying people's shopping bags and was able to personally finance his heroin addiction. In addition, a charitable and pious Gondal Chowdri had given Fazi a baby buffalo to rear, such that when the animal was fully grown, they would share the proceeds equally. An adult buffalo could be sold at about Rs. 80,000, allowing Fazi to reduce his debt by up to Rs. 40,000. However, there was an unfortunate setback: his sister contracted tuberculosis and her in-laws sent her back home because she had become a financial burden. Medical treatment was expensive and Fazi, who was desperate to repay his debt, complained that it was the duty of his sister's in-laws to take care of her and threatened not to make any monetary contributions towards her treatment.

V

CONCLUSION: POLITICAL MOBILIZATION AND ITS LIMITS

This article shows that changes in the regional agrarian economy largely resulting from the introduction of citrus orchards together with broader economic expansion in non-agricultural sectors resulted in the decreased economic dependence of rural labourers on the Chowdris. However, these changes in the regional economy were not matched by changes in the highly unequal political structure and the livelihood strategies of labourers continued to be circumscribed by the political influence of the Chowdris. Not only did the Chowdris control the means to physically coerce labourers, but they also had virtual monopoly over access to the state, giving them the power to grant and withhold patronage in ways that generally furthered their personal interests. Labourers continued to largely depend on the Chowdris for patronage in the form of mediation with state institutions, dispute resolution and for the extension of credit. Therefore, despite their dislike of the Chowdris, labourers undergoing periods of hardship were compelled to seek attached employment with them. Their dependence on the Chowdris was reflected in their behaviour which remained compliant and obsequious. Also, it was observed that having servants and dependents continued to be a political asset for the Chowdris because it allowed them to secure votes during elections and to mobilize the use of force in order to settle feuds. The relationship between labourers and Chowdris in the Pakistani Punjab therefore contained a strong political element.

I conclude with the suggestion that the principal reason for the lack of assertiveness of labourers in the Pakistani Punjab relates to the broader political evolution of Pakistan. The fact that Pakistan lacked a popular national political party at Independence, and that repeated military interventions over the country's sixty-year existence severely curtailed the possibility for the development of genuinely popular political parties later, had highly deleterious consequences for the country's social and political development. One significant consequence of this was that the Pakistani masses never witnessed the sort of political empowerment that some of their counterparts in India witnessed over the past couple of decades other than during a brief moment when Zulfiqar Ali Bhutto initially rose to power. Thus, the assertiveness of the Dalits described by Jeffrey and Lerche (2000) under Mayawati in Uttar Pradesh and the assertiveness of labourers in Gujarat described by Breman (1993) remained largely unthinkable for many labourers and *kammis* in much of the central

Punjab as well as southern and western Punjab. However, many labourers and *kammis* resented their subordination and their lack of assertiveness did not necessarily indicate that they fully acquiesced to it.

In fact, political developments in the 1970s indicate that, given a chance, the pent up frustration of landless labourers, artisans, and tenants could erupt into the political scene. Zulfiqar Ali Bhutto's promise of land and homestead reforms as well as the abolition of corvée labour (*begaar*) enlisted the support of tenants, landless labourers and village *kammis*. The poor rural voter hoped that the Pakistan People's Party (PPP) would pursue its interests against 'the classes and institutions that had weighed upon him so heavily and for so long—the *zamindariat*, the police, the bureaucracy and the courts' (Jones 2003: 362). According to Jones, the 1970 elections—the first national elections based on universal adult franchise—were the first time in the country's history when the have-nots erupted onto the political scene. These elections not only saw the emergence of horizontal, class-based ties of allegiance among urban voters but also among rural voters where historically the masses had 'been politically quiescent, conditioned by tradition and the local structure of power to follow their customary leaders—*ashrafi*-gentry *zamindars*, *pirs*, and clan *biradari* heads' (ibid.: 356). Because of the importance given to land and homestead reform in the PPP's electoral campaign, party affiliation was often divided along class lines between those who owned land and those who did not. Jones convincingly shows how, in villages across the Punjab, tenants and landless *kammis* emboldened by the mass support generated by Bhutto voted for the PPP against the wishes of the Chowdris who sometimes even set aside their longstanding feuds and rivalries in order to defeat the PPP. To this day, most tenants and *kammis* in the village of Bek Sagrana told me that if they had a choice they would vote for the PPP because it had historically been the party of the poor (*gharibon ki party*).

Subsequent political developments during the ten years of military rule under General Zia ul-Haq, and even during Bhutto's terms in office, neutralized much of the progress that had been achieved during the early 1970s.[23] General Zia pledged to protect the landlords from a second round of land reforms that had been planned by Bhutto and removed the ceilings on the amount of land owned. Under his regime, the courts once again reverted to being unsympathetic to the claims of tenants. On the political front, by undertaking large-scale repression of the political opposition spearheaded by the PPP and by holding non-party local body elections, the military regime ensured that the sort of mass mobilization that had occurred in Bhutto's time could not take place. Like his predecessor General Ayub Khan and his successor General Pervez Musharraf, Zia encouraged candidate-based as opposed to party-based electoral campaigns. According to Muhammad Waseem:

> Zia attempted to revert to the early colonial mode of district politics in which local influentials got elected into the legislatures on the strength of their respective support bases in the locality characterized by the ties of tribe, caste, faction or tenurial relations. The obvious target of this policy was the PPP which had continued to enjoy mass popularity ... The 1985 non-party elections localized politics, reinvigorated *biradri* [sic], cut across the potential though non-active lines of party support and decisively shifted political initiative towards electoral candidates. (Waseem 1994: 15)

Such policies implemented by successive military regimes in Pakistan resulted in fragmenting the political landscape, thereby forestalling the emergence of large-scale popular political movements such as the one witnessed during the rise of Zulfiqar Ali Bhutto in 1970. In this political scenario, politicians largely ceased to focus upon national issues, legislation, and policy making and became almost exclusively concerned with consolidating their position as local patrons.[24] One consequence of this is that rural strongmen in the Punjab, such as members of the Gondal *biradari* described in this article, consolidated their political and economic fortunes and continued to be the principal mediators between the have-nots and the state. There was no political party or organization based on either class or caste to which tenants and landless labourers could turn for patronage and they were therefore largely restricted to seeking patronage from local landlords. In this manner, political mobilization in much of the rural Pakistani Punjab remained factional, characterized by a vertical structure of power that cut across ties of caste and class.

ACKNOWLEDGEMENTS

For their comments and feedback on this article and other related work in progress, I would especially like to thank my PhD supervisors Professor Jonathan Parry and Professor Martha Mundy of the London School of Economics. I would also like to express my thanks to the editorial team at *Contributions to Indian Sociology* and, in particular, to Amita Baviskar and to the anonymous referee for their careful and considerate review of the article and for their invaluable suggestions which have been incorporated into the text.

REFERENCES

Brass, Tom (1999), *Towards a Comparative Political Economy of Unfree Labour*. London and Portland: Frank Cass.

Breman, Jan (1993), *Beyond Patronage and Exploitation*. Delhi: Oxford University Press.

Corbridge, S., Williams, G., Srivastava, M., & Veron, R. (2005), *Seeing the State: Governance and Governmentality in India*. Cambridge: Cambridge University Press.

Herring, Ronald J. (1983), *Land to the Tiller: The Political Economy of Agrarian Reform in South Asia*. New Haven, CT: Yale University Press.

HRCP (Human Rights Commission of Pakistan) (1995), State of Human Rights in Pakistan 1994. Lahore: HRCP.

Human Rights Watch (1995), *Contemporary Forms of Slavery in Pakistan*. London: Human Rights Watch/Asia.

ILO (International Labour Organization) (1993), *World Labour Report 1993*. Geneva: International Labour Organization.

Jeffrey, Craig & Lerche, Jens (2000), 'Dimensions of Dominance: Class and State in Uttar Pradesh'. In Chris J. Fuller and Veronique Benei (eds.) *The Everyday State and Society in Modern India*: 91–112. New Delhi: Social Science Press.

Jones, Phillip E. (2003), *The Pakistan People's Party: Rise to Power*. Oxford: Oxford University Press.

Rouse, Shahnaz. (1983), 'Systematic Injustices and Inequalities: Maliki and Raiya in a Punjab Village'. In Hassan Gardezi and Jamil Rashid (eds.) *Pakistan, The Roots of Dictatorship: The Political Economy of a Praetorian State*: 311–25. London: Zed Press.

Waseem, Muhammad (1994), *The 1993 Elections in Pakistan*. Lahore: Vanguard Books.

Wilder, Andrew R. (1999), *The Pakistani Voter: Electoral Politics and Voting Behaviour in the Punjab*. Karachi: Oxford University Press.

Zaidi, Akbar S. (1999), *Issues in Pakistan's Economy*. Karachi: Oxford University Press.

NOTES

1. See Human Rights Watch (1995: 64–65) for an account of this event. The Human Rights Watch report quotes newspaper articles stating that this jail was one of twelve such jails in the Sanghar district of Sindh.

2. See Wilder (1999): Chapter 3 for a general description of the geography and political economy of the different regions of Punjab.

3. See Zaidi (1999) for a discussion of the decline in agricultural sharecropping throughout Pakistan following upon the Green Revolution and the large-scale introduction of cash crops and orchards.

4. The names of the village and its dominant caste have been changed in order to protect the identity of informants.

5. Some Gondals had land holdings of up to 400 acres and were prominent politicians, lawyers and bureaucrats while the poorest had holdings of below five acres like other minor *zamindars* in the area such as the Lurkas, the Sagranas and the Mohajir Rajputs who on average owned less than five acres of land.

6. Some *kammis* including some village Lohars and Tarkhans were relatively well off thanks to the fact that they turned their traditional occupations into businesses. One family of village Tarkhans with seven siblings had a flourishing furniture business. In the village itself, *kammis* made up 35 per cent of the population but this proportion was much higher in the *deras*, clusters of houses surrounding a farmstead. In the *deras*, all houses other than that of the landlord were *kammi* households. For example, on the *dera* where I lived, sixteen out of eighteen households were *kammi* households.

7. Both terms were used interchangeably although the term *qaum* was more frequently used.

8. I was told that the drummers (*Pirhain*) were traditionally the ones who wove the strings onto the wooden frame of *charpais*.

9. For a sociological account of this trend in the district of Sargodha, see Rouse (1983: 320).

10. The involvement of the police in criminality in Pakistan was well known. I witnessed this on one occasion when an illegal gambling event was held in the village and a low-ranking policeman came to collect his dues in exchange for not interfering with proceedings.

11. Gunmen, who frequently landed in jail on behalf of their employers, told me that the experienced ones among them always carried opium to eat in case they were caught and subjected to beatings by the police because the opium would numb the pain.

12. Villagers particularly feared street-level lower ranking officers because they claimed that the officers planted drugs into unsuspecting people's pockets and then had them arrested in order to extort money. The victims of such practices were generally the poorest and most vulnerable since police officers knew that they could get away with harassing them, whereas harassing people with influence would be more risky.

13. In one instance, the driver of one of the Chowdris decided to personally file an FIR. With multiple trips to the police station and bribes to the clerks, he spent Rs. 1,500 which was equivalent to a month's wages for him.

14. See Rouse (1983: 323) for an account of the impact of homestead reforms in another village in the district of Sargodha.

15. During elections, Chowdris had various means to find out for whom their tenants and servants had voted. In the Union Council elections of 2005, for example, I witnessed Chowdris and their spies looking over people as they filled their ballots. Chowdris also had informants who told them who was planning to vote for or against them. Because of this, tenants and servants tended to vote for the candidate supported by their Chowdri.

16. An *urs* is a religious festival held annually to commemorate the unification with God of a Muslim saint upon his death.

17. See Zaidi (1999: 42) for an account of the decline of sharecropping from the 1960s.

18. It was also possible to cultivate both of these crops in the citrus orchards when the trees were small and did not stop the sunlight from reaching the crops.

19. The greatest display of influence and power was through armed gunmen. Having gunmen showed that a Chowdri was powerful and to be feared. These qualities were deemed to be necessary in a ruthless political environment where men considered to be weak could end up having their land and wealth taken away from them by more aggressive opponents.

20. There was a total of six Gondal Chowdris who had drivers in the village and its surroundings.

21. Most of the Chowdris owned some livestock in the form of cows and buffaloes for milk for domestic consumption.

22. It was possible for indebted labourers to leave their current employer so long as another employer was willing to purchase their debt.
23. The success of Bhutto's reform programme remains highly debated. Reports suggest that, following his rise to power in 1970, tenants could successfully appeal to the judiciary against evictions. However, restrictions on the size of land holdings remained ineffectual. Thus, Herring reports that, in 70 per cent of all cases of eviction, court judgements ordered the restoration of tenants (Herring 1983: 117). Since land ceilings were based on individual rather than family holdings, landlords could circumvent the law by transferring land titles to the name of close relatives.
24. See Wilder (1999: 204) for an account of why Punjabi politicians have ceased to be concerned with legislation and policy making.

CHAPTER 6

Bhadhal: Bonded Labour Among Fishermen on the Indus River

Ayaz Qureshi

This chapter presents an ethnographic study of bonded labour among a fishing community—known as the *looray*—of the Indus River in the Dera Ghazi Khan district of Punjab. These fisher people live in houseboats in three mobile settlements along the length of the river flowing through the district. They can be distinguished from the local villagers because of their darker skin complexion, so the villagers say, and their distinctive Sindhi accent. By their own account, the *looray* migrated to this area in their houseboats half a century ago from the district of Larkana in Sindh because of threats to their lives and property under an intensifying *dako raj* (lawlessness; lit., 'rule of dacoits') in the riverine tracts of that district. Known as *maachi* in Sindh, their main occupation was hunting crocodiles (*mung-machi/sesaar*) for their valuable skin, but as they migrated upstream, crocodiles were harder to find. Whilst they foraged the river for subsistence, the local villagers started calling them *looray*—purposeless wanderers (*loor loor karna*)—an identity that they gradually took upon themselves.

Fishing requires different skills and equipment than hunting crocodiles. After migration from Sindh, the *looray* learnt new skills and bought new equipment by borrowing money from local landlords. They were barred from commercial fishing because of government regulations which required bidding in order to win a contract for fishing rights. Due to their lack of capital they could not compete in the bidding process and were forced into working as hired labour for a local landlord who has held the contract for decades. Over the years, a relation of mutual dependence developed between the landlord-contractor (*thekedar*) and *looray*. They caught fish for him and he took care of their financial needs. Gradually, the landlord-contractor extended cash loans to buy more fishing boats and nets, and for ritual consumption such as on weddings and pilgrimage. As time passed, the landlord-contractor grip over their economic life tightened further, so much so that they came to see themselves as tied to him. At the time of this research every one of the *looray*, except the headman and two of his close relatives, was indebted to the landlord-contractor—a debt bondage that they described as *bhadhal* (a helpless state of being tied to something or someone). Whilst the amount of debt keeps mounting, the *looray* are bound to pay it back with their labour.

The *looray* were neither related through kinship ties to people in the surrounding villages, including the landlord-contractor, nor did they take part in agricultural activities or the village life in general. Instead, they are part of a larger endogamous group spread over the Indus River from Taunsa Barrage down to Larkana. Those working under one particular contractor in a given area of the river (i.e. district) call themselves a *raj*. The *raj* in DG Khan was divided into three groups, which comprised of three mobile settlements floating in the area of the river flowing through this district. These settlements were known by the names of their headmen, *Allahdad-alay*, *Haji Yousaf-alay* and *Khamesay-alay*, (*alay* translates as 'of someone, something, or somewhere'). A *raj*, therefore, is like a lineage, with divisions of sublineages or segments. However, the composition of these segments is more fluid, i.e. they do not strictly correspond to lines of descent. As with the *raj*, the composition of its three sub-divisions in these three mobile settlements was not permanent, as I explore in this chapter.

The research reported here was carried out among the *Allahdad-alay* in the summer of 2001. Located near Ghazighat Bridge on the Indus River in DG Khan, this group consisted of 20 households, their houseboats anchored at a seasonal island in the river. They comprised of 115 individuals in 20 houseboats. Almost half of them were under the age of 15 years, while only nine men and three women were above 45 years of age. They lived in 17 nuclear, two joint, and one extended family. Three men had polygamous marriages, with two wives each, living together in the same houseboat, and there were two cases of divorce. In addition to a houseboat *(gharoli)*, whose length could range up to 10.6 metres, some households also owned smaller fishing boats *(shikari-kishta)*.

The *Allahdad-alay looray* lived in both types of boats. Their way of living was impoverished and physically demanding. Their diet was simple, comprising of two meals a day. In winter, when fish was in abundance, they were allowed to keep some portion of the catch for their own consumption *(bhaji)* before handing the rest over to the landlord-contractor's agent *(munshi)*. In summer, some *looray* occasionally treated themselves to vegetable curries, but most of them ate *chapatti* with an onion and tomato gravy. None of individuals was literate, though a few could read the Quran. None of the community had ever attended a school or a madrassa. Common illnesses included malaria, diarrhea, and kidney pain. All three diseases can be attributed to the conditions of their livelihood; marshes which bred mosquitoes and contaminated river water used for drinking. The nearest government health facility, a Basic Health Unit (BHU), was said to have poor facilities. Therefore, they visited a private practitioner when required.

With their distinct origin and language and their waterborne lifestyle, *looray* live arduous and short lives in the midst of a *biradari*-based feudal agrarian setting. They are often held in contempt by the local villagers for their 'loose' morals, lack of religiosity, and even for their darker skins. For their part, the *looray* maintain minimum contact with people on land and in the surrounding villages, often limited to the landlord-contractor's men. Since they have hardly any cash at their disposal, as I will explain below, they seldom visit the town, and if they do, they are ridiculed for their 'backwardness' and lack of exposure to the modern world. Drawing their livelihood from *Darya Saeen* (or the Lord River, as they call it due to its mighty expanse and foreboding presence) involves risking their lives.

Economically, they are entirely dependent on their relations with the landlord-contractor, who has a monopoly over fishing rights in the river. In terms of their debt bondage, they are therefore different from agricultural labourers who may shift between agricultural and manual labour, migrate seasonally from villages to cities or have a number of different sources of livelihood within a single household (Martin 2009). Although they are paid at a piece-rate of 10 rupees per kilogram of fish they catch, the *looray* are also different from the labourers in football-stitching and bangle-making industries, where ties of common kinship, geography and class origin between labourers and employers might mitigate the chances of the system of advance *(peshgi)* developing into debt-bondage (Khan 2010). In terms of their labour relations, then, they are more like the *pathera* in brick kilns, studied by Ercelawn and Nauman (2004), who move from kiln to kiln with their entire families. An important difference, however, is that it is perhaps more common for the kiln worker to move from kiln to kiln, which tend to be located close by, where a neighbouring kiln owner might be willing to pay the debt to the current employer and transfer the bondage. In the case of the *looray*, however, changing employers is not feasible, if not impossible, due to the nature of their work and their riverine way of life. The landlord-contractor has a monopoly on fishing in a stretch of more than 90km of the river. He is also influential on the land. Where would a *loorya* go with his houseboat even if he managed to break free of his current labour relation? Buying off a *loorya's* debt, or even an entire *raj*, by a contractor is not unprecedented, but such an extreme situation would arise due to a change in the circumstances of contractors rather than those of the *looray*. *Looray* are dependent on the landlord-contractor not only for labour but practically all relations with the 'outside' world. This is what gives the landlord-contractor his enormous power over the *looray* and their subsequent immense vulnerability. He exercises this control through *munshis* (agents of the contractor-landlord) by using various strategies outlined below. A careful manipulation of relations between the *looray* and the villagers in the surrounding areas with the mediation of *munshis* is one such strategy.

What sets *looray* apart from other instances of forced or bonded labour in Pakistan is also the somewhat ironic fact that *looray* own part of the means of production. Unlike football-stitchers and bangle-makers, or even brick kiln workers, who own only their bodies and labour power, their employer does not provide the *looray* with raw material or half-made goods to turn into saleable products. He only holds the legal right to fish, and the rest is accomplished by the *looray* through their own physical labour, knowledge of the river, skilful fishing expertise and intergenerational experience of the work. All the fishing equipment belongs to the *looray* themselves. There is, however, a considerable differentiation of ownership of fishing boats and nets within the group, which adds a further dimension to the exploitation of asset-less *looray*, as I will explain below.

Of the 20 fishing boats that *Allahdad-alay* owned in 2001, the headman himself owned three and four of his close relatives owned two each. Nine households had one fishing boat each, and six had none at all. The smallest of these fishing boats was 2.4 metres long and the largest was 5.5 metres. Only three had roofs. The fishing nets (*narray/pattay*) also came in different sizes ranging from 15 to 50 metres in length and 15 to 18 metres in breadth. The total number of nets was 730 and they comprised of a mix of different sizes of the holes (*ghar*), ranging from 13 to 39 square centimetres. The maximum number of nets owned by a single household was 150. Again, this was the household of the headman. Six households did not have a single net, nine had between one to fifty nets, and the remaining four households had between fifty to one hundred nets. These differences in the possession of assets by households have important implications for the organization of fish catching and the distribution of income over the households.

FISH CATCHING

The area of the river that *Allahdad-alay* are responsible for fishing extends up to a length of 40 km. It includes two seasonal lakes as well as the mainstream river. Commercial fishing with nets was not permitted in the months of June, July, and August (*bandi da season*) because this is the breeding season for most species of fish. During these months they fish with *kundi* (a metal hook attached to a thread) using earthworms, but the catch from such techniques is negligible. From September to May, fish catching with nets takes place almost every day. The largest amounts of fish are caught in the months of November and December.

As the fishing season begins, *Allahdad-alay* start by sealing off the seasonal lakes with nets to confine the fish in them. Then they move on to their daily fishing routine nearer the place where the houseboats are anchored, gradually moving upstream in the north. With every passing day, their expedition takes them further away from the houseboats, until they reach the end of their allocated section of the river and start another cycle. In this way, they make up to four circular movements in their fishing boats in a given season. Whilst most fishing expeditions take more than a day's journey, the longest time away from houseboats can be up to two weeks. Only adult men fish from their fishing boats, leaving women and children back in the houseboats. A boy is considered an adult as soon as he is capable of pulling the nets in the water, at around 14 years. Women and children catch fish from their houseboats with a home-made trap called a *kurh*, which consists of a small piece of net attached to at the bottom of conical frame of wood sticks.

Fishing up and down the river, they follow a set pattern, except when the landlord-contractor requires them to spend more (or less) time on a particular spot. After reaching a designated spot, the actual process of catching fish starts with the appearance of the morning star. The *looray* would have already tied their nets together to form two large nets of length equal to the breadth of the water channel. These two nets are lowered in to the river at a right angle to the flow of water. The distance between two nets depends upon the breadth of the stream and the number of men involved in that day's labour. The greater the breadth of the water passage, the less the distance between the two nets. Usually, for a 200 metre-wide water channel, the distance between two nets is 900 metres. The nets are tied with stones at the bottom to weigh them down, and with pieces of white foam on the top to keep them visible and afloat. It takes up to two hours to lower the nets into the river, which is done by crossing it at a right angle in the fishing boats and lowering the nets gradually into the water. The nets are then tied on both ends to long ropes which are held taut by temporarily-erected poles on both sides. Once the nets have been lowered and the men have rested, they start pulling the northern net from both sides in the direction of the water's current. It is very heavy to pull, as, in addition to the catch, it drags along the weight tied to the bottom. Moreover, the net often gets stuck in the underwater wild growth, which they have to dive down to untangle. Therefore, pulling the net is not only labour intensive but a delicate process requiring a skill that only *looray* have mastered. It takes between 8 to 10 men on either side to pull at the long ropes tied to the net. They repeat the pulling after every 15–20 minutes and every time they manage to move the net a few metres closer to the other net on the southern side which remains in its place.

It takes between 8 to 10 hours to force the two nets together. As they come closer the fish trapped inside start to jump over the surface, trying to cross the net. The two nets are eventually tied from one end to make it into a single net, thus encircling the fish trapped between them. The ends of this big net are now on the same side of the river and are pulled vigorously. The trapped fish trying to escape through the holes of the net gets caught in it. If necessary, a second net with smaller holes is placed behind the main net to capture the smaller fish that escape. Once the nets are fully pulled out of the water, the fish caught in them are carefully removed and put into jute bags. The whole process is overseen by the *munshi* who arrives with a vehicle to transport the fish just before the nets are pulled out.

The fish caught by the men's collective labour is kept separate from that caught by women and children in the houseboats. The *munshi* supervises the weighing of the fish on the scales that he brings with him. He then writes down the amounts in his registers. The household catch is usually written under the name of the eldest woman. For the collective catch, the *munshi* writes down the total amount of fish, the names of all the men who took part in that day's labour, and the numbers of nets and boats with the names of their owners. As the fish is being weighed, some local villagers arrive on the scene to ask for some fish or even offer to buy some. Only the *munshi* can respond to such requests. A *loorya* can take home only a small portion to cook for the evening meal; he is not allowed to oblige any acquaintances or to sell it to anyone (this is strictly enforced by the *munshi*, as I describe below). After it has been weighed and the quantities entered in the *munshi*'s register, the *looray* carry the jute-bags full of fish on their backs to the *munshi*'s vehicle waiting at an accessible point near the bank. The *munshi* then takes it straight to a fish market in Multan.

THE ACCOUNTS

The money equivalent of the fish caught by the women and children, at the rate of Rs. 10 per kg, is noted down in their households' accounts straightaway. However, the recording of the money equivalent of the fish caught through collective labour follows a different method. The total amount is divided on men, nets, and boats which took part in the collective fishing on a given day. One third of the total amount goes to nets while the remaining two-third is equally divided on men and boats. All men, regardless of their age, status, or the amount of labour they have put in the collective fishing, get an equal share. The shares for nets and boats are written into the accounts of their owners.

In this whole process of noting down who earned how much, the money does not exchange hands but amounts are calculated and jotted down by the *munshi*. The *looray* keep verbal accounts, which sometimes do not match with amounts entered in the register. As for the conversion rate, there is an unwritten understanding between *looray* and the landlord-contractor that the landlord-contractor would pay workers at a rate of Rs. 10 per kg[1] for the fish they catch, that he would guarantee that no one other than them is employed for this purpose in their designated part of the river, and that he would prevent illegal fishing in the river. Another part of their mutual understanding is that if a *looray* tries to sell fish directly to anyone at any time of the year without the knowledge or permission of the landlord-contractor's *munshi*, he or she will be fined Rs. 1,000, which the *munshi* would add into his/her households debt. Where they are allowed to sell fish to a villager or a passerby, they must hand over the cash to the *munshi*, who would then record it in the household account at the rate of Rs. 10 per kg. There were three cases of a breach of this rule among the *Allahdad-alay* in one year, although none of these young men had been fined because the headman Allahdad intervened and pleaded on their behalf with the *munshi*. Disputes over discrepancies in amounts entered in the *munshi's* register and those remembered by individuals are also often settled between the *munshi* and the headman.

The amount of fish caught every day varies between 40 and 4,000kg, depending on the season, the number of men, the nets and boats involved, and the area of fishing. However, the average production is between 600 and 800kg, almost 80 per cent of which is caught by men through collective labour. At the household level, women and children manage to catch between 15–30kg at an average. The market price of these fish (*singhara* and *dhambhra*: local names) can be up to Rs. 120 per kg. With a huge difference between the market price and the rate given to *looray*, in their opinion, despite their labour and ownership of the nets and boats, it is the landlord-contractor who unjustly makes most of the profit. The *looray* believe that the river is a natural resource and that it should naturally belong to those who inhabit it, and that outsiders take advantage of the *looray's* financial inability to bid for commercial fishing rights. There is resentment against the situation the *looray* find themselves in but they have no means to break out of it. 'Stealing' small quantities of fish to sell directly to the villagers can be seen as a form of resistance, a 'weapon of the weak' (Scott 1984), but pilferage is punished with heavy fines. Likewise, foot-dragging is hardly an option because *looray* are 'paid' by piece-rate. However, *munshis* and the headman ridicule those individuals who are 'too lazy' and content with their low incomes. These are often the ones who fall sick often and miss too many days of collective fish catching, resulting in a missed share in the collective earnings and mounting debt. On the other hand, the fact that the landlord-contractor and his men maintain strict control over *looray*—in fact, their surveillance increases manifold in the fishing season—indicates that they have a strong distrust of the *looray*.

There is another disparity that is created within the *looray* community due to the system of compensation for the fish caught at the collective level. Under the current system of distribution of the total amount over men, nets, and fishing boats, a cycle of unequal benefit is perpetuated. The households that own nets and fishing boats end up getting a greater share, thereby reinforcing their assets, while asset-less households are left with a meagre income. A case study further clarifies this point. On 23 September, all the twenty households of *Allahdad-alay* participated in fish catching near their settlement. The numbers for the collective labour were 28 men, two fishing boats and 150 nets. The amount of collectively caught fish weighed 720kg and the amount caught by women and children at household level was 160kg. Adding these two amounts the total amount for that day was 880kg. Supposing that the market price that day was 120per kg, the total monetary worth of that day's catch can be calculated at Rs. 89,760. The amount noted down in *looray's* account as compensation for their labour, nets and boats was Rs. 8,800.

Fish caught by collective labour	720 kg
Fish caught at the household level	160 kg
Total fish catch	880 kg
Approximate price of fish in the market	880 x120 = Rs. 89,760
Looray's compensation	880 x(10) = Rs. 8,800
Landlord-contractor's share (before other expenses)	89,760 – 8,800 = Rs. 80,960

Now, the amount of money earned for collective labour was divided in two parts, one-third for nets and two-third for men and fishing boats, as illustrated in figure 1.

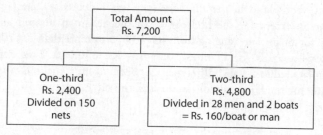

Figure 1: Showing the method of dividing the payments for the fish caught through collective labour on men, boats and nets.

To further understand the implications of this method, we can compare the two households of Allahdad and Deen Mohammad. Allahdad participated in the collective labour with his two sons, thirty nets and one boat, whereas Deen Mohammad does not own any fishing nets and boats and his household comprised of himself and his elderly mother. Moreover, Allahdad's two wives and younger children managed to catch as much as 30kg of fish whilst Deen Mohammad's mother could manage to catch only 6kg.

	Allahdad	Deen Mohammad
Share for men	160 x 3 =480	160 x1 = 160
Share for fishing boats	160 x 1 =160	Nil
Share for nets	16 x 30 = 380	Nil
Total share in collective catch	Rs. 1,020	Rs. 160
Household catch	43kg @ Rs. 10 = Rs. 430	6kg @ Rs. 10 = 60
Total earning for the day	1,020 + 430 = Rs. 1,450	160 + 60 = Rs. 220

Thus, from the way this system of compensation is organized it becomes clear that larger households which own more fishing assets benefit more from the collective labour than smaller households with less or no fishing nets and boats, even though individual labourers in both kinds of household provide equal amount of labour. (In fact, being the headman, Allahdad spent most of the time in the fishing boat supervising others, including Deen Mohammad, who did the back-breaking work).

Every household in the *Allahdad-alay* was indebted to the landlord-contractor, except for the households of the headman himself and two others, for an amount ranging from Rs. 10,000 to more than Rs. 100,000. The total amount for all households was Rs. 690,000. This debt had accumulated due to the difference between *looray*'s income from fish catching for the landlord-contractor and the credit extended to them in the form of cash, kind and services.

Households	Debt amount
8	Rs. 10–30,000
7	Rs. 30–75,000
2	> Rs. 75,000
3	Surplus or no loan

The maximum amount of debt for a household was Rs. 110,000. This was Bhudha's household which comprised of 14 persons, one houseboat, two fishing boats, one hundred nets, and two goats. The adult labourers comprised of three men and three women. This indicates that large families are difficult to sustain, especially those with large numbers of dependents who cannot contribute to household income and a greater number of women who are not part of the communal labour. Two households that did not have any debt on them at the time of the research were Deen Mohammad's and Jumman's. They consisted of two people and one person respectively, and neither of them owned any fishing boats or nets. Allahdad's household had accrued a surplus of Rs. 10,000. The household consisted of thirteen persons in the largest houseboat, three fishing boats and one hundred and fifty nets. The adult labourers in this household comprised of five men and two women. Though this was a large household, the earning members outnumbered the dependents. Moreover, most of the earning members were adult men (compare with Bhudha's household above) and greater number of fishing equipment meant more share for this household in the collective earning for the whole community.

The debts are accumulated mainly in lieu of food items, medical treatment, new boats and the repair of old ones, and cash loans for buying nets, spending on ceremonial weddings and circumcisions or emergencies that require visiting a specialist doctor, such as complications during childbirth, and other sudden serious illnesses. Everyday food items and medical treatment can be obtained on credit from a shopkeeper and a local dispenser that the landlord-contractor has specified. These providers maintain credit accounts for every *loorya* household, which is balanced on a monthly basis by the landlord-contractor's *munshi* who keep revising, from time to time, the standing instructions for the credit limit for each household. New boats are made and the old ones repaired by a local carpenter who is paid directly by the landlord-contractor's *munshi*. Similarly, if a *loorya* decides to buy new fishing nets, he must make a request with the *munshi*, who in turn discusses it with his manager or the landlord-contractor himself, as the case maybe. If the proposed purchase is approved, the *munshi* accompanies the *loorya* to Multan where they buy the net together. The *munshi* himself makes the payment for the purchase and notes it down in the account of that *loorya*, never letting the money fall into the *loorya's* hand, lest it be spent for a different purpose. Requests for cash loans on the eve of weddings or medical emergencies are also thoroughly scrutinized and dealt with differently for different households, depending on their earning potential. For weddings, the *munshi* often directly arranges for the tents (*shamiana)*, the cook (*charhoya*), the drum-beater (*marasi*), the priest/marriage registrar (*molvi/nikaha-khwan*], and the renting of video player and cassettes for entertainment. All expenses are written in the household account maintained by the *munshi*, and thus added to the debt accumulated by a household. This shows the degree to which the *munshi* mediate the *looray* contact with the outside world.

STRATEGIES OF CONTROL

Those households which have a greater number of labourers and fishing assets (boats and nets) usually have higher credit limits with the providers (shopkeeper, dispenser, and carpenter).They can also secure greater cash loans from the *munshi*. This is for the simple reason that due to more earning hands (and assets) they can balance the accounts by claiming a greater share in the collective fish caught. Thus, for example, with large households, the headman Allahdad and his brother Sher Mohmmad bring larger quantities of food items and feel less hesitant to demand cash loans from the *munshi*, yet Sher Mohammad's debt, at Rs. 40,000, is lower than the average for all households, and Allahdad has accumulated a surplus of Rs. 10,000. Though they feel bitter about it, the *looray* do not expect to be treated equally by the landlord-contractor when it comes to setting credit limits or extending cash loans.

The landlord-contractor's strategy of setting different credit limits and extending loans on the basis of a household's ability to pay back rather than its actual needs to subsist, works as a strategy of control in two ways. Firstly, it perpetuates the status quo of economic stratification among *Allahdad-alay* by making the earning-spending relation an unbreakable vicious cycle—i.e. those with more fishing assets can earn more, and therefore they can accumulate more assets, and so on. Whereas, with no alternative sources of income or loans, the poorer households are trapped in a state of perennial low income due to their lower productivity, which, in turn, is because of low assets (persons, boats and nets), even though they provide their full labour in the collective fish catching. The comparison between Allahdad and Deen Mohammad in the above case is again noteworthy here. Whilst Allahdad had more assets, not only in the form of boats and nets but also the number of labourers in his household, he could further increase this last asset by arranging a second marriage for himself in presence of the first wife and her children, and the landlord-contractor had no hesitation in lending him money for this purpose. Meanwhile, Deen Mohammad remained a widower, sharing his small houseboat with his elderly mother. He possessed no fishing boats or nets, neither could he raise enough resources to get married again. Deen Mohammad had no debt on him, not because he did not want one, to spend on his second marriage, for example, but because he would not get a large amount from the landlord-contractor due to his low productivity as the sole earning member of an unimportant household (an elderly mother and no fishing assets).

Secondly, while setting the credit limit with the shopkeeper, the consideration for the landlord-contractor is not the total amount of debt on a particular *loorya* household but its current ability to contribute in the collective labour. Moreover, these credit limits fluctuate with the fishing season. Thus, regardless of the total debt accumulated with the landlord-contractor, a *loorya* household could obtain greater amounts of food items from the shop in the months of increased fishing activity, whereas during the off-season months (June, July, and August) they find it very hard to meet even basic necessities due to the low credit limit set for them. Food is, therefore, rationed by the landlord-contractor in accordance with the year-long productive cycle, which in turn is based on seasonal changes and governmental regulations—none of which *looray* can possibly have any degree of control over. These fluctuations in the credit limits, which are done with no regard to the total amount of debt, work as incentives to work hard in the fishing season and are a kind of control in the off-season to force them to dispense with whatever savings they might have done in the preceding months. If, in the months of the fishing season, most of their labour went on paying back the debt accumulated over a long time, they would perhaps not be motivated to work hard, whereas immediate return in the form of increased credit limits and the ability to have greater quantities of food and cash loans incentivizes them to catch more fish for the landlord-contractor.

Being a big local landowner, the landlord-contractor has two managers and twenty-eight *munshi*s to run his farms and fishing business. Each of the three groups of *looray* working for him has one designated *munshi* who works as their manager as well as a channel of communication between them and the landlord-contractor and/or his two main managers. The *munshi*s are routinely rotated among not only the three groups of *looray* but also between fishing and farming businesses, so that they do not become too attached to one group or develop an independent relation. In the *Allahdad-alay*, the current *munshi*, Allah Diwaya, operates mainly though contact with Allahdad. He is authorized to extend a cash loan of up to a few hundred rupees. Any request beyond that limit has to be put to the manager at the farms. Even these small loans are not available equally for everyone. Allah Diwaya often makes such a decision only after consulting the headman. That is why the majority of *Allahdad-alay* often do not approach the *munshi*, the manager or the landlord-contractor directly. Those households who have greater amount of debt and have fewer fishing assets are more hesitant to make any move without involving Allahdad. Occasionally though, they go directly to the landlord-contractor at his farmhouse to ask for big loans for weddings and so on. He may oblige or refuse, may make a payment on the spot or refer them to his managers.

CASE STUDY

It was during the fishing season that Bhudha's wife suddenly fell seriously ill. He had to take her to a private clinic in DG Khan. The treatment was very expensive. He needed around Rs. 10,000 if he were to get that treatment for her. This was a large amount and Bhudha could not demand it himself from the landlord-contractor because he was already owed a considerable debt of more than Rs. 100,000. Instead, Allahdad requested the loan, which was paid in three installments over the whole duration of the treatment. In the meanwhile, the landlord-contractor made sure through his *munshi*s that the money was being spent on the treatment only.

On a different occasion, this time in the off-season during the month of August, one of Allahdad's wives became ill. Allahdad needed just Rs. 600 for her medicine. The *munshi* refused to give him that amount saying that it was off-season and that they were already short of money. Due to the urgency of the situation, Allahdad could not manage to meet the landlord-contractor himself or his two managers in time to complain about the *munshi* and ask for money directly from them; therefore, he had to sell his wife's gold earrings to pay for her medicine.

How much influence did Allahdad, the headman, have with the landlord-contractor and his men? On one occasion he got his fellow *loorya* as much as Rs. 10,000 from the landlord-contractor and on the other he could not manage to get just Rs. 600 for his own wife's medicine. The fact that Bhudda's need happened to arise in the months of fishing season and Allahdad's wife fell ill in the off-season is only one part of the story. This variable treatment of not just a common *loorya* but the headman, Allahdad, should be understood as akin to the policy of fluctuating credit limits in accordance with the fishing season, as discussed in the preceding section. The landlord-contractor and his *munshi*s send contradictory signals to the *Allahdad-alay* regarding the powers and approach of their headman. On the one hand, they control the whole group through him, and on the other, they make him an example of their own control over the entire group.

Another manifestation of the strategies of control was how a conflict between a *loorya* and the landlord-contractor's *munshi*, usually because the *loorya* accuse the *munshi* of manipulating the accounts, was dealt with. Typically if such a case was brought to the landlord-contractor or his manager, they would consult Allahdad as the headman before taking any decisions. The decision would usually be to order the *loorya* household that was involved in the conflict to move to one of the other two settlements to work under another headman with another *munshi*. This is an outcome which both Allahdad and his *loorya* would not want, but they had little choice but to accept. It is obvious again that, on one hand, the landlord-contractor endorses the unique status of Allahdad as the head of the group by consulting him, and on the other hand, he imposes the decision of his own choice resulting in the displacement of the household of the *looray* who brought the complaint. It is important for the landlord-contractor to have one political head in every settlement so that he can easily deal with all the *looray* through this person.

Relocating *looray* households between the three settlements and the relocation of each settlement between three sections of the river also works as a strategy of control. The composition of each of the three settlements (*Allahdad-alay, Haji Yousaf-alay,* and *Khamesay-alay*), in terms of the numbers of houseboats and the households it comprised of, was changed every year. A settlement might have 30 houseboats in one season and half that number in the next. Similarly, the houseboats of five brothers might be part of one settlement in one season and they might be spread over all three in the next. Take, for example, the *Allahdad-alay*. This settlement had 20 houseboats from September 2000 to June 2001, but with the start of next fishing season in September 2001, nine households were ordered to leave the *Allahdad-alay* to join the *Haji Yousaf-alay* in the south. These included the houseboats of Mahboob and Mureed who were Allahdad's brothers. Meanwhile, three new houseboats joined the *Allahdad-alay*. These included Ali Muhammad and his two sons, Hazara and Mukhtiara. Ali Muhammad was a brother of Haji Yousaf and the three households were previously part of the *Haji Yousaf-alay*.

The relocation of an entire settlement to a different section of the river or different spots within the same section also took place routinely. The *Allahdad-alay* and *Haji Yousaf-alay* exchange their designated sections of the river every year at the end of the fishing season upon receiving instructions from the *munshi*. Rotating their settlements on a yearly basis meant that their immediate contacts on land, apart from the landlord-contractor's men, also changed every year. This lowered the possibility of them building any permanent relations with local land people, which could potentially involve the exchange of fish for money or other favours.

Apart from this major relocation every year, the houseboats in each of the settlements did not remain anchored to one place throughout a year but kept changing their anchorage following instructions from the *munshi*. Thus, in the summer months when the flow of water was high, they were anchored to the western bank, and in the winter, when the flow was low and the fishing activity was at its peak, they were instructed to anchor at some suitable seasonal island in the river, inaccessible by land to of any the local villagers who might be interested in buying fish directly from them.

Households were relocated between three settlements even when there was no complaint or request by a household. It is noteworthy that when the landlord-contractor relocated a household to a different settlement on the request of the *looray*, he always consulted the respective heads of both settlements. However, when he did it with the stated purpose of achieving efficiency in the organization of labour through the entire length of the river under his control, he did not hold any prior consultation with the headmen or take their opinions into consideration, neither could they dare to oppose his decision. This is ironic given that it is the fishermen, not the landlord-contractor or his *munshi*s and managers, who know best about how to organize their labour most efficiently, and they already have an interest in catching greater quantities of fish anyway.

A closer reading of this practice suggest that the landlord-contractor's calculations in relocating *looray* households take into account more than the efficient division of the labour force at his disposal. Constantly changing the composition of these groups counters any collective challenge to the control of the *munshi*s over their labour and therefore the authority of the landlord-contractor remains strong. The *Allahdad-alay* identified themselves as part of a larger *looray* kin group, as members of their *raj* working under one landlord-contractor, and as belonging to a household within that *raj*. The identity through the settlement named after the headman was only a temporary one. This identity could change any time on the orders of the landlord-contractor. If they were not constantly relocated between the three groups under three different headmen, they would perhaps form a permanent identity as group of kinsmen under one head, working in their own section of the river with one set of surrounding villages and villagers. This could potentially harm the landlord-contractor's interest which lies in keeping them divided, dispersed, and disconnected within themselves and with the surrounding villages as much as possible and consolidate his control over their labour, similar to his monopoly over the other main factor of production—the river.

CONCLUSION

The case of the *looray's* economic dependence on the landlord-contractor is in contrast to what Khan (2010) has observed in bangle-making and football-stitching industries in Hyderabad and Sialkot. Khan argues that due to a common patrilineage (*biradari*) in the bangle-making industry, and a common geographical and class origin in the football-stitching industry, the system of advance payment or *peshgi* is unlikely to develop into debt bondage: 'the sense of shared origin amongst workers and employers can mitigate the factors that lead to a relationship of debt bondage' (247).

In contrast, the *looray* do not share *biradari* or class ties, or the links of shared geography with the landlord-contractor or his agents. In fact, they inhabit a completely different geography of the river, speak a different language, and have an entirely different way of life, living in their houseboats. They entered into an economic relation of hired labour with the landlord-contractor due to circumstances that were beyond their control. Gradually, they have drifted into a state of debt bondage. With few strategic exceptions, every *looray* household was indebted to the tune of tens of thousands of rupees. These debts gradually increased, whilst their everyday labour went into balancing what was needed for sheer physical survival. They were unable to break out of this cycle of misery because fishing as their livelihood required them to work for the landlord-contractor due to the legally binding 'license raj' imposed upon them by government regulation. Giving up this livelihood was next to impossible because fishing was not just a means of earning but a way of life in their riverine *habitus*.

Relocating to another *raj* is a possibility, but only if another contractor is willing to buy off the debt with the current landlord-contractor. Such a move may not bring any meaningful change because it would be changing one master for another. In other words, it would not bring any real change to the situation of being tied to or *bhadhal* of a contractor. The landlord-contractor has evolved a number of strategies to consolidate his control over the *looray*. He does that mainly through his *munshis* and the *looray* headmen through incentives and punishments. One of the strategies is the system of compensation for collective labour in fish catching. The total amount earned by their collective labour is distributed over men, boats, and nets. Consequently, the three strategic exceptions from debt were the households that also had greater fishing assets in the form of nets and boats. By no coincidence, one of these was the headman's and other two his close relatives. These were also the households which were set a higher limit to buy their groceries on credit and request cash loans. In comparison, the members of the households with no fishing assets were trapped in a cycle of low income and low expenditure—and virtually no asset-building, even though they put their full labour into collective fishing.

The system of credit instead of cash wages and the imposition of arbitrary limits on a household's ability to buy consumables was another strategy of control. This arrangement meant that money hardly went into their pockets and they were kept out of participating directly in the economy and society not only as producers but also as consumers. Another strategy of control was the relocation of houseboats away from each other and to various spots in the river. Although it was done in the name of efficient organization of labour, it was often done arbitrarily and without consulting the households or headmen of the settlements. This strategy of constantly changing the composition of all three groups countered the possibility of the *looray* forming any wider group solidarity.

These fishermen called themselves *maachi* before they migrated to DG Khan. They used to catch crocodiles, the biggest and most dangerous animal in the river, and sold them at a high price because of their valuable skin. They were an independent people. But after they relocated, the local villagers gave them the negative term *looray*. They had to change their occupation from crocodile hunting to fish catching and for that they acquired new skills and bought new equipment by accepting loans from a local landlord. The government restrictions on commercial fishing meant that they lost their independence. With the passage of time, the landlord-contractor brought them under his full control. They resented the circumstances which were beyond their control and which have turned them into *bhadhal* of the landlord-contractor. They are also aware that it is with their labour, special skills, and equipment that the fish-catching is made possible and that the landlord-contractor could not do anything with the river without them, despite his monopoly over fishing rights. They express bitterness over being tied to a landlord-contractor but find it impossible to break out of it, at least as long as he has the monopoly over fishing rights.

REFERENCES

Ercelawn, A. & M. Nauman (2004), 'Unfree Labour in South Asia: Debt Bondage at Brick Kilns in Pakistan.' *Economic and Political Weekly*: 2235–2242.

Khan, A. (2010), 'Peshgi Without Bondage: Reconsidering the Links between Debt and Bonded Labour.' *Cultural Dynamics* 22(3): 247–266.

Martin, N. (2009), 'The political economy of bonded labour in the Pakistani Punjab.' *Contributions to Indian Sociology* 43(1): 35-59.

Scott, J. C. (1985), *Weapons of the Weak: Everyday forms of Peasant Resistance*. Yale University Press.

NOTE

1. This rate had been raised only a year previously from Rs. 8 per kg, after much pleading before the contractor.

CHAPTER 7

Bonded Labour in Domestic Work and Begging

Haris Gazdar and Ayesha Khan

B onded labour constitutes one of the gravest violations of individual
human rights. Its presence in any society poses a serious challenge
not only to the people who are bonded, but also to all individuals
and institutions. Bonded labour is a coercive and oppressive labour
arrangement. It is perceived—both at the popular level, as well as among
legislators and the judiciary—as akin to slavery. Any labour arrangement
involving the loss of an individual's liberty and where physical restriction
and violence against the person are accepted norms is abhorrent. Some
types of personal abuse—such as child labour, sexual exploitation and
rape—must be explicitly included in the category of violence against the
person. These and other forms of abuse exist in Pakistan in a range of
social and economic relationships. They are not limited to instances where
people are held in chains, but also exist in less conspicuous settings where
the chains are the invisible ones of social control. This chapter is premised
on the understanding that bonded labour is usually disguised as legitimate
'voluntary' economic transactions. A range of activities with some level of
coercion might come under the purview of legalistic definitions of bonded
labour yet there are other activities that fall outside it. There also some
activities which fulfill the legal definition of bonded labour but may not
be particularly oppressive or coercive. The violation of the person is only
the most conspicuous and extreme form that 'bondedness' might take.
The main objective of this chapter, therefore, is to comment on a range
of labour, credit, and labour-credit arrangements that exist in domestic
work and begging and their social and political dimensions.

A common view on bonded labour is that it is a system based on the
interlocking of labour and credit arrangements. In addition to the

transaction in the labour market, a worker also transacts with the employer on the credit market, repaying the debt by working for the creditor. The employer-creditor enjoys monopolistic power vis-à-vis the worker-borrower and thus is able to impose exploitative terms and conditions in both transactions. The worker is considered a bonded labourer if the terms faced on either or both markets are extraordinarily exploitative, and allow no exit from either or both sets of contracts. This abstract model of bonded labour finds an apparently straightforward empirical counterpart in the *peshgi* system that prevails in many informally organized sectors in Pakistan. In the *peshgi*, or advance payment, system, a worker-borrower contracts a cash or kind advance—in the case of agricultural tenants the advance is in the form of a production credit—from the employer-creditor. The worker-borrower then works on a piece-rate or wage-rate basis, and a part (in some cases all) of earnings goes to repay the advance. The worker-borrower cannot change employers or locations as long as the loan remains unpaid unless the new employer takes over the loan, thereby becoming the creditor. The role of the *peshgi* system is thought to be crucial in the understanding of bonded labour in Pakistan. This chapter shows that the *peshgi* system exists in domestic service but not in begging. Cases of coercive *peshgi* contracts in the domestic work sector between employers and employees in rural areas, and between urban employers and employees of a common rural background are presented in some detail. The chapter argues that although labour bonding through *peshgi* is absent in the begging sector, some labour arrangements come very close to outright slavery.

The data was collected by using a number of qualitative research tools including community profiling, key informant interviews, informal and formal interviews, case studies, and observations. The geographic focus of the study were the districts of Lahore and Sargodha in Punjab, and Karachi and Sanghar in Sindh, and the fieldwork was carried out between December 2002 to January 2003.[1]

DOMESTIC WORK

Domestic work is often regarded as a sector in which workers are highly vulnerable to coercion and abuse. The international debate on forced labour pays a great deal of attention to the possible association of domestic work with trafficking, child labour, and physical and sexual abuse. In many countries young women migrants, the vast majority of domestic workers, are particularly vulnerable to abuse by employers and/or by the authorities if they are illegal migrants. They may also be cut off from their own families and social networks. Domestic work has the added complexity in that the workplace is someone's home. Unlike work that takes place in a recognized 'workplace' environment, domestic service occurs in an environment that is likely to be marked by highly personalized relations and extraordinary dependence between employer and employee. Formal laws as well as informal social norms governing employer-employee relations may have less significance than traditional and familial norms of behavior.

The Pakistani state is unable to implement existing labour legislation in the formal sectors and lacks the will and ability to monitor conditions in the informal sectors that are well beyond its current reach. Moreover, the private home is believed to be a female sphere, true to the structure of a deeply patriarchal state and society. The public sphere is male-dominated and the private sphere the realm of the female so it is inappropriate and undesirable for the former to investigate the latter's functioning too closely. Therefore, the domestic service sector remains largely undocumented and an informal part of the economy. Domestic work is performed by men, women, or children. It includes tasks like gardening, guard duty, driving, cooking, serving meals, cleaning, dish-washing, clothes-washing, sweeping, dusting, ironing, child-care, massaging. Domestic service is availed by the elite of a given community, be it a village, town, or urban neighborhood, and the service providers are among the poorest and most vulnerable in rural and urban society. The contractual agreement between the employer and the employee or his/her family is often unwritten, non-binding, and heavily biased in favour of the employer.

LABOUR ARRANGEMENTS

The labour arrangements in this sector vary according to rural and urban settings and the backgrounds of the employers and workers. Caste-based domestic service in the home of a landlord often involves bondedness and is regarded as the most oppressive of labour arrangements. Domestic service in urban centres offers some opportunities for advancement to those for whom the alternatives are begging, brick kiln work, or bonded labour in agriculture. In a large urban centre, it also becomes possible for some domestic workers to enter into a more organized sector through the mediation of domestic service employment agencies. The caste and class dimension play an important role in shaping the labour arrangements for both rural and urban domestic workers. Whereas this is true for urban-based domestic workers to some extent, in rural settings the workers have very little opportunity to explore other income-generating strategies or to change their employer in case of extreme exploitation.

In rural areas, domestic servants come from a caste-based or class-based community of agricultural workers who are dependent on their landlord. Exploitation of the workers stems from the absolute power and control wielded by the landlord. Sometimes, caste affiliations with the type of labour one is required to provide are hard to shed even after gaining employment in the government sector. For example, a doctor in Shahdadpur had a government job in the district health office. He was also a local landlord. He used another low-ranking government employee, who came from a low caste in his village, as his personal servant. They both drew their salaries from the government but neither of them performed their official duties. A common practice for compensation for domestic work in rural areas is to pay in kind, usually wheat at the time of harvest. A Makhdoom landlord *in* Sargodha who owned 16 *muraba* of land in his village had five full-time servants in his city house. All of them were compensated with fixed amounts of wheat per annum from his lands. Men and women domestic servants with non-landed employers also receive occasional food and clothing. However, this is not in lieu of their salaries, but in addition to their monthly remuneration.

Workers in these situations do not receive adequate remuneration for their domestic work to pay off their debt. They are, therefore, not free to choose their employers. They may be bought and sold by way of landlords assuming the loan arrangements from one another, without their participation in the decision. Debts are accumulated on the workers because of their need to borrow from the landlords on occasions like marriages. One rural Punjabi family of tenants/domestic workers got into debt because a relative demanded Rs. 50,000 before agreeing to a *watta satta* marriage. The family requested their landlord lend them the money. The landlord, in turn, arranged for another landlord to pay the sum in return for the labour of one of the young daughters of the tenants. The daughter was thus sent to this landlord's house as a domestic servant where she would work to pay off the family debt with her labour. In another household in Lahore, a 12-year-old girl worked for the landlord in his house and her father worked on the landlord's farms in Sargodha. They 'received' 20 *maunds* of wheat and 20 *maunds* of rice per annum for their combined labour, but the rice actually never given, was held back to repay the Rs. 60,000 loan on the father.

For young boys and girls, household chores at the landlord's house are sometimes combined with tending his animals. Landlords arbitrarily decide who among their servants would work inside the house or at the farms and who would be sent to a different landlord as a 'gift' or a bargain. Young girls among bonded domestic servants are said to be sent to other landlords as 'gifts'. For example, SH, aged 20, used to work for a landlord in a Punjabi village from the age of 4. At 15, her employers took her to Lahore with them against the wishes of her mother. SH moved between city and village twice over the next few years. Eventually her marriage was arranged by the landlords to a servant of another landlord in a different village. She could not refuse this marriage due to the fear of being beaten up. SH worked extra long hours as punishment for small mistakes and received beatings with sticks and horse-whips.

Case study 1: Rural domestic worker
N is a Musalli woman (Muslim Sheikh), illiterate, married, and working in the *haveli* of Z, a big landlord. Z owns N's home, although she built it herself. In her house, she has electricity but no other amenity. She has four daughters and two sons. Her husband, M, also works in Z's house. Two daughters live in Multan. N and her daughter, T, clean the floors, wash the clothes, and do the dishes in Z's house. Her husband looks after the animals and their sons water the lands. They work from five in the morning until eight at night. Their own house is right next to the *haveli*, so that they can be summoned in case work is needed at any time. Z's wife is particularly cruel, and hits them with her shoes. If they are sweeping she follows them around hitting them with her shoes, saying they are working too slowly or not doing the job right. Z also hits her husband and sons but N isn't sure for what reason.

N came here six years ago. Before that, she used to live in a village whose landlord, Chaudhry (landed employer), loaned her Rs. 80,000 to marry off her son and daughter. But it was very difficult to repay the loan, so the outstanding Rs. 60,000 was 're-financed'. That is, Z paid the amount to his friend the Chaudhry. In effect he bought them by taking on their debt and so they came to work with him. T says that if a flowerpot breaks during cleaning, and if it is worth Rs. 25, then it is added to the loan at a rate of Rs. 500. If an animal dies, its value is also added to the loan. It has gone from Rs. 60,000 to three lakhs.

This system of deducting money for every item damaged is called *parchi charhana*. By way of some compensation, every person is given 200 rupees and one sack of wheat. They use the wheat to reduce their loan and do not take it. Here, kidney and eye problems are common. T and her brother were married off in *watta satta*, but she got divorced and that is why she is back. Z often has men friends over who drink, and think nothing of bothering the Musalli girls.

In urban areas, labour arrangements in domestic service are such that the earnings from part-time work at more than one household yield higher income than full-time live-in domestic service with one employer. The advantage of part-time work for women is that they can return home to their household duties in the evenings. From the perspective of employers, part-time women workers are cheaper to hire than full-time male servants, thus making domestic help affordable for middle-income groups. Rates for part-time work vary in accordance with the type of task, e.g. gardening, ironing, cooking, cleaning, dish-washing, and cloth-washing. Men are better paid than women domestic workers. If the workers are absent or late from work they lose part of the remuneration.

Full-time domestic work brings with it more uncompensated labour. This is perhaps why it is preferable for many employers who can afford it. Working hours for live-in domestic servants vary but the servants are on call 24 hours a day. In many cases, when rural landlords migrate to cities they bring their domestic servants with them. Thus the caste-based bondedness in domestic service in rural areas replicates itself in domestic service in urban areas. The servants are made to work under conditions of long hours, virtually no pay or holiday, and often high abuse. One educated employer in Lahore whose husband worked in the Punjab Tourism Department employed a young boy, 12 years old. He worked full-time dishwashing and helping her in the kitchen, for which he received no remuneration at all. He was the son of a *muzara* (tenant) of her husband in a village in Bahawalpur. So the assumption was that his labour was in return for his father's continued employment and possible financial support. The same lady employed a part-time servant as well, a woman who came in briefly to do the cloth washing and cleaning and was promptly compensated for her service. By contrast to this case, an influential landlord in Karachi had a different kind of arrangement with his domestic servants. Most of his domestic servants belonged to his own caste. He considered them his relatives. Some of them had been working for him since they were children. He paid them in cash and gave them pocket money as well. He said he trusted them because they were his relatives. He strongly denied any suggestion that they might be bonded to him.

Case study 2: Part-time domestic workers

A, age 11, is from the Christian community and has been working in houses for the last three years. She goes to the residential Neelam Colony from her home every day and works in two houses, where she does cleaning and washing. Her mother and sister work nearby in other houses. She gets Rs. 300 and food and at times extra money, but if she is late or absent then she is severely admonished and in case of too many absences her salary is deducted.

She works from 8 am to 5 pm. If her work is finished early, she joins her mother and sister and helps them. When her mother is not with her, her *baji* makes her work more than usual. She makes her clean the ceilings and sends her to grocery stores and does not let her go early. She hands her the care of her children and takes a nap and keeps her late. A does not like cleaning, especially the toilets. The children of the house where she works are in her age group, but she is not allowed to play with them.

Case study 3: Part-time domestic worker

KM, age 45, migrated to Karachi from Gujranwalla 25 years ago. He was a brick-kiln worker in his native village, but in the city he began as a construction worker. Today, he lives in a rented house at Shah Rasool Colony for Rs. 2,500/month. His house has one bedroom and lounge, running water, gas, and electricity. He lives in the house with his wife, two sons, and two daughters. KM works as a sweeper with the Karachi Development Authority, for Rs. 2,200/month, from 6am to 2pm, with Sundays off. His job was arranged through a contractor and he is content to keep the arrangement. He makes extra money working as a gardener in the evenings in a private home, for which he is paid Rs. 500/month with Rs. 100 as a tip on Eid.

His wife, age 38, has been a domestic worker since she was very young. She used to earn Rs. 1,000/month working at multiple private homes, and now she has just one employer and earns Rs. 1,500/month, for working seven days a week, 8am to 1pm. One of her daughters used to work with her until she married a brick kiln worker. Her second daughter, age 16, has been employed since she was 10 years old at the home of an army colonel. She used to earn only Rs. 500/month and now gets Rs. 1,500/month. The two young sons do not work yet; one is studying the Quran and the other is in school.

KM says it is hard to manage his household on this income, and the worst disaster is an illness in the family. He would prefer it if his daughter did not work alone in a private home, apart from her mother.

Case study 4: Urban domestic worker

P, age 13, is a Musalli by caste. She has been living in Lahore for the last four years, since she arrived from the village Chak J near Sargodha. Her father runs a *tonga* and her mother used to work in the *choudhry's* (landed employer's) house in Chak J. P has six brothers and sisters. P works in the *choudhry's* daughter's house. She worked at the *choudhry's* house in the village before, but when his married daughter had a baby, P was sent to Lahore to work in her house. She looks after the baby boy and cooks. She used to do all the cleaning and washing work as well as the cooking but since her *baji* had her second child, a 10-year-old girl called D has been brought from Chak J to do the cleaning.

P does not want to stay with her *baji*. She says the husband scolds her and makes the servants work the whole day. If any guests come at night they are woken up to work, even at midnight, and even then they are scolded. The younger servant girl, D, is even beaten by *baji*. Nonetheless they have to stay here because their parents have borrowed money from the *choudhry*, although she does not know how much. P gets 800 rupees a month but does not get the money; it is deducted out of the loan. There is no extra money, but she gets transport money when she goes home to Sargodha. If a guest gives her any money as a tip she gives it to *baji* towards the loan payment. She is not stopped from eating anything she wants and receives new clothes from her employers. However, she wants to stay with her own family. There is no male in the house and if there is, then *baji* does not leave her alone in the house.

Urban domestic work, both part-time and full-time, involves a higher level of job insecurity. Workers have no binding contracts with their employers. If they are absent for too long or too often, as determined by the employer, or if they request an increase in their salaries, they run the risk of losing their jobs. In the urban context, advances are also not as forthcoming as they are in the rural setting under the *peshgi* system.

BONDAGE, HARASSMENT, AND VIOLENCE

Domestic servants are vulnerable to violence because of an unequal power relation with their employers in the private sphere away from the reach of legal redress. Reports of violence against domestic servants in rural areas are greater in number than in urban homes where women domestic servants complained consistently of being subjected to various forms of sexual harassment. In one Punjabi village, a mother and her divorced daughter worked together in the house of a wealthy employer. According to the daughter, the landlord often had male friends over who would get drunk and start bothering her and other Musalli girls; they would 'think nothing of it'. Other women domestic workers in Punjabi villages also complained of the drunken behavior of landlords and how they made them do 'strange' things. There were numerous stories of women who had returned from big cities like Karachi and Lahore because of the sexual abuse or harassment they experienced there. Sometimes, the women face hostility from their own men who accuse them of having illicit relations with the employers.

In urban centres, women domestic servants who travel on public transport and walk to and from work every day regularly experienced whistles, catcalls, and comments. Younger girls in particular were singled out for such treatment. Some women were sexually harassed by their employers when their wives were away. In Karachi, a sixteen-year-old girl got pregnant by the son of the employer. When the parents of the boy found out about it, they arranged for the girl to have an abortion, gave her some money, and arranged her marriage with her cousin. In a Punjabi village, an employer beats his male servants with sticks and the employer's wife hits her women servants with her shoes. On one occasion when one of the servants, a married Musalli girl aged 20, tried to protest against the employer's plans to remove her son from school and to put him to work with his father in the stables, he beat her up very badly. Violence like this is not limited to domestic worker in rural areas. Those in urban localities also talked at length about 'bad' *bajis*, ones who slap girls if not satisfied with their work or lose their temper on trivial matters. Servants in both rural and urban areas dreaded of being accused of theft which often led to police investigations, punishment, and loss of jobs.

Adolescent domestic workers, aged 10–24 years, enjoy neither the protection given to small children nor the powers of adults, yet they are expected to shoulder the same burdens as that of the adult domestic workers on one hand and on the other, they are treated as unknowing, gullible children. They suffer from exposure to physical and emotional trauma not only because they are overworked but also because they face punishment. When under-age boys and girls work, it cannot be assumed that they do so with their full consent. These workers usually, but not always, say that they would prefer to be studying at schools but their families cannot afford that. In most cases, the salaries of the under-age domestic workers are sent directly to their parents or next of kin; they have little say over the choice of the employers to work for, and they are expected to continue working until they get married or leave home. Young girls are particularly vulnerable to violence and harassment.

The landlords in rural areas, or those urban employers who like to live like landlords even after they have migrated to cities, tend to hire young girls and boys more often than do employers from professional urban backgrounds. These children work in return for little or no money and usually come from families who are bonded to the employers or their extended families in the villages. For example, in Sargodha, one educated woman whose husband was a government servant in the city and owned one *muraba* of land in his village had a full-time male servant for 25 years. This servant belonged to the village of the husband. He works as a watchman, gardener, and dishwasher. For all these services he received ten *maunds* of wheat per annum. In the same household, a 16-year-old married Musalli girl did the washing, cleaning, and cooking. This girl was 'given' to them by her former landlord. She could visit her husband and the rest of her family back in the village only when the master permitted.

Case study 5: child domestic worker
F is 14-years-old and works at *makhdoom's* (landlord) house. Her family belongs to a village near Sargodha. Her father was a labourer but was injured four years ago by fireworks during a wedding and now stays home; her mother works at a *tandoor* and her brother is a driver in the village at the *makhdoom's* house. Her brothers have studied up to the primary level, but her sisters have not. F cooks, cleans, and washes clothes in the house. She has been here for the last six years. The work has increased over time. She gets 36 sacks of wheat, about one *maund* per year, and no salary. Sometimes, when she is given a little cash handout, she buys tea and sugar for her family, since these items are expensive. Her employers give her old clothes and a new outfit for summer, winter, and Eid.

She would like to get 500 rupees because the work-load is heavy but she would not like to work anywhere else. She says her *baji* is nice, does not scold her if something is broken and pays for her medical treatment. F wants to study and has just started reading Urdu with her *baji*. She likes to watch television and also listens to music with *baji*. Washing pots and pans is tough work, she says, and so is making 20 to 25 *chapattis* a day. But there are all kinds of facilities here in the town, unlike the village where there is not even a toilet. Every two months she goes to visit her family.

BEGGING

Begging is a vast and complex informal work sector that encompasses a range of activities whereby an individual asks strangers for money on the basis of being poor or needing charitable donations. Beggars may also sell small items, such as dusters or flowers, in return for money that may have little to do with the value of the item for sale. The nature of activities and the range of people involved in begging are extremely heterogeneous and pose profoundly complicated questions of definition: To what extent is begging an economic activity? What constitutes a 'labour' arrangement? How might different forms of begging be related to other seemingly associated 'economic' activities, such as scavenging, sex work, entertainment, and other services? What is the interaction between begging and illegal activities such as petty crime and selling narcotics? The study of begging is further complicated by the fact that it involves the loss of status, is proscribed by law, and encompasses activities at the social, economic, and political margins.

Anecdotal evidence suggests coercive and abusive labour relations in this sector. Newspapers periodically run stories about 'beggar mafias' that exploit the 'labour' of street beggars, sometimes in collusion with police. There are also accounts of kidnapped children being maimed and used as beggars. However, the important issues like who begs, why, and under what circumstances are often ignored. The popular perceptions of begging are coloured by strong moral and religious views. The public is preoccupied with alleviating guilt through occasional handouts to beggars (particularly during the holy month of Ramzan), making judgments on the 'real' need of a beggar, or expressing strong opinions on whether begging should be permitted or not. On one hand, begging is viewed as a sign of growing poverty, or indigence, and as an occupation of last resort, but on the other, it is linked to crime and illicit activities.

Begging activities are not always organized by group, caste, or mafia, and there may or may not be intermediaries involved. Begging is best understood by observing its linkages or roots in socio-economic ciondintions. Some of these are rural-urban migration, urban unemployment, caste-based restrictions and opportunities, illegal businesses such as the drug trade and sex work, and the powerful role of *patharidars* in a range of mafia activities that include using children, elderly, and the disabled as beggars. A beggar's techniques and labour arrangements depend on how he or she came into this line of work. Whereas there is no clear-cut bondedness in the begging sector of the kind seen, for example, in the agricultural sector, this kind of labour is nonetheless coerced or forced through a severe set of circumstances.

LABOUR ARRANGEMENTS

Labour arrangements in begging are unconventional and difficult to categorize according to the usual notions of what constitutes work and how it is compensated. The popular view that begging takes place in the form of organized networks operating in their designated areas is contested as a falsely sensationalized picture in the media. According to some journalists who cover this issue and the beggars themselves, begging is hardly organized beyond family level and the older or senior beggars have very limited control over the younger ones. However, many commentators from the journalist community and government officials agree that beggars have close connections with organized criminal gangs and are often involved in sex work. Police officials concede the possibility of beggars working as occasional informants for criminal gangs but they also deny the presence of organized crime mafia behind beggars' day-to-day activities. In fact, the police accuse traffic wardens of taking cuts from beggars for allowing them to operate at traffic signals and intersections whereas the traffic wardens claim that the police is responsible for allowing begging on the streets and in some cases patronizing them.

Beggars can be divided in several categories. Seasonal beggars are those who visit big cities during Ramzan and Eid to make extra money. The rural-urban migrant beggars in both Lahore and Karachi come mainly from the impoverished areas of southern Punjab. Urban-based beggars are those who have 'purchased' prime begging locations from the police and effectively guard those spots against any intrusion by other beggars. Among these latter organized beggars, some interviews suggest the presence of a mafia that kidnaps children, including disabled ones, and maims them to use as beggars. However, this crime is on the decline due to effective police action and vigilance. In one case, an FIR (First Information Report) was registered with Karachi police regarding a missing child. A local police officer suspected a beggar of involvement and observed him for a few days. The police then raided the house of the beggar and recovered two kidnapped children. The beggars had chained and locked these children in a room and had sexually abused them repeatedly. Over a six-day remand with the police, he confessed to kidnapping these children from a neighborhood in Karachi and said that they were going to be sold to a mafia groups who would maim and use them as beggars.

Police officials were of the view that begging was organized more around the caste-system than criminal gangs. The main castes involved in begging were Bhatto (Punjabi Muslim), Bhagri (Sindhi Hindu) in Karachi and Mirasi (Rajasthani-origin Muslim) and Musalli (or Muslim Sheikhs) in Lahore. Begging in rural areas and small towns of Sindh and Punjab also appears to be caste-based. Caste-based beggars live in settlements with other extremely low-income communities. Most of the time, they are rural-urban migrants who were not beggars in their places of origin. Many come to cities to escape debt-bondage and harassment by the landlords in their villages.

Some women beggars sell flowers, *mehndi*, balloons, and *muswa* (sugared sweet). Children are often seen selling dusters, newspapers, and pencils and men combine begging with fruit and vegetable selling as well as working in the *mandi* (vegetable market) as labourers. Some Hindu women did not work as domestic servants because they feared that they would be accused of stealing because of being Hindu. In some cases women also worked at home to supplement their family income. For example Bhattos in Star Gate Karachi supplemented their incomes by sewing and quilting (*rilli*) even though begging was a major part of their earning. They claim that they resorted to begging after their men lost their jobs as porters at Karachi airport. This suggests that begging, even in those communities for which it is a traditional occupation, is an occupation of last resort.

Case study 6: A reluctant beggar
J, 35, has been married for ten years. She is a Marwari Hindu. She has eight children. Her husband used to be a construction labourer, but unemployment brought him to Karachi in search of better opportunities that have not materialized. Now he makes flower wreaths and she begs. Her husband does not like her to beg, so they fight over it, and now she does it when he is not around. She takes four or five of her children with her to make it easier. J makes 40–50 rupees a day, and her husband makes Rs. 80–90 a day selling flowers. He always brings a little home even on a bad day, but she has to beg for the household needs. She can earn through this work without spending anything herself. She started four years ago, and only goes in front of the Karachi University to beg because she is not familiar with routes and other parts of city.

> She only goes out to beg in the afternoon, and is afraid of her husband seeing her. J has brought her eight-year-old niece, P, from Tando Adam to beg here as well, as she feels it is better than her sitting at home with nothing to do and no food to eat. P earns well, up to Rs. 60 a day. She gives it to her aunt who saves almost all of it for her so that she can take it back to her parents in the village. She also wants her niece to take advantage of the *zakat* and ration distributed in the locality during Ramzan. When J goes to beg with her children she fears that her husband may see them. She also is frightened of crossing the road with them, in case of an accident. She would prefer to keep her children out of begging but now they have got into the habit and they even go out to beg without their mother. She suspects they enjoy it. Whatever they get, they spend on themselves, so J thinks it is better to keep them with her to keep control over the money.
>
> Ten people live in J's *jhonpri*. They own two *charpais*, some bedding, a box, a fan, a radio, and an urn for water. Their kitchen is a kerosene stove in the ground. The washroom is made of wood and bamboo covered by cloth. A fan and light-bulb run on electricity.

BONDAGE, COERCION, AND HARASSMENT

Begging presents itself as a profession of last resort. Mirasis in Punjab beg only when their singing does not earn them enough income: 'we are known as Mir Alam and society wouldn't accept us in another profession,' said one Mirasi in Lahore. As a result, it is not just singing but also begging that is associated with this caste. 'We beg because this is what our people do' is a commonly heard phrase among beggars belonging to various castes traditionally associated with begging. Thus children are born into begging as a way of life that offers no escape from it. However, a large number of those included in this study reported that they started begging only when their agricultural work, small shops, and odd jobs could not earn them enough to support their families. For example, *hijras* turned to begging and sex work when their role as ritual performers was gradually curtailed. Not all *hijra* or Bhattos or Bhagris or Mirasis are beggars but their caste association with begging results in a lower status in society. *Hijra* are further exploited by their gurus who force them into sex work, take heavy cuts from their earnings and control decisions in their everyday life, in return for protection and giving them their name. A *hijra* without a guru is a pariah to the *hijra* community.

Beggars in urban areas live in fear of their young girls being kidnapped and sexually abused. As a result, they hesitate to send their young girls out for begging which has the negative effect of reducing the family income for these poor families. Children safety on roads is another big concern for the parents. When they grow up, these children find begging a pre-determined line of work which they find difficult to break out of. Girls are sometimes forced into sex work by their family members to supplement their income. They are thus exposed to sexual violence and disease as are young children exposed to road mishaps and disability or death. At the same time, many parents desire more children in order to generate more income through begging. Some young girls may refuse to go out for begging after their marriage but they are reined in either through direct physical violence or through isolation and social pressure. Likewise, young *hijras* are sometimes coerced into castration and sex work by their *gurus*. Those who try to resist are subjected to social pressure and boycott by the entire community. Small children who have been kidnapped and maimed into begging are also sometimes encouraged to become drug addicts by their kidnappers or *patharidars*. They might even be inflicted with physical disabilities, such as amputated limbs, for example, to turn them into better earners.

Case study 6: Fear of kidnapping

F is a beggar from Khanewal. Her husband lost an arm in a land dispute. She has one son, married and educated, another unmarried, and one daughter who teaches the Quran in houses in the settlement. Her son earns Rs. 2,000 from his job in a nearby showroom but that is not enough, so she begs and earns Rs. 40–50 a day. She begs on the streets, and in addition to cash sometimes gets *sadqa* meat (religious charitable offering). She also sews *rillis* and earns Rs. 100/month for that work. She is unhappy with her work and says her boys earned better when they had jobs at the airport, where even though they had to give a cut to their contractor or *thekedar* (Rs. 50–100/month) they still earned enough.

Recently, she has put her daughters to work at home-based sewing because she is afraid of their being kidnapped. They sew dusters that they sell at Bolton Market for Rs. 13 for one dozen, or Rs. 2.5 for one. They also sell newspapers and get 50 paisas. She also worries about her sons being kidnapped while begging and sold for camel racing. She mentions a girl who was kidnapped and only escaped through the help of a teacher. The family income has been reduced because the girls are now sitting at home instead of begging.

Because beggars live in illegal settlements in urban centres, the security of their homes is dependent on patronage of the authorities. Residents complain of police harassment and threat of evacuation by the local administration. Sometimes they are arrested in police action against beggars and have to pay heavy fines for their release. In rural areas landlords demand *wangar,* from the beggars and tenants, i.e., a whole day's labour in return for just a meal. If they do not comply with the landlord's demand, they may face physical violence and eviction from his land.

CONCLUSION

The insights from this study of domestic work and begging can be summed up as following. Firstly, the precise economic role of *peshgi* in an inter-locking labour-credit contract is not straightforward. The classic account of labour bonding under inter-locking labour and credit transactions is neither an exclusive nor a sufficient model for understanding the diverse forms of coercive labour arrangements in Pakistan. In some cases, it is not even clear whether the employer or the employee is the real creditor in economic terms. There are many contracts, for example, where a worker is remunerated towards the end of the contract period. Even if s/he now takes an advance from her/his employer, in strictly economic terms s/he might still be a net creditor. Secondly, dispensing with the idea of inter-locking labour and credit contracts, it is possible to hypothesize that *peshgi* provides a lever or a legitimizing mechanism for employers to exert control over workers. This interpretation of *peshgi* also requires qualification. Workers who are socially much weaker than their employers—either because they belong to social groups (or caste-based communities) at the lower end of the social hierarchy (such as the Musalis in Punjab, or the Odhs in Sindh) or because the employers enjoy a local monopoly of socio-political power—are vulnerable to coercion and abuse under the *peshgi* system. But these workers are vulnerable to abuse even in those situations where the *peshgi* system is absent. Other workers who enjoy greater social parity with their employers, such as the glass bangle workers (See Khan, this volume), are less vulnerable to abuse even when they take *peshgi.*

Thirdly, in virtually all sectors, both workers and employers face uncertainty and insecurity in the enforcement of contracts. Workers in the 'freest' segment of the labour market—say, daily wage-rate construction labourers—fear that their employers (the contractors) might renege on payment for services rendered. Many of the employers, on the other hand, fear a high probability of worker default, and cite this as a reason for not advancing loans to workers. These observations give rise to an alternative, potentially powerful, interpretation of the *peshgi* system—that it represents one way in which workers can secure advance payment for their services, which they fear might go unremunerated if their accounts were settled only at the end of the contract period.

In conditions where the general contractual environment is insecure, workers who are socially weak compared to their employers are likely to be fearful of employer default. Workers who enjoy similar levels of social power to their employers are likely to be more confident of recovering their arrears. The *peshgi* system, according to this view, is not a credit arrangement designed to ensure labour supply. Rather, it is an assurance device that allows workers to enter a contract in an otherwise insecure contractual environment. Those workers who are vulnerable to employer default are the socially weak, and therefore also vulnerable to other forms of coercion and abuse. The key to ending bonded labour—according to this interpretation—lies not in improving poor people's access to credit, but in improving the overall contractual environment and reducing social hierarchy.

The issue of social hierarchy—either in the generalized sense of 'high' and 'low' castes, or in the localized context of the political monopoly of an individual employer—is important in all instances of coercive and abusive labour arrangements. The social hierarchy in terms of caste/ kinship community is important in the rural areas in both Punjab and Sindh in the extraction of unpaid labour, physical and verbal abuse, vulnerability to sexual exploitation, and the danger of bondedness. An inter-sectoral perspective allows some insights into the significance of caste and social grouping in this regard. Caste or social grouping, and networks are important features of the labour market in all sectors, regardless of the existence of hierarchy or abuse. For example, a large proportion of the people involved in marginal activities such as begging are identified by specific ethnic, caste, and kinship identities. Groups such as the Bhattos or Bagris, for example, have a significant presence in the begging sector across cities and provinces. Caste and kinship-based social networks, therefore, were found to be crucial in the operation of labour arrangements in general.

The manner in which these group identities operate in various sectors and for various people, however, differs. In some sectors and in some labour arrangements, there is no strong social hierarchy in the relations between employers and employees. Caste or kinship-based social networks either appear to be one more form of organization without any added significance in the employer-employee relationship, or these networks generate some level of solidarity between employers and employees.

Instances where the social distance between employers and employees is wide, however, are those where the danger of coercion and abuse is the highest. There are a number of groups—such as the Musalis and Masihis and other *kammi* castes of Punjab, or Bheels, Odhs, and Bagris of Sindh, or the 'nomadic' Riasatis (from south Punjab) in Karachi—at the margins of economy, society, and polity. These groups are vulnerable to abuse across sectors, across contractual arrangements, and even across locations. In some cases, a group that is 'socially weak' in one location appears to be relatively 'strong' in another—for example, the Odh/Rangar of Punjab appear stronger than their Odh counterparts in Sindh. A clearer understanding of the systematic nature of coercion and abuse, therefore, requires a great deal of attention to social as well as economic relations.

Cultural mechanisms may exist whereby individuals belonging to a particular social group remain associated with a particular type of economic activity. Social perceptions—even if not based upon empirical evidence—can lead to the reproduction of social hierarchy. If employers generally perceive people from a particular group to be suited for certain types of jobs, individuals from that group will be largely excluded from other jobs. The social perception might also become a self-fulfilling prophecy if the group in question acquires and maintains special knowledge and ability with respect to that particular job. Individual members of the group may themselves believe their economic options to be limited to the jobs assigned them in social perceptions. This form of adhesion by a social group to an economic activity might well be regarded as a form of bondedness, characterized by a psychological dependence, particularly if the job in question is a low-paid, hazardous, and unpleasant one.

NOTE

1. This chapter is based on the findings of a Rapid Assessment (RA) research project commissioned by Bonded Labour Research Forum in Pakistan with the financial assistance of the International Labour Organization.

CHAPTER 8

Constructing a Culture of Fear: The Role of Gender Based Violence in Controlling Bonded Labour in Pakistan

SADAF AHMAD

The literature on bonded labour in Pakistan highlights a number of reasons that have collectively contributed to the existence of this system and sheds light on the factors that have prevented bonded labourers from successfully challenging those who exploit them. The threat of violence or the experience of violence contributes to the culture of fear that bonded labourers live in and is one of the factors that reduces the likelihood of their challenging the asymmetrical power relations that they are caught in. Violence therefore serves as a mechanism of control, one that facilitates the continuance of the system. This chapter engages with this idea but also draws upon case studies of those working in debt bondage in brick kilns and the agricultural sector to build upon it and suggest that violence is differentially effective when it targets bodies that are culturally inscribed in a particular manner in a patriarchal society.[1]

Bodies are cultural texts and can be viewed as a 'surface on which the central rules, hierarchies, and even metaphysical commitments of a culture are inscribed' (Bordo 1989: 13). Michel Foucault (1979) refers to these constructed bodies as 'docile bodies', bodies which he asserts have been disciplined by a range of institutions in modern society. Foucault's account is useful in identifying the manner in which human bodies become a product of hegemonic institutions and a text of culture. However, others have built upon his work and shown how this text may differ for different segments in society, men and women being two such segments (Bartky 2003). Adrienne Rich, for instance, refers to a woman's body as 'the terrain on which patriarchy is erected' and it is in this context that we see the meanings inscribed on women's bodies differing from men's in a patriarchal set up (cited in Thornham 2000: 159).

Pakistan's hegemonic cultural and nationalist discourse portrays women as 'the weaker sex' who also embody the honour of their households and their nation. This honour is tied to their 'sexual purity' (Saeed 2001; Haeri 2002) and any act that mars this purity is popularly believed to shame and dishonour them, their family and the larger community/ nation. Protecting *his* women (not just his own mother, sisters, and daughters but also his nation's) from all kinds of harm in general and from sexual violence in particular is thus one of the acts of a *ghairatmand* or honourable man, and ties to his gendered desire to keep women safe and their collective honour intact. It is this context, one in which women's bodies and their protection are inscribed by very specific gendered meanings, that I suggest that violence or the threat of violence against women in bonded labour has the potential of being differentially effective in maintaining the status quo.

It is important to understand the context in which women work as bonded labourers to fully appreciate the importance of violence as a mechanism of control. I therefore begin this chapter by providing a brief overview of bonded labour in Pakistan and highlight the various factors (that include but are not limited to violence) that play a role in reproducing this system. I then focus on the relationship between gender based violence and control, and move onto delineating the multiple ways in which the former serves as an agent of control; an agent that is as effective but differentially so when it is directed towards women's bodies.

BONDED LABOUR IN PAKISTAN: A MANIFESTATION OF INTERSECTING VULNERABILITIES

Debt bondage is considered to be a form of slavery and it is estimated that twenty million people are enslaved in some form or the other across the world (Human Rights Watch 1995; BBC News 2004). It is estimated that up to two million people are in debt bondage in Pakistan (US Department of State 2010). They can be found in a range of industries that include but are not limited to carpet-weaving, domestic work, mining, and fisheries, with the heaviest concentration in agricultural work in interior Sindh and southern Punjab followed by brick making in Punjab (Human Rights Watch 1995).

Debt bondage is a condition that typically arises when a man takes an advance or *peshgi* from his employer and pledges his, and oftentimes his family's, labour in return. The debtor, and those whose labour he pledges, are then compelled to keep working until that debt is paid. However, the probability of paying off the debt is small. The wages these workers earn are low to begin with. Regular deductions—to pay back the *peshgi*, and in many sectors like the brick kilns, to pay for their accommodation, electricity, and any fines incurred—means that what they end up with is lower still. As savings are an impossibility when their wages are barely enough to meet their basic needs, many in debt bondage often find themselves in a position of asking their employers for even more loans for expenses related to illnesses or life events like marriages. The amount they owe, especially if it is large to begin with, thus only increases with time and it is not difficult to find families who have been working under conditions of debt bondage for more than one generation. The debt does not end with death but merely gets transferred to other family members (Ercelawn and Nauman 2001, 2004).

Although poverty plays a critical role in determining whether or not people end up working as bonded labourers, a historical overview of changing policies and cross sector research reveals that the state of bondage is the result of intersecting vulnerabilities. People's economic vulnerabilities have been compounded because of a number of reasons. Structural changes, inaccessibility to social networks, not having national identity cards and illiteracy are the most pertinent ones and I will go over each of these briefly below.

Structural inequalities have played a critical role in increasing the gap between the 'haves' and the 'have-nots' and ensured that those seeking justice find it difficult to do so (Human Rights Watch 1995). Policies introduced in the first couple of decades of Pakistan's existence, such as the Essential Services Maintenance Act of 1952 and the Land Reform Act of 1959, for instance, systematically undermined workers' rights and favoured those who already possessed land. Many *haris* or agricultural workers found themselves unemployed in the aftermath of the green revolution of the 1960s that sought to industrialize the agricultural sector. They became further marginalized in the subsequent land reforms that made land distribution even more inequitable than it already was, and their vulnerability to exploitation increased in a context where a capitalist mode of agricultural production weakened the traditional relations between landowners and workers (Human Rights Watch 1995).

Migrants, working as brick kiln or agricultural labour, also occupy a vulnerable position because they find themselves in a space where they have no access to social networks that they can draw upon in times of hardship. As such, they find that turning to their employers for monetary assistance in the form of loans is their only choice, especially when there are no alternative credit facilities available (Ercelawn and Noman 2001). They are thus more likely to find themselves in debt bondage and to pledge their and their families' labour against the amount they borrow in comparison to their fellow workers who are from that region.

Not having a national identity card is another source of vulnerability. Workers without these cards cannot take advantage of social protection or income support schemes where they do exist, and are thus more likely to seek loans (Awan 2010). Illiterate workers are also more susceptible to becoming trapped in the web of bondage as they cannot read their contract or the record of how much they owe their employer when such contracts and records do exist (ILO 2002). This is particularly significant in a context where 'most if not all creditors fiddle the accounts in every way possible' (Ercelawn and Nauman 2001: 17; Human Rights Watch 1995).

People's poverty and their subsequent need to grab onto work whenever the opportunity arises can also make them more susceptible to exploitation. Shirmati Dhori, a *hari* in debt bondage in Sindh, admitted that 'at that point we needed the work so badly that we started immediately without asking too many questions' (Mehergarh 2007: 39). People's desperation in conjunction with their illiteracy increases their vulnerability and their chances of entering a situation where they can be exploited.

COERCION AND THE CONTINUATION OF BONDED LABOUR

While there are intersecting factors that push individuals and families into a state of debt bondage, a host of other factors facilitate their remaining in that position. Their inability to return their *peshgi* is the most obvious reason for the continuation of their state of bondage but this inability is itself rooted in exploitative practices. The cycle of low wages, fines and additional loans to meet incurring costs make loan repayment challenging enough. Withholding pay on all kinds of pretexts makes it even more so; having to give birth in the middle of a work day and unable to complete the daily quota of moulding bricks is an example of one such pretext, according to Azra Shaad, the chairperson of the Women Workers Help Line. Furthermore, financial manipulation, where it exists, worsens the situation significantly. 'We were sometimes drawing 2,000 rupees and they were writing 5,000 down in the book' shared one man who used to be in debt bondage (BBC News 2004). In another instance, Veeru Kohlan, a forty-year-old *hari* who had been in debt bondage in interior Sindh for more than seventeen years managed to run away and collect the 60,000 rupees her family owed the landlord from a number of her relatives. She shared that she was shocked when the people she had sent to the landlord with this money returned and told her that the landlord claimed that they owed him 800,000 rupees (Mehergarh 2007). Apart from financial manipulation, pay is often also withheld on all kinds of pretexts.

Many workers are also not allowed to work elsewhere once they have completed their responsibilities in the field or the brick kilns. Not being able to avail other opportunities for income generation becomes a deterrent in their ability to pay back their loans and ensures that they remain under the control of their employers for a longer period of time (Human Rights Watch 1995; Ercelawn and Nauman 2001; ILO 2002). Not paying their employees for extended periods of time also serves the same purpose and prevents them from leaving. Shirmati Dhori and her husband worked for their landlord for a year without getting paid. They wanted to leave at that stage but found it difficult to 'walk away from hard earned income' (Mehergarh 2007: 40).

The fact that employers usually get away with holding workers in bondage and exploiting them is often seen as a manifestation of the state's complicity in a system that sustains a number of its members and is considered to be one of the key reasons for its continuation (Human Rights Watch 1995). However, even when some political actors have pushed for the implementation of the Bonded Labour (Abolition) Act of 1992, the local administration has not been interested in doing so. Their lack of enthusiasm or outright complicity has been explained through their connection with the elite in their regions and their disconnect from the workers who—as migrants or minorities in terms of religion or ethnicity—have a very different social profile and are often looked down upon (Ercelawn and Nauman 2001).

Owners have also been proactive in ensuring that the system continues relying upon and propagating a romanticized tradition of patron-client relations that is 'integral to the culture' as a 'self serving veil for perpetuating extremely inequitable economic and social arrangements' (Ercelawn and Nauman 2001: 2). The fact that land and brick kiln owners are already in a powerful position in comparison to their workers in terms of the resources they possess and that their economically vulnerable workers are dependent upon them is enough to give the owners sufficient power and control over the latter. That many of these owners also have (or are perceived to have) connections with the police or army officials, and either belong to political families themselves or have connections with political families only adds to their power and ability to control those in bondage (HRCP 1998; Ercelawn and Nauman 2001, 2004; Mehergarh 2007). Policemen, for instance, paid off by the owners, have been known to refuse to register cases against them and have arrested workers who have run away, imprisoning them on false charges on their owner's behest and/ or beating them for doing so. 'Attempt[s] to organize other workers, leave their place of work, or [being] disliked by a particular employer' are other reasons for their being arrested by the police (Human Rights Watch 1995, 97; Mehergarh 2007).

Furthermore, landowners usually give their *kamdars* or managers full authority to control their labour by taking whatever steps they deem necessary. *Jamadars* or contractors enjoy similar authority in brick kilns. Both minimize the chances of bonded workers running away by taking a number of steps to control them and their mobility. These include assigning guards to them, putting fetters around their feet, separating the men from the women at night and locking them in separate enclosures, or denying them permission to travel to other villages to meet their relatives. On the occasion when permission to travel is granted, some family members may be kept behind as 'collateral' to ensure that those who have gone come back (Human Rights Watch 1995; ILO 2002, 2004; Ercelawn and Nauman 2004; Mehergarh 2007). Taking their workers' national identity cards at the time of employment is yet another way to control them and prevent them from running away (Awan 2010). Such measures are particularly common if the amount the workers owe is high and when there in an overlap between the workers' residence and workspace (Ercelawn and Nauman 2001, 2004). The overlap is the greatest in the agricultural sector and this facilitates the easy surveillance and subsequent control of the work force.

Workers find it difficult to successfully challenge the exploitative conditions—the low wages, the long hours, the work induced health issues, the violence, etc—they work in, which serve to both maintain and reproduce the status quo. Violence, in particular, plays a critical role in sustaining the asymmetrical power relations that permeate the system and is heavily relied upon for this end. The rest of this chapter will illustrate this point by focusing on violence directed towards women who work in the agricultural sector and the brick kilns.

GENDER, VIOLENCE, AND THE CONTROL MOTIVE

Different industrial sectors have different worker profiles. The mining sector is largely made up of men, for instance, while child workers dominate the carpet-weaving industry. The brick making and agricultural sectors are primarily worked by families and have a high number of women workers. These women find themselves in a state of bondage for a number of reasons. According to Nasira Chaudhry, a senior manager at Bunyad Foundation, an organization that operates in twelve brick kilns just outside Lahore, many of the women in these brick kilns were born in bondage. Other women may be married into a family of bonded labourers or their fathers or husbands may pledge their and their families' labour when entering into a labour arrangement or seeking a loan. The women usually have little to no say in these negotiations (Mehergarh 2007; Awan 2010).

Women primarily work as *patheras* or brick moulders at the brick kilns. It is the most labour intensive yet the lowest paid job at the kilns (Awan 2010). Their work in the agricultural sector involves helping cultivate the land, milking the cattle, cutting grass, removing weeds, collecting wood for fuel, digging irrigation canals, picking cotton, fetching water, etc. (HRCP 1999; Mehergarh 2007). Apart from working as labour in the brick kilns or engaging in agricultural activities for landowners, women are also responsible for the chores at home, such as cooking, cleaning, and taking care of their children. A woman's workload, made up of their reproductive labour and their productive labour both inside and outside the house, is seldom recognized and manifests in their being embroiled in webs of power where patriarchal and class interests intersect. That these power dynamics are often not recognized—at least not until the abuse is blatant—speaks to their hegemonic nature. A group of teachers working at Bunyad Foundation, and who have interacted with the women at the brick kilns, highlighted this point when they spoke of the complacency they saw among these women workers. They did not, they claim, recognize that they were being abused and exploited by their husbands and by those whom they worked for. People's internalization of a system usually makes it invisible, and helps reproduce the skewed power dynamics and maintain the status quo. It is this kind of power that Foucault associates with modern states.

Foucault (1979) speaks of the exercise of power in pre-modern and modern times to illustrate how it is brought to bear upon individuals in significantly different ways in these time periods.

Those engaging in gender and power studies in the last few decades have relied upon his understanding of the contemporary form of power, where it is anonymous, diffused, and invisible, to shed light on the proactive role women unknowingly play in sustaining patriarchal ideologies and systems (Bartky 2003). It is in this context, for instance, that a lot of work has been done on how patriarchal and corporate interests have intertwined and promoted hegemonic standards of beauty, and how this has resulted in many women subjecting their bodies to multiple disciplinary techniques that include but are not limited to extensive dieting and plastic surgery (Bordo 1989; Morgan 2003). They unwittingly collude in the sustenance and reproduction of a larger system through their actions. However, the pervasiveness of modern forms of power as explicated by Foucault does not mean that the pre-modern forms of power, that take the form of physical violence, no longer exist (Westlund 1999). They do so, in abundance, in a variety of contexts in both the public and the private sphere. And although both forms of power serve to control individuals, it is this visible form that it is directed towards women to control them and their community, that is the subject of this chapter.

The control of others has long been established as a common motive for violence. There is an abundance of literature on the varied reasons different individuals and groups have had in using violence, such as protesting inequity, seeking justice and punishing and controlling others (de la Roche 1996; Felson and Messner 2000). Literature stemming from empirical studies on women's abuse in intimate partner relationships, in particular, clearly shows that perpetrators' use of violence is linked to their desire to dominate and control women (Westlund 1999; Felson and Messner 2000; Johnson and Ferraro 2000; Amnesty 2004). The Duluth Domestic Abuse Intervention Project, for instance, engaged in a comprehensive examination of the dynamics of abusive relationships and developed the power and control wheel, a well-known tool for those who work on issues of gender based violence. It is a diagrammatic illustration of how perpetrators use a range of violent tactics—such as intimidation, coercion, and threats—in addition to violence itself, to gain power and control over others in intimate relationships.

Violence or the threat of violence and the fear this generates among women, their families, or both, has also been known to affect their behaviour in instances where the perpetrators are strangers and where the latter may or may not intend for their behaviour to lead to such consequences. Research done among the Pakistani community in

Bradford, for instance, tells us of a woman whose father asked her to stop going out in the evenings because of the sexual harassment women faced in public (Macey 1999). In a similar vein, Jillian Foster's account of her stay in Tajikistan reveals how she, too, became affected by the climate of fear that the other women lived in. As she explained, 'in Tajikistan, women are controlled by the fear of an attacker hiding in the dark waiting to grab them in very unwelcome ways if they stay out after 9 p.m.' This— despite her cognitive refusal to be 'controlled and silenced by fear'— eventually had an impact on her as well and resulted in her controlling her mobility[2] (2011: 2, 4). The personal experience of being on the receiving end of violence was not required in these two instances; belief in the threat of violence served as an effective mechanism of control.

Similarly, literature on bonded labour also refers to violence and the threat of violence as one of the means through which workers in debt bondage are controlled and can be drawn upon to see how 'a consistent pattern of physical, sexual, and psychological abuse' and the resultant fear can prevent them from challenging the asymmetrical status quo (Human Rights Watch 1995: 22). Women in particular are especially vulnerable to sexual abuse and there is evidence of such abuse in both brick kilns and the agricultural sector. Some of these 'women' are as young as fourteen according to Mehmood Butt, who has dealt with many rape cases at the brick kilns through his affiliation with the Bhatta Mazdoor Union. Their experiences are drawn upon to shed light upon the numerous ways in which violence can sustain the system of bonded labour.

VIOLENCE AGAINST WOMEN AND THE MAINTENANCE OF ASYMMETRICAL POWER RELATIONS

Prior research on bonded labour tells us that the threats or acts of violence that women in debt bondage face are enacted to meet a variety of specific goals. Violence, after all, 'rewards the perpetrator in ways other than, or in addition to, simply exercising power over his or her target(s)' (New World Encyclopaedia 2009). An overview of these goals—each of which directly or indirectly creates or heightens fear among bonded labourers and makes them more susceptible to being controlled—is given below.

COERCIVE POWER AND THE EFFECTIVENESS OF THREATS

The threat of violence, as mentioned above, is often enough to control behaviour. This is especially so when the person who makes the threat is believed to possess coercive power (Felson and Messner 2000). Labourers believe that landowners, brick kiln owners, and their men possess such power because of the reasons mentioned earlier. Their threats thus prove to be effective.

Some threats of violence, often left deliberately vague, are made to meet a desired goal. Veeru Kohlan, a *hari* in Sindh, disclosed that her landlord's men would frequently threaten her and the other women workers with a 'you better work hard or else' (Mehergarh 2007: 29). However, those in power may not just use violence or the threat of violence to meet an immediate goal but may also do so to 'influence future behaviour—that is, to deter the target from repeating a specific behaviour or to produce general compliance' (Felson and Messner 2000: 86). Threats such as the one Veeru Kohlan and the other women received not only served the immediate goal of increasing agricultural productivity but also instilled fear among all the labourers, hence facilitating the fulfilment of a long term goal, that of sustained maximal output.

The threat of violence directed towards women was not just made to the women in question, in order to control their behaviour. Men were also threatened with harm befalling women for the same reason; to control them. A common threat took the form of men in debt bondage being told that the women in their families would be sold to others if they thought of running away. Another common threat took the form of 'just wait and see what we do to your women' (Mehergarh 2007). Such threats proved to be effective in controlling men's behaviour.

The examples above clearly illustrate that the goal of each threat was to seek immediate compliance that would either result in the facilitation of a behaviour or lead to its prevention. The fact that physical violence had been witnessed or experienced in the past made the workers take these threats more seriously (Westlund 1999). However, even when violence is not directly experienced or witnessed, the awareness of it in other localities can, hypothetically, serve the same purpose, i.e. gaining immediate submission and increasing the chances of long term compliance which would, in turn, keep the system intact (Ercelawn and Nauman 2004).

Actual violence also served the same purpose and was also frequently employed, as is illustrated in Marwa's story. Marwa and her family worked as *haris* in Sindh. The *kamdar*, she relates, gave the women labourers impossible tasks and then had his men beat a few of them with sticks when they were unable to complete them. This would happen on a daily basis. These men would 'terrorize us and make us work harder,' she continued (Mehergarh 2007b). Although set up for failure, the regular abuse the women faced in the guise of punishment resulted in their working as hard as they were able to and also increased the climate of fear through which their behaviour was then subsequently controlled. 'The politics of bonded labour revolves around fear' shares Fouzia Saeed, the director of Mehergarh, whose work on sexual harassment led her to interact with women who used to work as bonded labour in the agricultural sector. As such, women were often subject to violence for the sole purpose of keeping the fear level high.

PUNISHING 'DEVIANCE'

An overview of the cases of bonded labour reveals a clear pattern in which *kamdars* and *jamadars* always act swiftly in response to 'deviance'. The latter includes a range of acts that those in power want to curtail immediately. Examples of these behaviours include challenging the authority of the owners or their representatives, or reporting their behaviour to the police when the exploitation becomes unbearable. Such behaviour was severely punished.

Marvaan Kohlan and her family worked as bonded labourers on a farm in Sindh for twenty-two years. One of the stories she shared involved one of her neighbours filing a police report against their landlord. All the women workers were forced to work naked in the fields as a punishment. Luxmi Kohlan's story reveals the same pattern—she and her family had run away from their landlord but were soon captured and brought back. The men and women were separated and the women were subjected to systematic rape over an extended period of time (Mehergarh 2007). Each of these punishments was linked to a clear message, that there would be no mercy for those who tried to run away or engage in any activity that challenged the system and the power dynamics on which it was based.

The power that is unleashed in the form of violence in these contexts is a clear manifestation of an authority figure punishing those who have attempted to challenge this figure. It is marked by 'a spectacle not of measure, but of imbalance and excess ... there must be an emphatic affirmation of power and of its intrinsic superiority ... [manifest by] the physical strength of the sovereign beating down upon the body of his adversary and mastering it' (Foucault 1977, as cited by Westlund 1999:

1048). The purpose is not merely to punish the person or group that acts 'inappropriately', but equally importantly, it is to use the opportunity to make an example out of them. This is one of the reasons why the abuse often takes place in front of other family or community members.

Violence has been used as a strategy to keep others in check in other parts of the world as well. Guatemalan women's efforts to organize themselves into trade unions, for instance, resulted in their being kidnapped and raped on the orders of the owners of the assembly plant where they worked under exploitative conditions (Amnesty 2004). But no matter where it takes place, letting people experience or witness the consequences of breaking 'the rules' increases their fear, reduces the probability of others engaging in similar behaviour in the future and thus serves as an effective technique of control that, once again, sustains the system.

POWER PLAYS

The violence that women bonded labourers face sometimes has little to do with punishment per se and everything to do with the enjoyment of those who have power over them. Shrimati Dhori, who used to be a *hari* in bondage in interior Sindh, narrated a story about how her landlord noticed her beautiful daughter and made arrangements to have both her daughter and her son-in-law shifted closer to his residence, where the daughter was given household chores. The proximity made it easier for him to abuse her on a regular basis (Mehergarh 2007). There are countless examples of *kamdars* kidnapping women who catch their eye. These women are usually taken to the *auttack*—the guest house where the guests of the landlord are entertained—and are raped over a period of a few days before they are returned. Saeed points out that 'their fear of being noticed is very high. This fear results in their behaving in ways that they believe will prevent them from standing out, and subsequently, from being abused.' The common strategies they rely upon in this context include their huddling together in a group whenever they can and not making any smart rejoinders whenever the *kamdar* makes inflammatory comments. Those who are attractive make an extra effort to not bring attention to themselves and hide their faces whenever they can.

Saeed also points out that although the landlord may have women brought to his house or the *auttack* for himself or his friends upon occasion (as is also documented elsewhere, for instance, see Human Rights Watch 1995), women face more frequent abuse at the hands of the *kamdar* and the guards. *Kamdars* often rape women in the fields, sometimes in isolation and sometimes in the presence of other women or their husbands (Human Rights Watch 1995; Mehergarh 2007; HRCP 2010). Women also told Saeed that if a *kamdar* visited a woman who was alone in her hut while her family was working in the fields, she knew that '*us kee shamat ayee*' (she was in for it). Incidents of being sexually assaulted at home while other family members were out working have also been documented at the brick kilns. Mala's narration of being restrained while a *jamadar* sexually assaulted her teenage daughter in their home near Hyderabad in Sindh is one such example (Human Rights Watch 1995).

Cases such as these illustrate that women are perceived as nothing more than objects and possessions, to be used for the amusement of their owners and their men whose enjoyment lies in manifesting their power over those they can control. After all, 'sexual abuse is less a matter of lust than instilling terror and helplessness into their victims' (Ercelawn and Nauman 2001: 8). Seeking pleasure and satisfaction in demonstrations of dominance and control is something that is well documented in studies done on perpetrators of gender based violence. That their actions instil fear into those who are abused as well as their families and the larger community, and becomes a means through which their control becomes more effective, is an additional bonus.

Although this chapter focuses on violence that is directed towards women, anyone who engages in a brief overview of the literature on bonded labour in Pakistan will see that men are equally vulnerable to threats and acts of violence and these too serve to control them and their family members.[3] There are many cases like that of a group of brick kiln workers who were hung upside down and beaten with sticks because they had begun to organize themselves in an attempt to seek redress, or of another group of men who were beaten by hot iron rods and shovels because they were suspected of helping a fellow brick kiln worker escape. Some land or brick kiln owners have been known to operate private jails and imprison workers—men, women, and children—for extended periods of time in order to discipline and punish them by meting out severe physical, sexual, and psychological abuse. Broken bones, being beaten unconscious, or being deprived of food are common punishments that aim to decrease or prevent the frequency of any behaviour that attempts to challenge the status quo in that moment and, by generating fear among the workers, in the future as well (Human Rights Watch 1995). And sometimes, as was seen in the case of women earlier, the purpose of violence is nothing more than creating fear. In the words of Veeru Kohlan:

'sometimes they would beat up our husbands in front of us on purpose ... No reason! They just wanted to control our lives and keep us living in fear' (Mehergarh 2007: 29). However, violence that is specifically directed towards women does not just create fear. It is also likely to lead to other cultural responses, like shame and/or a feeling of being dishonoured, which makes it a differentially effective mechanism of control.

THE DIFFERENTIAL MEANINGS OF VIOLENCE

Pakistan, like many other countries, is one in which a woman is believed to embody honour. 'Honour, symbolized in the female body and reduced to women's sexual purity, is perceived as a "natural" foundation for social and moral order'[4] (Haeri 2002: 36). A woman is believed to be sexually 'pure' and thus embody honour when she only engages in sexual activities within the bounds of marriage. Thus any sexual conduct (or perception of such conduct) outside these bounds is seen as a loss of her honour. Furthermore, since no distinction is made between consensual and non-consensual sex, rape is also believed to lead to such a loss. The term *izzat lut gayee* (honour has been lost) is a common euphemism for rape in Pakistan. This link between rape and dishonour or impurity helps explain why women in different parts of world have been stigmatized (Mookherjee 2004). Thousands of women who were raped in Bosnia-Herzegovina in the 1990s, for instance, have been viewed as 'tarnished' and 'fallen' by many in their region (Amnesty 2004: 44).

However, it is not just a woman who is said to lose her honour. Like their counterparts in many other parts of the world, Pakistani women are believed to embody the honour of their family, community and ultimately their nation; the loss of honour is thus theirs as well (Amnesty 2004; Foster 2011). Furthermore, 'women's loss of honour—whether by force or choice—bears directly on the honour of those primary male kin who ... [are] the presumed custodians of women's chastity' (Haeri 2002: 36). Dishonouring one's enemy by raping his daughter, sister, or wife— something which has been witnessed in the context of warring nations at a global level—is an old technique and one that continues to be relied upon to this day in Pakistan (Haeri 2002). Many men have attempted to reclaim their honour and get rid of the shame attached to its loss by killing these women. Eight hundred and sixty-nine Pakistani women were killed in the name of honour in the year 2013 alone (HRCP 2014). These examples are a testament to the meaning that is inscribed on a woman's body and the importance this meaning has in this cultural context. It is here that we see how these docile bodies are different from those of men and why they can become a differentially effective means of controlling both women and their families.

While both men and women bonded labourers have been known to suffer their supervisors' beatings, it is the women who are sexually assaulted and raped on a regular basis. This form of violence is imbued with cultural meaning and therein lies its impact. The threat of rape and its actual occurrence both become very effective means of control because it is not just physical harm that the workers fear; they also fear the helplessness, sense of violation, dishonour, and shame that is tied to this act of violence.

Even if a family does not subscribe to the hegemonic association between rape and dishonour, men are still likely to have undergone a gendered socialization that makes them responsible for protecting women from a very young age, when they are not even capable of taking care of themselves. Being able to do so is one of the markers of South Asian masculinity. Case studies done on Bangladeshi men whose wives were raped in war, for instance, therefore reveal their feeling of shame and a sense of emasculation because they had not been able to protect them (Mookherjee 2004). Similarly, conversations with and research done among the *haris* who used to be in debt bondage in Sindh suggest that the raped woman's family members may have, on some occasions—for instance, when she is taken away or raped in front of them—felt helplessness and shame for their inability to protect her. This is illustrated in the following account that Shrimati Dhori shares. The landlord that she and her family worked for dropped by their hut one day and told her son that he wanted his wife for some chores at his house. 'We had to send her,' she explained and then continued:

> He [the landlord] was very powerful. I could see my son's face getting red but he didn't say anything. She [the wife] looked at her husband, to get a clue about what she should do. He lowered his head. She looked at my husband and then at me to see if we would say something to stop the landlord from taking her. We looked away. We knew that he would not forgive us for disobeying him. She left with him and was brought back after two days. (Mehergarh 2007: 41–42)

The literature on violence directed towards women in brick kilns is sketchy but what is available suggests that patriarchy has a much tighter control over the lives of the brick kiln workers in Punjab in comparison to their *hari* counterparts in Sindh (Awan 2010). Discussing the reasons for this is beyond the scope of this chapter but generally speaking, Punjab is a more conservative province than Sindh. Furthermore, this emerging pattern seems to be in line with the general cultural differences that exist between rural and urban settings. Rural women, be they in Sindh or Punjab, are relatively more independent and assertive than women who live in small towns and on whom patriarchy has a much stronger hold in terms of their gender roles, mobility, dependence upon men, decision making, etc. Most brick kilns are set up in or near small towns.

Women at the brick kilns seem to face the risk of being sexually assaulted by the men in their own communities as well as by the kiln owners and their men, and are more likely to be·blamed for bringing shame to their families if they are raped. The shame that men in these communities may feel over this dishonour is also likely to be intertwined with their feeling that they have been unable to control 'their' women's sexuality, something which may decrease their social standing and make them vulnerable to ridicule. That *haris* in rural Sindh are relatively less stigmatized when raped may also be connected to the frequency with which *kamdars* use rape as a tool for control, and/or a strong feeling of helplessness over the course of events in their life. But regardless of where it takes place, what is clear is rape is not just an act of violence that physically violates the person who is raped. It has many cultural connotations attached to it. *Kamdars* and *jamadars* are aware of these cultural connotations and know what kind of impact their commonly made threat—'just wait and see what we do to your women'—is therefore likely to have.

BREAKING THE CYCLE OF FEAR

Hearing threats and either witnessing violence, experiencing it, or both instils fear among bonded labourers, and this fear proves to be effective in gaining their compliance and preventing them from challenging any act of exploitation or violence that is directed towards them. A joint survey conducted by the Human Rights Commission of Pakistan and the ILO among 100 freed *haris* revealed that seventy-nine respondents had never complained about their working conditions because they were afraid of their landlords, had been threatened by their landlords, had been tortured, and because they believed that their landlords were influential and that their complaining would make no difference. *Hari* Shirmati Dhori's neighbour once called the police in an attempt to stop their landlord from harassing his wife but he ended up spending years in jail because of false allegations made against him by that landlord. And so 'no one dared to stop the landlord ever again,' she concluded. 'He would tease any woman in the village' (Mehergarh 2007: 41).

Thus violence and the fear it generates becomes one of the means through which the system, which is based on asymmetrical power relations, reproduces itself. However, violence and coercion are not always effective mechanisms of control in the long run; being the recipient of exploitation and violence is also what motivates many workers to run away. The stories of their experiences reveal that attempts to run away were undertaken when the fear they lived in was surmounted by the reality of the violence they faced, particularly if it was extreme, sustained over a long period of time, or both. It was when the experience of violence eclipsed the fear that many stopped caring about the consequences of being caught and actively began looking for opportunities to escape. And while violence or the stories of violence have proven to be effective in the continuation of the system, hearing stories of successful escapes has also increased the hope of those who are currently in debt bondage and has encouraged them to attempt to do the same.

REFERENCES

Amnesty (2004), *It's in Our Hands: Stop Violence Against Women*. Oxford: Alden Press.

Awan, S. A. (May 2010), 'Gender Dimensions of Bonded Labour in Brick Kilns in Punjab Province of Pakistan'. Available at http://www.ciwce.org.pk/Publications/bonded_labour/Gender_dimensions_of_bonded_labour_in_brick_kilns_in_Punjab-province_of_Pakistan.pdf. (Accessed 15 July 2011)

Bartky, S. L. (2003), 'Foucault, Femininity, and the Modernization of Patriarchal Power', in *The Politics of Women's Bodies*, R. Weitz (ed.). New York: Oxford University Press.

BBC News (25 November 2004), Life as a Modern Slave in Pakistan. Available at http://news.bbc.co.uk/2/hi/south_asia/4042207.stm. (Accessed 1 August 2011)

Bordo, S. (1989), 'The Body and the Reproduction of Femininity: A Feminist Appropriation of Foucault' in A. M. Jaggar and S. Bordo (eds.) *Gender/Body/Knowledge:Feminist Reconstructions of Being and Knowing*. New Brunswick: Rutgers University Press.

Chakravorty, B. (2004), *Gender Issues in Bonded Labour: A Study of Rangareddy District, Andhra Pradesh*. Geneva: ILO.

De la Roche, R. S. (1996), 'Collective Violence as Social Control', *Sociological Forum* 11.1: 97–128.

Ercelawn, A. & M. Nauman (2001), Bonded Labour in Pakistan. Geneva: ILO.

Ercelawn, A. & M. Nauman (2004), 'Unfree Labour in South Asia: Debt Bondage at Brick Kilns in Pakistan'. *Economic and Political Weekly*.

Felson, R. B. & S. F. Messner (2000), 'The Control Motive in Intimate Partner Violence'. *Social Psychology Quarterly* 63.1: 86–94.

Foster, J. (28 April 2011), 'Quietly Resisting in Tajikistan'. Available at http://www. heptagonpost.com/node/66. (Accessed 22 July 2011)

Foucault, M. (1979), *Discipline and Punish: The Birth of the Prison*. New York: Vintage Books.

Haeri, S. (2002), *No Shame for the Sun: Lives of Professional Pakistani Women*. Syracuse: Syracuse University Press.

HRCP (1998), State of Human Rights in 1997. Lahore: HRCP.

HRCP (1999), State of Human Rights in 1998. Lahore: HRCP.

HRCP (2002), State of Human Rights in 2001. Lahore: HRCP.

HRCP (2010), State of Human Rights in 2009. Lahore: HRCP.

HRCP (2014), State of Human Rights in 2013. Lahore: HRCP.

Human Rights Watch (1995), *Contemporary Forms of Slavery in Pakistan*. New York: Human Rights Watch.

ILO (2002), Survey of Bonded Labour in Two Sectors in Pakistan: Brick Kiln Workers (Punjab) and Sharecroppers (Sindh). ILO.

ILO (14 September 2004), 'Combating Bonded Labour in Rural Pakistan'. Available at http://www.ilo.org/global/about-the-ilo/press-and-media-centre/insight/ WCMS_075594/lang--en/index.htm. (Accessed 15 July 2011)

Johnson, M. P. & J. J. Ferraro (2000), 'Research on Domestic Violence: Making Distinctions'. *Journal of Marriage and the Family* 62: 948–63.

Macey, M. (1999), 'Religion, Male Violence, and the Control of Women: Pakistani Muslim Men in Bradford'. *Gender and Development* 17.1: 48–55.

Mehergarh (2007), *Women in Bondage: Voices of Women Farm Workers in Sindh*. Islamabad: Mehergarh.

Mehergarh (2007b), *Marwa's Story: A Farm Worker Living in Bondage*. Islamabad: Mehergarh.

Mookherjee, N. (2004), '"My man (honour) is lost but I still have my iman (principle):" sexual violence and articulations of masculinity', in R. Chopra, C. Osella and F. Osella, *South Asian Masculinities: Context of Change, Sites of Continuity*: 131–59. New Delhi: Women Unlimited.

Morgan, K. P. (2003), 'Women and the Knife: Cosmetic Surgery and the Colonization of Women's Bodies' in R. Weitz (ed.) *The Politics of Women's Bodies*. New York: Oxford University Press.

Nasir, Z. M. (2004), *A Rapid Assessment of Bonded Labour in the Carpet Industry of Pakistan*. Geneva: ILO.

New World Encyclopedia (13 January 2009), 'Domestic Violence'. Available at http://www. newworldencyclopedia.org/entry/Domestic_violence?oldid=901166 (Accessed 21 July 2011)

Saeed, F. (2001), *Taboo! The Hidden Culture of a Red Light Area*. Karachi: Oxford University Press.

Saleem, A. (2004), *A Rapid Assessment of Bonded Labour in Pakistan's Mining Sector*. Geneva: ILO.

Thornham, S. (2000), *Feminist Theory and Cultural Studies: Stories of Unsettled Relations*. New York: Oxford University Press.

US Department of State (14 June 2010), Trafficking in Persons Report 2010 – Pakistan. Available at http://www.unhcr.org/refworld/docid/4c1883d1c.html. (Accessed 5 August 2011)

Westlund, A. C. (1999), 'Pre-Modern and Modern Power: Foucault and the Case of Domestic Violence', *Signs* 24.4: 1045–1066.

162 Bonded Labour in Pakistan

NOTES

1. The primary research for this paper is based on conversations with women who used to work as bonded labour in the agricultural sector in Sindh and on semi-structured interviews with key people in Bunyad Foundation, Mehergarh, the Bhatta Mazdoor Union, and the Women Workers Help Line—organizations that either directly work with bonded labour or that interact with them in the course of their work. However, challenges in directly accessing women who are currently working as bonded labour, a challenge that researchers have elaborated upon in their own work on bonded labour in the past (for instance, see Ercelawn and Nauman 2001; 2004; ILO 2002; Nasir 2004; Saleem 2004) has meant the arguments that are made in this chapter are also significantly based on secondary data.

2. It is important to acknowledge the fear of being stigmatized as a 'bad woman' (which can also result in their being the recipients of violence-as-punishment) is as effective in controlling women's behavior as is violence, and often results in determining how women dress and behave, who they interact with, etc. (Macey 1999; Saeed 2001; Amnesty 2004; Foster 2011).

3. The relationship between violence and control has been witnessed in other parts of the world as well. Threats of violence by employers, for instance, have been identified as one of the factors that ensure that men in bonded labour keep reporting to work regularly in India (Chakravorty 2004).

4. The control of women's sexuality for the purpose of maintaining a patriarchal and patrilineal society has been the subject of much feminist discourse and can be found to exist to various degrees across the world (Saeed 2001).

CHAPTER 9

Bonded Labour Without Bondage: Reconsidering the Links between Debt and *Peshgi*

ALI KHAN

D ebt bondage has come to be inextricably linked with the ubiquitous advance or *peshgi* as it is widely known in Pakistan. Wherever there is evidence of *peshgis* it is assumed that debt bondage will inevitably follow. And yet it has been pointed out (Ercelawn and Nauman, 2001) that if we include as bonded all those workers who have had at some point taken an advance, the size of the estimate would expand immeasurably. This article looks at how, despite the presence of *peshgis* and other features that would normally promote the existence of a debt bondage relationship, there is in fact no evidence of such a system in the two particular sectors being analysed.

Using examples from the glass bangles industry in Pakistani Hyderabad and the football-stitching industry in Sialkot, it will be argued that mediating factors, primarily a feeling between workers and employers of a shared common origin, has a positive effect on worker–employer relations. Patrilineage (*biradari*) ties in Hyderabad and shared geographical and 'class' origins in Sialkot have led to the avoidance of antagonistic relations and have promoted a more balanced and supportive relationship between worker and employer. This in turn has allowed the existence of credit relations without the resulting spectre of debt bondage and its related features of violence and oppression of workers. Moreover, this points to the fact that indiscriminately linking *peshgis* with bondedness is an inaccurate basis for analysis but one that has been used regularly in the past.

Fieldwork carried out in Sialkot during the course of one year forms the basis of the research for this article. The city of Sialkot, located at roughly 220 km from Islamabad, off the Grand Trunk Road, is considered a prominent industrial centre of Pakistan. However, Sialkot is home to mostly small-scale and cottage industries rather than medium- or large-scale industries. Sialkot's industry also draws its strength from local Sialkoti entrepreneurs and industrialists who went from initially being artisans to becoming industrialists, rather than drawing its strength from Muslim industrialists who migrated to Pakistan at Partition. This has led to a strong feeling of pride and ownership amongst the local Sialkoti industrialists and artisans of the skills that they possess and the industries that they have set up (Khan 2007).

During fieldwork in Sialkot, I relied on my close association and contact with the organization Bunyad, which was actively involved with football stitchers in Sialkot, to gain access to football stitchers, artisans, industrialists and others. Employees of Bunyad also provided me with detailed information on Sialkot and introduced me to the people who I needed to interview for my research. Early into my fieldwork, I realized my research would not focus solely on Sialkot city itself as decentralization of the football industry has led to stitching centres being based in the surrounding villages. The villages where Bunyad had identified significant numbers of football stitchers and had set up informal schools were the ones that I decided to focus on during the course of my fieldwork, these being located evenly in the tehsils of Pasrur, Daska, and Sialkot. However, I also visited villages with football stitchers where such informal schools had not been set up. I started off by interviewing a core group of child stitchers who were attending non-formal schools and, through these children, I then gained access to their parents and others in the community. I not only interviewed child stitchers and their parents but also those children who had dropped out of the non-formal schools, industrialists, subcontractors, and others involved in the football-stitching business. As the issue involved was a deeply sensitive one and it could hurt the interests of the informants to provide certain information, I needed to gain the trust of my informants to attain in-depth information. To this end, I decided not to use cameras or dictaphones in my interviews. I also participated in children's activities such as sports events, school plays and others to build a rapport with and gain the trust of the child stitchers (Khan 2007).

As far as bangle-making is concerned, Hyderabad city is one of the main centres of bangle production in Pakistan. Much of the production of bangles in Hyderabad takes place in the areas of the Sindh Industrial and Trading Estate (SITE), the old city districts and Latifabad. SITE, an industrial zone with a large number of factories, is the area where raw materials are initially processed and it is home to roughly 35 large bangle factories, each covering an area of a few hundred square metres. On the other hand, bangle-making in the old city districts and Latifabad is mostly carried out in small workshops and in homes, resembling a cottage-industry form of production. It is in the old city, and specifically in the areas of Churi Para, Noorani Basti, and Ilyasabad, that most of the contractors and workers are located and work. These areas have narrow lanes and small houses, with many houses consisting of one or two rooms, and it is in these houses that much of the home-based bangle-making work takes place. Initial bangle-making processes, such as melting glass bottles to get molten glass, that require large furnaces, take place at the factories located in SITE. Bangle-making processes requiring less heavy equipment take place at homes and workshops in the old city and Latifabad, as will be explained in more detail later (Collective for Social Sciences Research 2004).

Before going further it may be useful to define, for the purposes of this paper, what a *biradari* is. The relationship between *biradari* and caste, or *zaat* as it is locally known, is complex and is further complicated by discussion over whether caste even exists in Muslim societies. Without going into details of this[1] debate, it is sufficient for this analysis to point out that if caste applies to a hereditary non-corporate category then *biradari* can be considered the local manifestation of caste in that it is the minimal patrilineage.

Blunt defined *biradari*[2] as a fraternity, a group of caste brethren who live in a particular neighbourhood and act together for caste purposes: 'it is *zaat* (caste) in action' (quoted in Dumont 1980). It is the *biradari*, rather than the wider notion of *zaat*, which is the primary factor amongst the primordial loyalties that govern social organization in Punjab villages. *Biradari*, if we use this definition, refers to a minimal patrilineage. As shall be discussed later in the article, it is the notion of belonging to one particular *biradari*—the Ferozabad Siddiquis—that has created harmonious worker–employer relations in Hyderabad's glass-manufacturing industry.

In Sialkot almost all *biradaris* are to be found stitching footballs today but the notion of employers emerging from within this group of workers remains strong and is something that employers continue to propagate and foster for their own benefit. Over the years the international success of Sialkot's sports industry—particularly of football stitching which increasingly dominates the entire sector—has also helped Sialkotis come to see the sports manufacturing occupation as being their own—typically 'Sialkoti'.

HISTORICAL DEVELOPMENT: SIALKOT'S FOOTBALLS AND HYDERABAD'S BANGLES

In order to understand the absence of debt bondage in Sialkot and Hyderabad it is essential to be aware of the specific historical development of both the football-stitching and the glass bangles industries, respectively. As a result it is necessary to provide a brief history of these two sectors.

SIALKOT

Sialkot's sports industry was not indigenous to the region, but likely began as a response to British demand for the repair of their sports goods—mainly rackets, cricket bats, and footballs. Gradually it moved from repair to manufacturing. Much of the transition came about through an injection of capital into the fledgling industry around the 1870s. The majority of this investment came from Sialkot's indigenous Sikh and Hindu entrepreneurs, the most famous of who were the Sikh brothers Ganda Singh Uberoi and Jhanda Singh Uberoi. The brothers became involved with the sports manufacturing industry as letter-writers—Ganda Singh Uberoi, a teacher by profession, used to write letters on behalf of the illiterate Muslim carpenters turned sporting goods manufacturers—but soon became the middlemen of the system, buying tennis rackets from the Muslim carpenters and selling them through their own contacts, first throughout the Subcontinent and soon after that to England and other points in the British Empire.

By 1883 the Uberoi brothers turned from being middlemen to setting up their own production and, by 1946, four large workshops, including two run by the Uberoi brothers, were registered under the Factories Act. These four units employed 947 workers of which 752 or just over 80 per cent were Muslim. However, few units were as large as Uberoi Ltd, and most engaged between five and eight workers and continued to work in a more informal set-up, with Muslim artisans manufacturing the goods and Hindu and Sikh middlemen selling the products on. A further 4,000 workers were estimated as being employed by cottage units (Anwar and Abdul Aziz 1956). The figures reflect the overwhelming number of Muslim artisans who worked in the sports industry as well as the fact that even at this stage the informal dwarfed the formal sector in terms of the sheer number of workers.

Though Muslims were becoming increasingly literate, the Hindus and Sikhs continued to maintain a strong hold over exporting networks and other middlemen activities. The Muslims had historically been seen as being poor handlers of money, preferring to spend when money came in, rather than save judiciously, like the Hindu traders. Moreover, in the Punjab, Muslims had tended to invest only in agriculture and simple trading, often citing that usury was forbidden in Islam. The Hindus and Sikhs faced no such religious bar. In addition, Saberwal (1976), writing on the tendency of Sikhs to respond to entrepreneurial opportunities, stated that this characteristic came from their psychological openness to change and an emphasis on individual achievement. The Sikh community was often the most literate in the Subcontinent and they made special efforts to maintain a wide network of contacts. As a result of these traits, the Sikhs were well placed to capitalize on the opportunities that came their way. Similarly, Hindus from the trading castes had generations of experience and a vast network of contacts to build upon.

It was only after Partition that Muslims came to be in possession of their own manufacturing units. Following Partition in 1947, the majority of Sikhs and Hindus migrated to India, taking with them their capital to purchase raw materials, their extensive contacts to facilitate the export of items and their acumen for quality control. Markets for the disposal of finished goods also vanished. With the forests of Kashmir becoming unavailable to Sialkot's industries, much of the immediate raw material supply was also disrupted. Sialkot's location quickly became a negative factor. Not only was it some distance from the main transport artery, the Grand Trunk Road, but it was also close to the disputed border with India. As a result, businessmen and financiers immigrating to Pakistan during Partition went elsewhere in the country. The new government was also wary of investing in the border district.

This disruption, however, created a space for local craftsmen to become industrialists. Many of those who had previously worked as labourers, often in the pioneering Uberoi Ltd, now became the driving force for industry. To date, with a few exceptions, sporting goods companies currently operating in Sialkot were started by men who had previously been labourers. Whereas, elsewhere in Pakistan, new industries (including Hyderabad's glass bangles industry) were largely based on those founded just after Partition by Muslim businessmen immigrants from India, in Sialkot the craftsmen-turned-industrialists produced a very different structure. Sialkot's industries organized around the new entrepreneurial class and their biological kin.

Initially in Sialkot, small groups of patrilineally related craftsmen made tables and chairs together and then made cricket bats and tennis rackets together. Now craftsmen started up very small-scale manufacturing units employing no more than two or three workers and were able to expand very gradually in the following years. It was essential that the new entrepreneurs cooperated closely and in this they were greatly assisted through the use of existing social networks. Business relations were based on kinship and family ties and these bound the new entrepreneurs together, forming an industrial cluster. Being part of this larger cluster provided the myriad small producers with access to economies of scale and scope, as well as lower factor costs through reduced search and transaction costs.[3] Without being part of a local network in which firms specialize and complement each other, it would have been extremely difficult for Sialkot's firms to compete in the export market niche. Despite intense local competition, Sialkot's new entrepreneurs were characterized by their ability to cooperate for the overall benefit of the cluster.

Since a very high level of specialized skill is not required for football-stitching (particularly not for stitching low-grade footballs) and it is easy to pick up the skill of football-stitching, a wide range of casual and irregular stitchers overwhelmingly dominate football-stitching. Moreover, there has been no evidence of any particular *biradari* monopolizing the football-stitching business and I met football stitchers from a wide variety of *biradaris*, including the highest status Sayyeds, Mughals, and Sheikhs, as well as the Jats and Arain, and the lowest status Lohars, Nais, and Fakirs. Interestingly, as a result of the wide variety of *biradaris* involved in football-stitching and the fact that no single *biradari* monopolizes this skill, football-stitching has come to signify a skill that Sialkotis as a whole 'own'. Moreover, the achievements of Sialkot's football industry and the long history of this skill in Sialkot also give rise to feelings of collective ownership and pride amongst Sialkotis in their football-stitching skills (Khan 2007).

HYDERABAD

In Hyderabad's glass bangles industry the situation is somewhat different but with important points of similarity. Unlike Sialkot's sports industry, which—post-Partition—was carried forward by an indigenous class of craftsmen, the Hyderabad glass bangles industry was established by a group of entrepreneurs who had shifted to Hyderabad at Partition. This group—which forms the core of the glass bangles sector in Hyderabad—consists of Urdu-speaking migrants from the area of Ferozabad in western

Uttar Pradesh in modern-day India. Moreover, they all also trace their roots to a patrilineal group known as the Ferozabad Siddiquis.

At Partition, the Ferozabad Siddiquis from India migrated to various locations in Pakistan, including Lahore, Shikarpur, Sukkur, Rohri, and Hyderabad in Sindh, where they soon took up their traditional work of making glass bangles on a small scale. Hyderabad proved to be an area with good potential, since it already had a glass factory, and because it provided better access to markets than the other smaller towns of Sindh. It was also said that some leading members of the Ferozabad Siddiqui patrilineage had prior links with the existing glass-manufacturing industry in Hyderabad.

Thus, Hyderabad's glass bangles industry follows the more conventional post-Partition occurrence of 'migrant' Muslims establishing industry in the cities of Pakistan and bringing with them a degree of expertise that they had already developed in India. In Sialkot neither employers nor workers were migrants but what was similar to Hyderabad was the influence of a class of entrepreneurs who traced their roots back to some shared origin—in terms of place (Ferozabad) and occupation (glass bangles manufacturing)—with that of their workers.

Historically, then, all of the various classes of people involved in the bangles sector—from workers and subcontractors through to factory owners—belonged to a particular kinship-based community: the Siddiquis. There was—in Ferozabad and there still remains in Hyderabad—a strong sense in the glass bangles sector that the work is a traditional profession which the migrants brought with them from Ferozabad, much of it requiring a degree of skill and learning that can only be imparted within this kinship group. The Siddiquis in Hyderabad continue to trace their descent to the town of Ferozabad in India where the community is still known for their work manufacturing glass bangles.

In Hyderabad the feeling of group inclusion and solidarity is strong, based as it is among a tightly knit patrilineal clan of Siddiquis. In the Subcontinent, patrilineages do often act as combined mutual aid societies and welfare agencies, for example, frequently contributing collectively towards dowries and wedding expenses. In Sialkot those who initially made cricket bats and tennis rackets together and then stitched footballs came from a much more diverse range of patrilineages or *biradaris* as they are known in Punjab.

PRE-CONDITIONS FOR THE PROLIFERATION OF *PESHGIS*

Having provided a brief historical background for both industries, let us now look more specifically at the question in hand—i.e. the specific conditions within the industries in question that would typically lead to the proliferation of advances or *peshgis*.

The proliferation of *peshgis* in any sector of the economy is dependent on a number of variables, the most fundamental of which is the proviso that the majority of the work activities in the sector are undertaken in the unregulated (informal) sector of the economy. This in turn typically means that much work is home-based, wages are low, and that legislative measures do not apply to these activities. Moreover trade unions are absent and collective action on the part of workers is lacking. It also means that agreements are not formally recorded or written, and there is the danger of arbitrary interpretation on the part of the employer. There are two further key factors that promote the incidence of *peshgis* in certain sectors, namely:

• the extensive use of subcontractors;
• work within the sector being characterized by seasonal demand.

Many of these aforementioned variables are present in both the football-stitching and glass-bangle manufacturing sectors. How they precisely promote the incidence of advances is best explained through an analysis of the structure of the industries in Sialkot and Hyderabad.

STRUCTURE OF THE INDUSTRY: GLASS BANGLES AND FOOTBALL STITCHING

In both the Sialkot football industry and Hyderabad glass bangles industry a small formal sector is supported by a much larger informal sector but the division between the two is far from rigid. Since the time that Hart (1973) first talked of the informal sector in his seminal work on traders in Ghana the concept has evolved to encompass not two separate sectors of activity but a much more fluid concept whereby the boundaries between the two often blur and cannot be easily separated.

As mentioned earlier, the sports industry was initially dominated by an informal sector that dwarfed the more formal part of the industry. In Sialkot the industry did go through a period of 'consolidation' in the 1970s when Zulfiqar Ali Bhutto[4] came to power in Pakistan on the basis of an Islamic socialist manifesto.[5] In the years that followed a tightening of labour laws and unions demanding increased representation, higher pay, and better working conditions led to several organized strikes at Sialkot's factories.

Labour laws, of course, were not applicable to units employing less than ten full-time workers and as a result factory owners decentralized their operations, thereby pre-empting the possibility of any further dissent. Work was increasingly done at home and by a female labour force. The result was a return to a distributed cottage industry relying not on a fixed labour force but on a casual and cheap pool of workers. This also allowed industrialists to avoid large capital outlays, overheads and providing workers benefits such as medical coverage, educational benefits, and old age pensions.

Similarly, in Hyderabad, a small formal sector was always supported by a much larger informal sector based in homes and small workshops where much of the handwork was undertaken. The glass bangles industry was never formalized and the labour force remained decentralized except for the very initial steps in the process.

There are other features inherent in both the football and glass bangles industries that made them suitable to the decentralized, informal format. Seventy-five per cent of work in football stitching and glass bangle manufacturing is done by hand, making it extremely labour-intensive. For both the football-stitching and glass-bangle-making sector the formal industry dominates only the initial stages of production. This involves converting the basic raw material (recycled glass or sheets of synthetic leather) into the main working material (open bangles, panels for stitching). In the case of glass bangles this is done through the application of high temperature to different forms of glass through the use of large high-intensity furnaces. This is feasible only in a factory environment. In football-stitching large machinery is required in order to cut the panels into standardized sizes and shapes, stamp the logos on the panels and for the final testing of the product.

Even within the factory premises, however, labour arrangements are subdivided vertically. The factory owners are exclusively responsible for the operation of the furnaces and the stamping/cutting machines. Once the glass wire spirals or the panels leave the factory premises the primary responsibility for the material as well as the work passes to a private subcontractor. Factories, therefore, typically employ permanently only those workers directly connected to the operation of the factory and the handling of material before it leaves the factory.

In the glass bangles industry in Hyderabad, processing of glass bangles takes place in three main stages. The first stage takes place in factories (located in the SITE area) where raw material, mostly in the form of glass bottles, is melted in furnaces to make molten glass. This molten glass then trickles in fine wires which are shaped into spiral forms through the use of rolling pins. Once the molten glass cools and the spiral shapes harden, they are then snapped to make open bangles which are put into bundles of around 300 bangles each, known as *toras*. These *toras* are transferred from the factories to the old city and Latifabad where additional processing takes place in homes and small workshops. Great skill and concentration is required to complete this entire process. In the first stage, factory owners are in charge of running the furnace and making molten glass. Once the molten glass is made into spirals and hardens, private contractors then become responsible for all the other processes involved in bangle-making. The second stage of the bangle-making process involves straightening the bangles and closing the ends and this takes place in houses and workshops located in the old city and Latifabad. Ovens, open flames and stoves are used for this additional processing. Women and children are also involved in doing this work (Collective for Social Sciences Research 2004). According to one survey, the number of children working in the bangle industry of Hyderabad is approximately 9,584 and of these around 86 per cent work in the bangle-making profession full-time (AKIDA 2004). The third stage involves processes such as cleaning, polishing, reshaping, and dyeing the closed bangles so as to bring them to their final, complete form. This, too, is done in workshops and at homes with the help of women and children. The only production workers who are on the factory payroll are those men who operate the furnace and who manage the molten glass. Even the workers who remove the glass wire spirals from the rolling pin, although employed by the factory, may actually be daily wage-workers. The processing done at stages two and three of bangle-making by workers in workshops and at homes is remunerated at a piece-rate basis by the subcontractor. The subcontractor and the workers generally belong to the same kinship, Ferozabad Siddiquis, and might also often be relatives or neighbours. Bangle-making work done in workshops and at homes is considered less skill-intensive than work done in operating the furnaces in factories and hence is also paid less than factory work. In general, wages in bangle-making are low and the work involved is often hazardous (Collective for Social Sciences Research 2004).

In the case of football-stitching a small number of permanent employees are maintained on the factory payroll to check for quality, to convert sheets of synthetic leather into panels and to stitch the highest quality footballs—which usually constitute only 20 per cent of total footballs produced but which are always stitched within factory premises and almost always by adult male stitchers. Well-known brand manufacturers such as Saga Sports and Sublime in Sialkot have established large, modern stitching centres with supervision to ensure that children are not involved in the stitching process, since the implementation of the 1997 Atlanta Agreement aimed at eliminating child labour from Sialkot's football industry. A few stitching centres for women have also been established. Smaller, non-brand manufacturers who have agreed to abide by the Atlanta Agreement have established small stitching centres in villages, mostly consisting of one or two rooms with a few light bulbs and fans. Each of these smaller stitching centres can accommodate around 15–20 stitchers at a time. As a significant number of home-based football stitchers prior to the implementation of the Atlanta Agreement were women—according to a survey by Save the Children (Voices of Children 1997) 58 per cent of football stitchers were women—and since working in stitching centres is not viable for many women for cultural and other reasons, women were amongst the hardest hit by the restructuring that took place under the Atlanta Agreement. To soften the impact of the Atlanta Agreement on women, they were allowed to set up home-based stitching centres. Three or four women could get together, set up a stitching centre at home and register it with the ILO and the manufacturer. Home-based stitching centres are usually located in small, one- or two-room houses. More than 500 home-based stitching centres have been established, with roughly 2,000 women working in these centres.

Despite the restructuring that took place under the Atlanta Agreement and the setting up of stitching centres that could be monitored, children are still involved in stitching footballs, although the number of children involved has significantly declined. Manufacturers who have chosen not to join the Atlanta Agreement and are not registered with the ILO still rely on subcontractors to distribute football panels for stitching and children often end up stitching these footballs. Companies exporting footballs to countries which are not concerned about child labour also use children for stitching footballs. Moreover, stitching centres set up by companies that have registered with the ILO sometimes leak football panels to home-based stitchers which include children. In stitching centres located in far-flung areas where monitoring is less strict, footballs are sometimes stitched partly at home and partly at the stitching centre. In order to keep costs low and meet tight deadlines, subcontractors also sometimes provide football panels for stitching to home-based stitchers, including children. Moreover, companies open up new stitching centres at times of high demand and close down stitching centres when the demand goes down so there is no fixed number of stitching centres and this makes monitoring harder. While a 2006 ILO-IPEC report (ILO 2006) claimed that fewer than 5 per cent of the stitching centres are not part of the monitoring programme and still use child labour, a report by the Clean Clothes Campaign suggested that 'child labour in the football goods industry is still alive and thriving in Pakistan, despite efforts made by the sporting goods industry, the International Labour Organization (ILO), and numerous other actors' (Clean Clothes Campaign 2002). My own fieldwork leads me to conclude that children are still involved in the football industry of Sialkot, although it is difficult to accurately estimate the percentage of children still stitching footballs.

Once the panels for stitching are cut, work shifts to homes and to smaller stitching centres where workers only require a few basic tools in order to stitch a whole football. At home families work as a unit, with children gradually taking on more complex tasks, graduating from putting glue on the thread used in stitching to stitching a few panels to half a football and ultimately to a complete football. But generally children will complete easier tasks, with the more experienced, older stitchers completing the process. For example, a 12–year-old child may stitch a few panels and pass them on to an older sister or mother who will put the panels together to form a half. The halves are then passed on to the master stitcher who will complete the most complex task of stitching the two halves of the ball together.

The fact that most work can be done by hand at home without the use of heavy machinery makes both football-stitching and glass bangles manufacturing particularly suitable to the home-based environment.

But the two additional key features identified earlier, namely (i) seasonality of demand within the sector and (ii) the extensive use of subcontractors, are crucial both to the structure of the industry and the existence of credit relations within the sectors. These factors need to be examined in some detail.

SEASONALITY OF DEMAND

Seasonality provides, prima facie, some grounds to expect a highly active informal credit market in the sector and, thus, some scope for the presence of bonded labour. Other sectors such as agriculture that are marked by seasonal incomes are associated with periods over which workers incur debts, followed by periods when debts are paid off. *Peshgis* are used to cover expenses in the fallow period.

In the football trade seasonality is based on the scheduling of large tournaments like the World or European Cups. In the glass bangles sector demand peaks before the two Muslim Eid[6] festivals and during the traditional wedding season in winter. The level of activity in the sector goes up dramatically two months before Eid-ul-Fitr and remains high until the festival of Eid-ul-Azha—covering a period of around four months.

According to some workers in the glass bangles industry, their total earnings in the four-month busy season equal their earnings during the rest of the year. In Hyderabad, the high seasonal demand for labour is met by longer hours worked by existing workers, as well as seasonal workers. Seasonal workers, however, are not, by and large, people from other communities or localities coming to work in the glass bangles sector. Rather, the influx appears to come from people in families already involved in glass-bangle-making, or those leaving other casual jobs or looking for additional work.

In the case of football-stitching, the seasonal demand meant that workers rarely stitched all year round. Most stitchers would stitch footballs in addition to other employment such as agricultural work. Stitching was used especially at times when the family required extra income—such as weddings or festivals like Eid when individuals buy new clothes and families distribute sweets and food to neighbours and relatives. Football-stitching, therefore, came to be seen as a convenient supplementary source of income on which few families solely relied rather than a 'formal' industrial occupation.

This means that in both sectors work comes intermittently rather than on a regular basis and correspondingly labour demand is highly seasonal. The use of an irregular non-permanent workforce means, for employers, that whenever demand increases, more workers can be added. When demand sags, workers can be released without any obligations. For workers this irregularity often translates into having to take advances in order to cover expenses incurred during the slack season.

THE ROLE OF THE SUBCONTRACTOR

The role of the subcontractor was crucial both in the decentralization—and therefore informalization of the industries—and in the presence of informal credit relations as it is through the subcontractor that the advance from an employer typically passes.

In Sialkot and in Hyderabad subcontractors worked both as recruiters of labour and as conduits for passing on skill. *Thekedars,* as they are known in Hyderabad, and *makers* as they are known in Sialkot typically receive large amounts of raw material—i.e. panels for stitching or unfinished bangles—from factories and subsequently take them to homes for completion. In both cases the subcontractor would provide some kind of surety to the factory owner, either in the form of credit relations or payment upfront. From that point onwards the subcontractor handles all labour arrangements, with the factory owner being at least one step removed from the workers.

The subcontractor is also involved in credit relations with his workers, giving *peshgis* on footballs and bangles to be completed. In Sialkot and Hyderabad workers take *peshgis* ranging from a few hundred rupees to several thousand rupees from their employers (via their subcontractors). These *peshgis* are taken against the understanding that the worker-borrower will pay back the amount by deducting the *peshgi* from his or her wages. A worker is obliged to work for his creditor until the advance is cleared. A new employer may clear the advance and then enter a labour-credit relationship with the worker. Once work has been completed the subcontractor returns the completed products to the factory owner and settles accounts with him. The process then repeats.

Typically, then, a subcontractor was a stitcher or a home-based bangle maker who usually, through his own initiative, contacts, and/or the injection of some capital, was able to take on the new role of supervising workers and ferrying material between factories and homes and back to factories. It is, for example, still a common sight in Sialkot to see *makers* with sacks full of material or completed footballs riding motor bikes with their load.

As trust and social capital are essential aspects in both the industries' structures, the most successful subcontractors would have worked with and developed a close relationship with their 'employers' and their workers.

Typically, then, a subcontractor was someone who had prior linkages with both his employer and his workers. In Hyderabad the *thekedars* were usually from the same kinship community (the Siddiquis) as the workers, and were often their relatives and neighbours. There was also likely to be some distant relationship with employers who were also largely from the same Siddiqui patrilineage. But while the economic and social distance between *thekedars* and workers was often relatively small—*thekedars* usually lived in the same localities as workers, sent their children to similar schools and lived in similar houses—this was certainly not the case with reference to *thekedars* and employers, where the social and economic difference in class was much more noticeable. But as Lefebvre (1999) points out, entirely rich and poor patrilineages do not exist, but within each is found a continuum of households at different levels on the economic scale. So with the Siddiquis there existed a range of households at different levels of the economic ladder.

In Sialkot *makers* and workers do not necessarily come from the same *biradari* as any particular caste association with the industry broke down decades ago—if it ever existed. All castes appear to be involved in football-stitching. But, as in Hyderabad, the subcontractor was someone who had prior linkages with both employer and workers. This could initially have been through *biradari*. *Makers* tended to be from the same *biradaris* as their stitchers but as the demand for footballs and the required labour force grew *makers* began to recruit neighbours and villagers as well.

As in Hyderabad, the social and economic distance between *makers* and workers was much more muted than that between workers, subcontractors, and employers. This means that while relatively subdued hierarchy between industrialists and their employees (subcontractors and through them football stitchers) may exist at the workplace, this does not extend to social spaces or occasions. Intermarriage is ruled out and while the industrialists may maintain houses in their native villages (and many make it a point to do so, further re-inforcing their local influence and identity as Sialkotis), these houses are usually ostentatious mansions compared to the modest two-room dwellings of their employees. Children of the industrialists are often educated in foreign universities while those of the workers are lucky to receive any education at all.

Despite these differences there is a common feeling of belonging that binds workers and employers together in both Hyderabad and Sialkot. In Sialkot the points of reference are the shared geographical area of origin, the common 'class' roots—even though the employers have now moved beyond their humble origins—and a feeling of a shared history that has culminated in Sialkot emerging as a world-class manufacturer of footballs. In Hyderabad there is similarly a feeling of a shared history, 'traditional' occupation, and origins in a particular geographical area. If anything, the feeling of solidarity is stronger as it involves a smaller, more homogeneous group of related kinsmen.

This recourse to shared background is a powerful bond between the three groups (workers, subcontractors, and employers) and the ability to maintain the support of workers through timely reminders of shared roots and history is essential to the industrialists' strategy of maintaining a loyal, skilled, and cheap labour force.

Within this industry structure it appears that many of the factors that promote the proliferation of *peshgis* and the incidence of bonded labour are present. Clearly the influence of subcontractors and seasonality—as already discussed—are key factors. Moreover, the sectors are to be found largely in the informal part of the economy. This means the absence of social security, old age benefits, and regular wages. It also means that wages are rarely at a subsistence level. The ensuing shortfall that the family faces is almost always met by recourse to loans. In neither the bangle industry nor in the football-stitching industry were wages sufficient to cover basic expenditures, except for the workers at the top of the hierarchy. Moreover the fact that work in both sectors is home-based and often undertaken by women who have few other options for work ensures low wages throughout the home-based sector. Women are willing to take on work at extremely low rates of pay because even a marginal increment to earned income is welcome. Since these women are also busy maintaining their households, this implies that women's leisure time has an extremely low value (in economic terms).

The absence of social security also makes families particularly vulnerable to expenditure 'spikes' that invariably occur. Even those families which are able to subsist on the meagre income of their individual members cannot cope with the costs related to a sudden illness or death. In the absence of this social security *peshgis* are often the only way to make ends meet at times of high expenditure. Similarly, life events such as weddings and funerals demand considerable expenditure. For example the expenditure associated with a wedding can easily exceed the annual earnings of a family and the failure to arrange an 'appropriate' wedding leads to an immediate loss of face (*izzat*) for the family in the larger community and may also result in an unsuitable match for daughters.

In fact the *peshgi* system is active in both Hyderabad and Sialkot and resembles the classic labour–credit interlinkage observed in other sectors of the economy. In both Hyderabad and Sialkot around half of all workers or more in the industry were involved in credit relations with their employers. In fact *makers* and *thekedars* often stated that, unless they had *peshgis* to offer, stitchers/bangle makers would not accept work from them.

The International Labour Organization (ILO) defines debt bondage as a specific form of forced labour in which a worker renders service under conditions of bondage arising from economic considerations, notably indebtedness incurred through the provision of a loan.[7] The conventional view on *peshgis* therefore is that once an advance is taken and the worker falls into a cycle of indebtedness, debt bondage and its associated implications will inevitably follow. The most serious of these implications are the exercise of coercion, which refers to the menace of penalty, and the denial of freedom, which refers to the involuntary nature of the work. In sum, the leverage provided by indebtedness allows the creditor to exercise non-economic coercion, typically in the form of violence, imprisonment, and financial penalties, in order to ensure that the worker is forced to continue on the terms imposed by the employer.

And yet despite the fact that both the glass bangles and the football-stitching industries were characterized by a proliferation of *peshgis,* there was scant evidence of the debt bondage and the extra-economic coercion that appears to characterize other sectors where *peshgis* are taken. Why is this the case?

SHARED HISTORIES

I believe the answer lies in the mediating effect that the notion of a shared history and background has had in both environments. In Sialkot and Hyderabad the unique historical development of the industries has meant a less antagonistic relationship between employer and employee.

In Sialkot, the emergence of employers and *makers* from within the group of workers—many of today's industrialists in Sialkot worked their way up from being artisans—has, in fact, led to the formation of a relatively supportive employer–subcontractor–worker relationship.

During fieldwork in Sialkot, it was often pointed out by both workers and employers that one of the major reasons for the success of the sports industry was that the industrialists were familiar with every process involved in the production of goods. This not only improved quality control but also meant a very hands-on approach by employers who would often spend time on the work floor passing on advice to their workers. The result has been a labour dynamic that promotes a relatively close and non-antagonistic employer–employee relationship. The fact that *makers*, stitchers, and owners all emerged from the same class of artisans has played down divisions that are often highly visible in other industries.

In Hyderabad the group providing workers, subcontractors and employers all belonged to the Siddiqui kinship group and while there were clear economic and social differences within this group there was also a strong notion within the community of the more fortunate members having obligations towards the less fortunate—the notion of the patrilineage acting as a mutual aid society.

This feeling of a common origin and heritage in both sectors promotes a degree of trust, solidarity and mutual understanding between the different economic actors. There is social capital that the community can call upon.

Normally, the fact that employers and employees are from different castes—employers from the higher castes and workers from the lower, servicing castes—as in tanneries, agriculture, and brick making—means that relations often become antagonistic and are marked by dominance on one side and submission on the other. But in both Sialkot and in Hyderabad there was little sign of the antagonistic relationship described by Ong (1991), for example, in her description of the intimidating relations between the Korean supervisors of a multinational company and the local Indonesian workers. Nor is there the hostile arrogance that Punjabi Hindu employers show towards the caste of Jatav craftsmen involved in the Agra shoe industry of India (Knorringa 1996, 1999).

As a result, relations between owners, subcontractors, and workers tend to be more supportive than in other sectors. The fact that in both cases the industry is confined to one city (Hyderabad) or district (Sialkot) also promotes a feeling of it being owned by the community. Thus rather than being based on coercion, the 'hold' of employers over workers was through recourse to notions of community solidarity and socially sanctioned mutual obligations.

OTHER FACTORS

Apart from the major mediating factor just described there are other aspects that have contributed to the lack of bonded labour in the two sectors. In the case of Sialkot, the hold of landowners has historically been weak. The region has long been an industrial centre and this has meant that the worker population has never been overly dependent on landowners for their livelihood, therefore not making them reliant on any one form of work. It has also meant that traditional relations of exploitation based on caste relations were not strengthened or replicated in other sectors.

In Hyderabad the fact that the glass bangles industry was urban-based did mean that the long-standing relations of exploitation that are typical of a rural setting were absent. Moreover, many of the industries that did develop in Hyderabad came to be owned by a class of migrant that shifted from India and as such did not come from the landed classes.

There are other important reasons for the absence of debt bondage. Significantly, loans in both Hyderabad and Sialkot tend to be calibrated to earning power. Workers who take or are offered the largest loans are the highest skilled workers—who in both cases will be permanent factory employees who happen to be the highest paid workers in the sector and the elite few who form part of the formal workforce. Overwhelmingly the master craftsmen are adult males and can have debts in the range of 20,000 rupees or more.

Adult male workers who work in the small-scale sector can run up debts of upto 5,000 and 10,000 rupees but usually debts tend to be smaller. In Hyderabad female workers generally avoided taking advances, and their debt rarely went over a few hundred rupees. The usual practice for obtaining a loan was to give a few days prior notice to the employer. If a worker wanted to leave employment, s/he also had to give notice of a few days. At times, the advance was small enough for it to be covered by work already done. In cases where the outstanding debt is larger than the work done for a particular employer, the process of debt transfer did not appear to be particularly troublesome for the worker.

In Sialkot home-based workers did take advances but they remained small—a few hundred rupees at a time and were therefore manageable. In Sialkot advances were made for a family usually on a weekly basis and the loan rarely amounted to a few hundred rupees at a time. Taking an advance to stitch six footballs would come to around Rs. 200. Again paying back or transferring debts appeared not to be overly problematic in most cases.

In both Sialkot and Hyderabad it was also common to find workers working for a number of different subcontractors simultaneously or changing subcontractors, implying that there was little or no compulsion to work for a particular *thekedar* or *maker*. Again the main factor appears to be that the amount of the loan was seldom higher than what may be cleared within a season.

Moreover, terms of loan repayment were usually agreed between employers/subcontractors and workers. Employers/subcontractors appear not to be too apprehensive of worker default, since they share social proximity. Workers are also aware that they have to ultimately return to their community. In Hyderabad the social sanction is that much stronger as the bangle industry involves a single community that is concentrated in one part of the city. In Sialkot there is more of an onus on the subcontractor to pressurize his 'workers' through his extensive kinship linkages with them.

When asked about the options available to the subcontractors in the event of a worker's default, subcontractors and workers gave similar responses stating that very little could be done against a worker, except in the way of social sanctions on the part of the community. Moreover, it was felt that there were clear obligations on both sides that had to be respected.

Clearly this is very different from the large *peshgis* that are offered at the brick kilns or carpet-weaving and agricultural sectors where labour is bound for years.

Finally, according to informants, the credit transaction is not regarded as an essential feature of the labour contract. A significant number of workers in both industries do not take loans. When queried about the seasonal nature of the sector, those in the bangle industry replied that many people accumulated savings during the busy cycle and were able to smooth their consumption over the rest of the year by drawing on these savings. In Sialkot, football-stitching was rarely looked at as a full-time occupation and was undertaken at times when extra income was required. It also represented an ideal source of income for household-based women and therefore was seen as an additional—almost bonus—form of income. Most families had at least one or two male members who had other sources of income that could be tapped into.

This points to the fact that *peshgis* in Hyderabad and Sialkot did not lead to a situation where the obligation of labour was backed up by non-economic coercion. Non-economic coercion usually comes in the form of surveillance, physical confinement of labour, and the use of the threat of violence as well as the actual use of violence. Thus bondage may be instigated through indebtedness (economic coercion) but it is made effective through the additional application of non-economic forms of coercion. Neither in Sialkot nor in Hyderabad were there any accounts of physical violence used against defaulters. Even instances of verbal abuse were rare.

These factors—the agreed terms of repayment and the calibrated loans—are made possible because they exist in an environment where the relations between the actors involved in the industries are supportive rather than hostile. Again this is based on the shared histories and origins of the groups that constitute the football-stitching and the bangle-making industries.

But that does not mean that the *peshgi* did not provide any leverage to the employers and it would be incorrect to overly romanticize the relationship between workers, subcontractors, and employers in Sialkot and Hyderabad. Rather than use violence and confinement as non-economic forms of coercion, employers used a more subtle form of control based around the very factor that mediates relations—the notion of shared origins and belonging to a particular community. This leads to the effectiveness of the social sanction and the maintenance of patron–client relations amongst workers, subcontractors and employers.

CONCLUSION AND FUTURE DIRECTIONS

In neither Sialkot nor Hyderabad does debt bondage appear to be substantive, despite the presence of *peshgis* and other factors that would normally be associated with sectors where relations of bondage are common. In both cases what we find is the frequent taking and returning of *peshgis*.

It is the contention of this article that it is therefore inaccurate to jump to the conclusion that where there are *peshgis* there is debt bondage. This remains an inaccurate basis for the analysis of debt bondage and yet the assumption that where there is *peshgi* there is bondage is common. For example, Sydney Schanberg, a prominent American journalist writing for *LIFE* magazine discusses bonded labour, and he finds the *peshgi*[8] system as common in the football industry as 'the flies that swarm about the faces of workers'. He goes on to reveal the appalling conditions that he witnessed: 'Children as young as six bought from their parents for as little as $15, sold and resold like furniture, branded, beaten, blinded as punishment for wanting to go home, rendered speechless by the trauma of their enslavement' (Schanberg 1996). Similarly, Jonathan Silvers who also wrote a piece on Sialkot's football industry found evidence of debt bondage in the sector. Both writers err in their understanding of the *peshgi*–debt bondage relationship, taking it as one-dimensional and lacking in complexity.

Instead of this situation we find that *peshgis* do not necessarily bring about the extra-economic coercion that characterizes a debt bondage relationship. In Hyderabad and Sialkot, there are in fact few options open to those who give *peshgis* when return is demanded, pointing to the fact that employers may actually find it difficult to retrieve outstanding loans.

This may also be a further reason that employers do not usually offer large loans in either the glass bangles or football-stitching sectors.

We thus see, both in the case of Hyderabad and Sialkot, that taking *peshgis* does not translate in to a cycle of debt bondage. Nor is there any evidence that suggests that factory owners take advantage of the asymmetrical balance of power and use violence to subdue workers into accepting low wages and poor working conditions. Violence and physical coercion, however, are not the only tools that can be used to generate a compliant workforce—social linkages and mechanisms can play an equally important role.

Ironically enough, it seems that the strong sense of solidarity within both communities that keeps violence at bay is the same tool that can be used to manipulate workers in to accepting low wages without creating resentment and protest. As mentioned earlier, the football industry in Sialkot was initially developed by a group of indigenous craftsmen who were initially stitchers themselves, and there was and still remains a great sense of pride within the community at being able to develop a world-class industry from such humble beginnings. Not only does this create a sense of solidarity within the community but it acts as an inspiring tale for other football stitchers and craftsmen.

Yet at the same time, this sense of a community can be used in a Gramscian sense to manipulate the workers and exert control over them. Stressing their own humble beginnings and creating a sense of solidarity between themselves and the workers also serves as an effective tool for ensuring a harmonious relationship with the latter despite the low wages and poor working conditions.

This does not imply that the stitchers or bangle-makers do not gain any benefits from this relationship. It has been documented that *makers* and *thekedars* are at times extremely generous in terms of bestowing economic favours upon workers. Workers, in this regard, feel indebted to the owners for making such compensations. This bond between the stitchers and *makers* and bangle-makers and *thekedars* of unequal reciprocity—where the former feel indebted to the latter for all the favours bestowed upon them—corresponds with the characteristics of a classic patron–client relationship.

Though patron–client relationships are more commonly found within patrilineages, the shared notion of history present in the football-stitching industry gives the community *biradari*-like ties where there are vertical linkages between powerful and less powerful actors. This sense of indebtedness makes it extremely difficult for the workers to break out of this dyadic relationship and start demanding increased wages and other labour rights. Moreover the provision of *peshgis* to individuals helps maintain vertical segmentation within society so that, as Hamza Alavi (1988) points out, power and authority are vested at the top with a patron and rather than class conflict there are vertical cleavages that work against horizontal solidarity.

The patron–client relationship in the football industry hinges on the sense of community that exists between the stitchers and *makers*. References to shared origin can thus be used to continue a patron–client relationship within the community where workers feel that they cannot let down 'their community' and feel indebted to the factory owners and therefore accept low wages without much protest.

The situation in Hyderabad is similar, where a community of migrant bangle craftsmen developed the entire industry. Even though the bangle industry has now expanded to include workers from other ethnic backgrounds, owners and workers both continue to regard bangle-making as the traditional profession of Ferozabad Siddiquis and there is a strong sense of community within the bangle industry. It is this sense that makes social sanctions against workers who do not pay off their loans as effective a tool as using force. However, further expansion in both industries may change the dynamic as it has in other industries where other castes and communities have joined the workforce—such as the power loom industry in Tamil Nadu where relations between loom owners and workers became especially hostile after a new entrant previously unconnected to the industry, the Gounders, entered the market and changed the delicate existing relationship balance (De Neve 1999). As workers from different castes and communities enter the workforce, it may become difficult to maintain the same notion of a community and other forms of control may have to be used.

There are already indications of a growing rift between workers and factory owners in Hyderabad where, although the Ferozabad Siddiquis remain the core community in the glass bangles sector, people from a number of other communities have also entered the sector as workers, subcontractors, and traders. The new entrants—who have increased in numbers over the past decade or so—are from diverse ethnic, caste, and *biradari* backgrounds, including Sindhis, Punjabis, Rangars, as well as Urdu-speaking communities other than the Ferozabad Siddiquis. Despite this the shared community identity of the Ferozabad Siddiquis had remained strong but of late there have been indications of growing resentment between workers and factory owners.

In 2005, factory owners closed down factories and laid off all employees as a response to workers' protests for higher wages, better working conditions, social security and rights under the prevalent labour laws and factory act. Though this issue was resolved in a couple of weeks, the resentment against the factory owners remains and workers often accuse them of understating their profits as a justification for low wages.

In Sialkot too a new generation of employers is bringing about a change in the dynamic between worker and the employers. The new generation of employers does not share the same history with the workers as the previous generation did. Also, as the industry expands exponentially, more and more individuals and groups that do not share the same sense of community are entering the market. There are signs of growing polarization between employers, *makers* and stitchers and the references to shared origins are beginning to run thin as workers and subcontractors increasingly see where the profits are pocketed.

REFERENCES

Ahmad, I. (1973), *Caste and Social Stratification Among the Muslims*. New Delhi: Manohar.

Ahmad, S. (1971), 'Social Stratification in a Punjabi Village'. *Contributions to Indian Sociology* 4: 105–25.

Ahmad, S. (1974), 'A Village in Pakistani Punjab', in C. Maloney (ed.) South Asia: Seven Community Profiles. New York: Holt, Rinehart & Winston: 131–72.

Ahmad, S. (1977), Class and Power in a Punjabi Village. New York and London: Monthly Review Press.

AKIDA Management Consultants (2004), 'Baseline Survey Report on Child Labour in Glass Bangles Industry Hyderabad'. Unpublished.

Alavi, H. (1972), 'Kinship in West Punjabi Villages'. *Contributions to Indian Sociology* 6: 1–27.

Alavi, H. (1988), 'Introduction to Sociology of the Developing Societies', in T. Shanin (ed.) *Peasant and Peasant Societies*. Harmondsworth: Penguin.

Anwar, A. A. (1953), 'Effects of Partition Industries in Border Districts of Lahore and Sialkot'. *Board of Economic Inquiry Punjab (Pakistan)* 105: 56–105.

Barth, F. (1960), 'The system of social stratification in Swat, North Pakistan', in E. R. Leach (ed.) *Aspects of Caste in India, Ceylon and North-West Pakistan*. Cambridge: Cambridge University Press: 113–45.

Clean Clothes Campaign (2002), Executive Summary of the Global March Report on the Football Stitching Industry of Pakistan. http://www.sweatsoap.com/news/clean-clothes-newsletter-24/1156-executive-summary-of-the-global-march-report-on-the-football-stitching-industry-of-pakistan. (Accessed June 2010)

Collective for Social Sciences Research (2004), 'A Rapid Assessment of Bonded Labour in Hazardous Industries in Pakistan: Glass Bangle-Making, Tanneries and Construction' (March). Unpublished.

De Neve, G. (1999), 'Asking for and Giving *Baki*: Neo Bondage or the Interplay of Bondage and Resistance in the Tamilnadu Power-Loom Industry', In: J. P. Parry, J. Bremanand,

and K. Kapadia (eds) *The Worlds of Indian Industrial Labour*. New Delhi: Sage Publications: 379–406.

Dumont, L. (1980), Homo Hierarchicus. Chicago: University of Chicago Press.

Ercelawn. A., Nauman, N., (2001) Bonded Labour in Pakistan. Geneva: International Labour Organization.

Fischer, M. D. (1991), 'Marriage and Power: Tradition and Transition in an Urban Punjabi Community', in D. Hastings (ed) *Economy and Culture in Pakistan*. Basingstoke: Macmillan: 97–123.

Fuller, C. J. (ed) (1996), *Caste Today*. Delhi: Oxford University Press.

Hart, K. (1973), Informal Income Opportunities and Urban Employment in Ghana. *Journal of Modern African Studies* 11: 61–89.

International Labour Organization and International Programme on the Elimination of Child Labour (2006), *Combating Child Labour in the Soccer Ball Industry in Pakistan: From Stitching to School*. http://www.ilo.org/global/About_the_ILO/Media_and_public_information/Feature_stories/lang--en/WCMS_071247/index.htm. (Accessed July 2010)

Jalal, A. (1995), *Democracy and Authoritarianism in South Asia*. Cambridge: Cambridge University Press.

Khan, A. (2007), *Representing Children: Power, Policy and the Discourse on Child Labour in the Football Manufacturing Industry of Pakistan*. Karachi: Oxford University Press.

Knorringa, P. (1996), *Economics of Collaboration: Indian Shoemakers Between Market and Hierarchy*. New Delhi: Sage Publications.

Knorringa, P. (1999), 'Artisan Labour in the Agra Footwear Industry: Continued Informality and Changing Threats', in J. P. Parry, J. Breman, and K. Kapadia, (eds) *The Worlds of Indian Industrial Labour*. New Delhi: Sage Publications, 303–28.

Lefebvre, A. (1999), *Kinship, Honour and Money in Rural Pakistan*. Richmond, Surrey: Curzon.

Lindholm, C. (1986), 'Caste in India and the Problems of Deviant Systems: A Critique Of Recent Theory'. *Contributions to Indian Sociology* 20: 61–96.

Nadvi, K. (1990), *Employment Creation in Urban Informal Micro Enterprises in the Manufacturing Sector in Pakistan*. New Delhi: ILO-ARTEP.

Nadvi, K. (1999), 'Shifting Ties: Social Networks in the Surgical Instrument Cluster of Sialkot, Pakistan', *Development and Change*. Oxford: Blackwell Publishers Ltd, vol. 30: 141–75.

Ong, A. (1991), 'Gender and Labour Politics of Postmodernism', *Annual Review of Anthropology* 20: 279–309.

Saberwal, S. (1976), *Mobile Men: Limits to Social Change in Urban Punjab*. New Delhi: Vikas Pub. House.

Save The Children (1997), *Stitching Footballs: Voices of Children*. London: Save The Children.

Schanberg, S. H. (1996), 'Six Cents an Hour', *Life Magazine* (June): 38–45.

Shaw, A. (1988), *A Pakistani Community in Britain*. Oxford: Basil Blackwell.

Silvers, J. (1996), 'Child Labour in Pakistan', *Atlantic Monthly* (Feb.): 79–92.

Talbot, I. (1998), *Pakistan: A Modern History*. London: Hurst & Co.

Werbner, P. (1989), 'The Ranking of Brotherhoods: The Dialectics of Muslim Caste Among Overseas Pakistanis', *Contributions to Indian Sociology* 23(2): 285–315.

NOTES

1. For further information on the existence of caste in Muslim societies, see, I. Ahmed (1973), S. Ahmed (1971, 1974, 1977), Barth (1960), Dumont (1980), Alavi (1972), Lindholm (1986), Shaw (1988), Werbner (1989), Fuller (1996).
2. For a fuller discussion of caste and *biradari* see Alavi (1972), Shaw (1988), Fischer (1991), Werbner (1989).
3. For a detailed discussion of this see Nadvi (1990, 1999)
4. Z. A. Bhutto—President 1971–73, Prime Minister—1973–77.
5. For a political history of Pakistan see Jalal (1995), Talbot (1998).
6. There are three Eid festivals during the Muslim year celebrating the end of the month of fasting (Eid-ul-Fitr), the prophet Muhammad's birth anniversary (Eid-i-Milad-un-Nabi) and the commemoration of Abraham's sacrifice of his son (Eid-ul-Azha).
7. 'The term forced or compulsory labour shall mean all work or service which is extracted from any person under the menace of any penalty and for which the said person has not offered himself voluntarily'—ILO Convention 29, 1930.
8. The term *peshgi* refers to an advance of money and the *peshgi* system therefore implies a bonded labour system.

CHAPTER 10

Brick Kilns Revisited

ALI KHAN, LAILA BUSHRA, AND HAMID SULTAN

May 2015

F ew aspects of the Pakistani economy have attracted as much
international interest as the prevalence of bonded labour in its
different sectors. The phenomenon is identified as the primary
factor in perpetuating both the underperformance of the economy, and
the suppression of workers' rights. The sectors that have been identified
for their reliance on bonded labour include, but are not limited to,
agriculture, brick kilns, domestic service, carpet-weaving, and mining.[1]
Several reports commissioned by international agencies invariably reach
the conclusion that replacing bonded with 'free' labour would address
both the economic and socio-ethical issues in the Pakistani labour market.

This chapter aims to contribute to the debate on the prevalence of
bonded labour in Pakistan by analysing its functioning in the brick
making sector. Based on a survey of brick kilns in the district of
Gujranwala in the province of Punjab, we discuss the mechanisms and
institutions through which certain sections of labour become 'bonded' to
their employers, and how the arrangement is reproduced over time. A key
instrument of labour bondage is the practice of taking an advance on
payment—called *peshgi* (plural: *peshgis*)—through which workers become
indebted to their employers until the debt is paid off. During this period
of indebtedness, restrictions on taking on other employment, accepting
wages below the market rate, and being subject to physical and verbal
threats become part of the employer–employee relationship.[2] We discuss
the contours of *peshgi* within the overall functioning of brick kilns, and
the various features of the mutually-bound labour-capital arrangement
engendered by the practice of *peshgi*.

Brick kilns constitute a sizeable sector of the Pakistani economy given the centrality of fired bricks for the construction industry. It is also one of the least mechanized sectors, and is well-noted for its reliance on bonded labour. The estimated number of brick kilns in Pakistan ranges from eight to ten thousand, employing around one and a half million men, women, and children. Almost half of these kilns are located in the province of Punjab.[3] A detailed analysis of the structure of kilns in Punjab would not only shed light on the prevalence of bonded labour in this sector, but also provide a framework for analysing the broader issue of bonded labour in a developing country like Pakistan.

RESEARCH DESIGN

This chapter draws on research conducted at fifteen brick kilns in the district of Gujranwala in Punjab for two months in 2013. We used a questionnaire of sixty-three questions to interview owners, workers, sub-contractors, and managers at each kiln. This was supplemented with quantitative data on the rate of wages and *peshgis*, as well as the overall economic structure of the kilns.

ANALYTICAL FRAMEWORK AND CHAPTER ORGANIZATION

There are two dimensions to the term 'bonded labour' as a particular type of employer—employee relationship. The first dimension refers to the fact that the arrangements between capital and labour are forged outside the domain of the 'free' market wherein skills and wages would be negotiated and exchanged without interference of any non-economic—particularly coercive—factors. Given that all states have legal injunctions[4] against any kind of forced or bonded labour, such arrangements by definition operate in sectors and regions outside the purview of state institutions. In addition to operating outside the 'free market' then, bonded labour also operates beyond the direct control of the state in the informal sector. This 'informality' of the socio-economic context constitutes the second dimension of bonded labour. Along these two dimensions, the actual processes and institutions through which the employer-labour relations are established and reproduced on a 'non-economic' or 'unfree' basis in 'informal' settings are quite diverse.

Informality or the absence of state control characterizes the entire Pakistani economy rather than any particular business or industry. State control of even the largest and most visible sectors is precarious at best, and even sectors with an outwardly formal structure rely on an informal workforce.[5] This informality provides fertile ground for the forging and institutionalizing of a number of unfree, non-economic, even illegal labour arrangements. For brick kilns, as we shall see, informality is the central factor accounting for the existence and resilience of bonded labour arrangements through *peshgis*. But labour arrangements at the brick kilns also underline how informality or lack of state control does not always imply the existence of coercive or violent mechanisms. Contrary to the standard image of violence associated with bonded labour in Pakistan, as we shall see, 'bonded' arrangements on kilns are founded and reproduced entirely on economic foundations without recourse to coercion or other 'non-economic' measures. And the labour-capital relations respond to opportunities and constraints of the 'market'—economic factors in other words—no less than sectors in the formal and/or free part of the economy. Our findings suggest that these economic factors include the issues of subsistence wages and job security for the workers, and labour supply for the employers.

The following discussion is organized in four sections. The first section discusses the overall economic and labour structure at a typical brick kiln in Punjab. The second section discusses the types and functions of *peshgi* payments. The third section is dedicated to what we consider to be the most important role of *peshgis* for both the employers and the workforce at the kiln. The concluding section offers some tentative thoughts for a broader discussion of the issues of subsistence and security of employment in informal settings without any 'non-economic' constraints.

WORK AND WAGES AT BRICK KILNS

The process of brick making relies entirely on manual labour, carried out by teams of *patheras* (responsible for preparing, moulding, and trimming bricks), *jalaiwalas* (responsible for firing and baking in the kiln), and *bharaiwalas* and *nikasiwalas* (in charge of stacking, loading, and unloading of bricks). Even if it is not entirely visible to outsiders, there exists skill-based differentiation within the kiln, where *jalaiwalas* are at the top of the hierarchy followed by the *bharaiwalas,* the *patheras,* and finally the *nikasiwalas.*

These workers are recruited and supervised by the sub-contractor. The kiln operation is supervised by a full-time manager called a *munshi.* In some instances, the *munshi* and sub-contractor might be the same person. In general though, the two positions are separate. The kiln usually also has some ancillary staff like watchmen. For the manual workers, all family members (parents and children) work at the kiln, although certain tasks are reserved for the adults. The average size of each family is four to six individuals.

The production of bricks on the kilns follows both a seasonal and a monthly cycle. Brick production is halted for at least two periods every year because of the rainy season. The two off-seasons last roughly from early January till mid-February, and from early July till mid-September. The average daily output of a family of *patheras* is 1,500 to 1,800 bricks, and a kiln produces around 650,000 bricks per cycle.

In the operation of the kiln, the owners rely on a small core of salaried employees with a large number of contractual and seasonal workers. The *munshi* (manager) enjoys a salaried position with compensation ranging from Rs. 12,000 to 20,000 (US$120–200). The small number of *jalaiwalas* and ancillary staff members like watchmen also tend to be salaried employees. Aside from the *jalaiwalas*, all the production workers (*patheras*, *bharaiwalas*, and *nikasiwalas*) are hired by the sub-contractor. Each of these labour categories has a separate sub-contractor. The sub-contractor for the *patheras* works on a commission—he is paid Rs. 20–30 (US$2–3) per thousand bricks. In addition to recruitment, the sub-contractor is also responsible for arranging workers' accommodation on behalf of the owner—these are usually makeshift mud huts built on the premises of the kiln. Utilities like electricity and water are usually provided by the owner, while food and medical bills are the responsibility of workers themselves.

The two most important members of this workforce are the *patheras* and the sub-contractor. The latter—in his capacity as the labour agent—forms the most crucial link between the owners and the workforce. Kiln owners have little or nothing to do with the recruitment of labour, apart from the few regular employees mentioned above. It is the sub-contractor who accepts payments for the delivery of bricks, and is responsible for the recruitment, management, and supervision of workers. He decides the structure and form of labour compensation, and has to ensure that the work is completed to the owner's satisfaction. The owner does not deal directly with the workforce, and accepts no responsibility for the working conditions and salary arrangements of the largest component of 'his' sub-contracted workforce. Through the sub-contractor then, the kiln-owner is able to pass on a disproportionate share of uncertainty and risk to the workers.

The sub-contractor, who takes on responsibility for the workers he recruits, and for distributing advances on behalf of the owner, needs to be able to reduce the chances of non-accountability of labour. Ensuring compliance is easier when he enjoys previous links with his workers. Specifically, he can locate workers in the event that they do not 'honour' their commitments. He is also the first point of quality control for the moulding and baking of the bricks. For these reasons, the sub-contractor often recruits workers from his own extended kinship group or village. This allows him greater control over the workforce, and also enables him to 'oblige' his kin members by providing them employment. As a typical patron, the sub-contractor is seen as the one extending a favour to his 'clients' who then feel obliged to him, whereas in fact the flow of services, in the form of cheap informal labour, is in favour of the labour agent.

It is also important to underline that the sub-contractor frequently participates in the manual job of brick-moulding himself, and does not enjoy his high position in the labour hierarchy at the kiln owing to his skills or formal qualifications. He is usually the 'first amongst equals'—a person who has managed to take on the role of a sub-contractor through the injection of cash from his extended kin group and recruiting a sizeable number of *patheras*.

The *patheras* form the largest group of manual workers. They are predominantly Muslims and Christians whose low-caste Hindu ancestors had converted to Islam or Christianity to escape institutionalized caste discrimination. A survey conducted by the Federal Bureau of Statistics in 2002[6] found that almost half the surveyed households of *patheras* were from Christian or Muslim Sheikh castes.[7] Most *patheras* are migrants from central and south Punjab. There are some Afghan migrant workers in kilns of northern Punjab districts like Rawalpindi, although their numbers have declined in recent years. Most of the *pathera* families have been in the profession for generations. Others have recently moved from agriculture to brick making. This movement from agriculture to brick kilns is not unfamiliar and the first *patheras* were probably all agricultural workers who had been displaced from their lands as more landowners mechanized their farms and became owner-operators (see Ercelan and Nauman this volume). *Pathera* families tend to move from kiln to kiln on a fairly frequent basis. The participants of the present study included both Christians and Muslims, with little difference in terms of socio-economic status or educational credentials. Almost all of them were illiterate, economically in the lowest strata and shared the typical profile of *patheras* outlined above.

COMPENSATION AND *PESHGIS*

The typical mode of payment to the *pathera* is piecemeal, and the average compensation ranges from eight hundred rupees to nine hundred (US$7.7–8.7) per thousand bricks[8] (see Table 1 below for the overall economic model of a typical brick kiln). The regional variations in the rate of compensation per thousand bricks reflect the relative scarcity or availability of *patheras* in different parts of the province. Overall though, the piecemeal system is particularly advantageous for the employer when it is used in conjunction with *peshgi* or advances. If advances are combined with wages not based on a piece rate, workers have less incentive to ensure that their output remains high, particularly if they are unsupervised. This can lead to a slow-down in worker output once an advance is obtained. However, if workers are paid on a piece rate basis, the ability to repay a *peshgi* is directly linked to the workers' productivity and thereby the kiln's total output. The piece-rate serves as a mechanism of quality as well as labour control. The combination of piece-rates and advances serve as incentives for high output whereby the workers can only repay the advances by maintaining productivity.

Peshgi is used as a catchall term referring to advances against salary. In practice, however, *peshgis* cover a broad spectrum both in terms of the amount and time frame of the loan. *Peshgis* are taken on long-term as well as short-term basis, and the amounts vary from a couple of thousand rupees to around fifty thousand. The two most frequent categories are short-term, subsistence loans, and large loans covering a longer period. Small subsistence loans (small in relation to the workers' earnings) are usually in the amount of one thousand rupees (US$9.6) or less. These are availed by all workers to meet short-term income shortfalls. Such loans have a rapid circulation, being taken and returned on a fairly regular basis. Some of these, however, can and do accumulate to form larger debts if not repaid in the short turn.

In a general discussion of *peshgi*, these small loans do not appear to have the serious implications associated with long-term indebtedness. The latter refer to large advances (again, larger in relation to the earnings) that turn into *substantive* bondage—a condition leading to long-term indebtedness with no real option for debt redemption. The only three options for the workers in this condition are continued work for the same employer, labour flight, or transfer of debt to another owner but only at the discretion of the current one. It is here that *peshgi* can become an economic instrument of coercion that increases the leverage that the employer has over the indebted worker. These large *peshgis* are relatively less frequent than the small, short-term loans, and the group most commonly associated with these substantive *peshgis* are the *patheras*.

REASONS FOR RECOURSE TO PESHGIS

Peshgis are taken for a number of reasons and most previous reports have identified three major factors. The first is low wages that force the labourers to take *peshgis* to meet their subsistence requirements. The second reason is the 'seasonal' nature of work in sectors like brick making, whereby workers depend on *peshgis* during the 'dry' or 'off' seasons. The third function that *peshgis* perform is helping workers deal with certain inevitable life-course 'expenditure spikes'.[9] Each of these explanations has some merit, albeit with some qualifications, as discussed below. However, these studies do not address what we argue is the one crucial function that *peshgi* performs for both the employers and the workers, i.e., that of providing a regular and predictable labour supply for the owner and employment for the workers. We cannot adequately understand the functioning of brick kilns and the role of *peshgis* therein without taking account of how both the employers and their workers view and approach the *peshgi* system.

NOT SUBSISTING AT SUBSISTENCE WAGES

The most widely reported reason for recourse to *peshgis* is that wages are rarely paid at the subsistence level and the ensuing shortfall that the family faces is met by recourse to loans. To appreciate this factor, it is important to critically examine the issue of minimum wages in Pakistan and not be misled by figures. Some critics of *peshgi* have argued that the *pathera* families earn almost twice the minimum wage[10] (at 1,500 bricks/day, the family can earn Rs. 22,500 [US$220]) and the short-term loans reflect reckless and 'irrational' expenditures on part of the *patheras*. These arguments are disingenuous at best. To begin with, the minimum wages are determined for individual workers, while these earnings are those of the entire family. Second, minimum wages are by definition implementable only in the formal sector, which is of negligible size in Pakistan. And finally, even the assumption that the minimum wage in Pakistan actually does ensure 'subsistence' is highly questionable. The overwhelming majority of the working population supplements the 'minimum' wage with informal and after-hours employment by the family head as well as the rest of the family members.

SLACK SEASON

A second reason that is often given for the taking of *peshgi*s involves the seasonal nature of brick production. As we saw in the first section, brick production is halted for at least two periods every year because of the rains, and *peshgi*s help workers tide over the slack season when they are not receiving regular wages.

Patheras actually do take up other jobs at the kiln during the slack season. The most common off-season job available to *patheras* is the loading of baked bricks on trolleys or trucks for onward transportation, or transporting the already baked bricks around the kiln. But the income from those jobs is neither adequate nor regular. Some *patheras* also return to their villages, or travel to other parts of Punjab to do farm work. Since the off-season coincides with the rice-growing season, and wages for short-term employment on rice fields or farms are actually higher than those at kilns, some *patheras* do leave the kilns to work in the fields with permission from the subcontractor and the kiln owner. But agricultural income is itself vulnerable to seasonal cycles, and *peshgi* seems to be the only means of ensuring a stable income throughout the year. Indeed, the pattern of *peshgi*s clearly follows the seasonal cycle of employment at the kiln: they spike during the 'off-season' and decline significantly during the functional months at the kiln. In most cases indeed, sizeable (and long-term) *peshgi*s decline to zero during the functional cycle. We can see the clear correlation of *peshgi*s with the slack season in Table 2.

EXPENDITURE SPIKES

The third reason for taking *peshgi*s and occasionally letting them turn into long-term substantive loans is to try and cover expenditure 'spikes'. These spikes refer to occasions requiring expenses that cannot be met with the regular income, which is barely enough for subsistence. These include weddings or deaths in the immediate or extended family, sickness or health emergencies.

Even those families that are able to subsist on the income of their individual members cannot cope with the costs related to a sudden illness or death. It is important to remember that the public health system in

Pakistan is woefully inadequate, and private medical services are expensive. And the informal labour force is ineligible for unemployment benefits, health allowances or any other social benefits by the very virtue of its informality. In the absence of this social security *peshgis* are often the only way to make ends meet at times of high expenditure. A protracted illness can involve considerable expenditure for the family. The situation is made more acute if it is the main earner who is incapacitated as this means expenditure on treatment as well as the loss or reduction of his/her income.

As most of the *patheras* are migrants, they also need to contribute to their extended family funds in native villages when their relatives visit the cities for medical situations. In the cities, medical emergencies are the most frequent occasion when the workers need to borrow sums of money often two or three times more than their monthly incomes. Childbirth is one such occasion entailing large expenses, but protracted illnesses are not uncommon either. Other occasions that entail extra expenses are religious holidays and family travel.

Similarly, life events such as weddings and funerals demand considerable expenditure. The failure to arrange an 'appropriate' wedding leads to an immediate loss of face (*izzat*) for the family in the larger community. It may also result in an unsuitable match for daughters. The expenditure associated with weddings can easily exceed the annual earnings of a family, coming to between Rs. 100,000 and 150,000 (US$1000–1500) per wedding.

There are also a series of other ceremonies and occasions that workers spent considerable amounts on. These include child-birth and carnivals (*melas*). Participation in these community ceremonies is an important part of the workers' social universe. Some *patheras*—indeed most members of this socioeconomic group—also regularly visit at least one Sufi shrine annually. These are the key (indeed only) sources of recreation and relaxation available to socio-economic groups at the bottom rung of the social ladder. They also act as occasions for showing the family's standing within the community.

Low-income groups have often been blamed for not developing a culture of 'savings'.[11] This is frequently a charge made against the *patheras* as well. These 'evolutionist' arguments attribute the inability to save to the 'primitiveness' of the *patheras* behaviour and their inability to grasp the intricacies of modern social and economic organization.[12] This backwardness allegedly ties them into a relationship with intermediaries (the sub-contractors in our case) who can too easily exploit them. This argument is weak on both empirical and analytical grounds.

To begin with, the kiln earnings are barely sufficient to cover living costs and expenditure spikes. Expecting workers to accumulate savings while trying to eke out a living reflects an inadequate understanding of their socio-economic situation. Second, being illiterate persons with irregular employment, *patheras* do not have recourse to banking and credit facilities (like house or car loans, loans against salaries) that salaried members of the middle class access to tide over their expenditure spikes. The only credit facilities they can and do access are the *peshgis* advanced by the sub-contractors at their workplace. There are also psychological factors that work against the accumulation of savings. Amongst these, as Kanlan (2010) points out, is the natural tendency to prioritize the present over the future[13] and what he refers to as 'status quo' bias—people may plan to change what they want but one of the best predictors of future behaviour is our current behaviour. People not saving now are likely to continue not saving in the future.

Last, to the extent that *patheras* do find themselves with extra liquidity, it is common and socially important for them to share the extra income with their immediate and distant relatives. Social pressure towards kin demands the sharing rather than hoarding of extra income as and when it becomes available.

The last explanatory factor related to the practice of *peshgis* that is largely ignored in the literature is the provision of security to the employers and the workers. This factor is important, and merits a detailed discussion in the section below.

SECURITY OF EMPLOYMENT AND PRODUCTION

The least analysed factor in the prevalence of *peshgis* is the provision of regularity and predictability for both the employers and the workers. We start this discussion with observations from the fieldwork that question some of the widely-held assumptions about *peshgis* and kiln operation.

While the owners' use of the principle of *peshgi*-cum-piece-rate may be to ensure high productivity on part of the workers, actual findings suggest that this strategy is not necessarily effective. During fieldwork undertaken in the district of Gujranwala, it was actually observed that when cuts were being made from wages for return of *peshgis* worker output dropped substantially. The total output for the first week when partial *peshgi* repayment was deducted from the wages was 171,500 bricks. In the following week when no deductions were made, the output increased to 283,000. In the fourth week when the deduction was re-started the production decreased to 152,300. The fifth week saw an increase to 223,000 when deductions were again not taken.

This observation raises two questions. First, if the wages are actually paid on a piece rate, why do workers not increase their output (and hence income) to pay off their loans? Second, if productivity actually does decline with *peshgi*s, why don't the employers find an alternative method for meeting the workers' extra needs? It would appear that neither the employers nor the workers seem interested in eliminating *peshgi*s despite their apparent disadvantages. The answer to both questions is tied to the long-term concerns of both protagonists wherein *peshgi* plays a crucial role.

The fact that the workers do not actually want to pay off their outstanding loan is related to job security. The loan, after all, is one of the few guarantees that the employer will continue to give them some work. As soon as the loan is repaid the bond between employer and employee—not dependent on a contract and completely informal—is broken. In a highly insecure working environment the outstanding loan is one small guarantee of continued work. So the worker is not overly concerned or burdened by the loan that has been taken and in fact may view it positively.

THE BONDED OWNERS

For the kiln owners, to begin with, the *peshgi* system allows them to pay a lower wage rate. As we have seen, all kilns where *patheras* receive *peshgi* pay a lower wage rate. As we can also see from Table 2 and Figure 1, kiln owners receive an interest rate of around 14.5% on the *peshgi*s, and the outstanding principal debts remains the same. Arguably, the low cost of labour is an important explanatory factor for the lack of mechanization in the brick making sector in Pakistan.

However, the real function of *peshgi* for the kiln owners is not financial. Other operational costs of the kilns, like fluctuations in coal prices or litigation, actually cost the owners more in financial terms than the higher wages in the absence of a *peshgi* system. Indeed, the cost of recovery of *peshgi*s may well exceed their cost for the owners (as an example, see Table 3).

The most effective function performed by *peshgi* for the employer is to ensure a steady supply of labour, and to provide an effective means of labour control. *Patheras* constitute the largest workforce on a kiln, and the seasonal nature of brick production gives the *patheras* important leverage, as the employers place a high premium on the availability of workers during the peak season. In addition, the brick making sector has high start-up costs implying that the costs of interruption are particularly high for employers. It has been argued that one important technological explanation for the existence of *peshgi*s in the brick kiln sector is the presence of high start up costs for employers.

There is usually an assumption that *patheras* constitute an unskilled labour force. But this is not really the case. Brick moulding is not a skill or a profession that all labourers are willing or able to do. Therefore, the *peshgi* is used in order to attract and retain a skilled, and more importantly, available labour force. *Patheras* actually enjoy high bargaining power in both the market and the workplace, especially in the larger and economically well-off districts in Punjab where more employment options are available, and labour mobility is therefore higher than other parts of the country.[14] As the kilns cannot operate all year round, owners need to ensure continuous operation during the functional months to generate revenue. And since most *patheras* tend to be migrants, owners rely to a significant degree on a steady and reliable supply of labour. *Peshgi*s are the only (albeit imperfect, as we shall see below) means of ensuring a continuous supply of labour during the functional months. And retention appears not to be based on physical coercion but because the *peshgi* is a facility that *patheras* are attracted by. It is seen as a benefit of the job.

Indeed, *peshgi* loses its utility to the creditor when it is returned on a regular basis, as is common with the smaller loans. When *peshgi*s are returned they can lead to an increase in the bargaining power of the worker who can subsequently ask for larger advances. Repayment decreases the leverage that a creditor has over labour. So the utility of the *peshgi* for the employer lies in its ability to assure a labour supply for the busy season and also ensure that this labour remains in place during the off-season through the incentive of easily available credit.

A similar argument has been made for the pattern of advances in the power loom industry in Tamil Nadu by Geert De Neve (1999), who has argued that advances were used by employers to ensure a regular supply of skilled labour in an environment where skilled labour may be in short supply.[15]

In fact, in an environment of labour demand and its relative shortage, *peshgi*s can become more problematic for employers than for employees. The labour shortage immediately improves the bargaining position of the worker. De Neve emphasises this point by stating that in such situations it is the employer who may find himself bonded to the worker. He quotes an employer in the power loom industry of Tamil Nadu:

'Once they [the workers] have received an advance, they keep asking for more money. And if we refuse, they simply walk out and look for work in another factory, and on top of that they will not even return the advance they previously took from us. We are powerless.' (De Neve 1999: 396)

The current fieldwork indicates a similar situation. Many of the implications of taking a *peshgi* appear less serious than in other sectors. For example it is usually considered that once a *peshgi* is taken that a worker cannot move from the current employer without repaying the advance in full. This means that the possibility of availing better opportunities is forfeited. However, it was not uncommon for *patheras* to take another advance from an alternate creditor to pay off the original loan and then move to a more favoured employer. Moreover, this was not a last resort strategy but in many cases seen as a preferred one.

FREEDOM IN BONDAGE?

In literature, it is often believed that if bondage is to be *effective* along with being *substantive* (long-term indebtedness) then the obligation of labour should be accompanied by the threat of non-economic coercion i.e., it should be seen as enforceable (see Ercelan and Nauman this volume). Non-economic coercion comes in the form of surveillance, physical confinement of labour, and the threat and/or actual use of violence. Thus bondage may be instigated through indebtedness (economic coercion) but it is made effective through the additional application of non-economic forms of coercion. But not necessarily. In the example quoted from De Neve's work the economic coercion was clearly not backed by other forms of coercion.

Our research did not find evidence of the systematic use of non-economic (violent or otherwise) coercion either.[16] Part of this may simply be because the kilns are located in accessible sites rather than remote locations where labour could be isolated and the reach of the media reduced. Moreover, on at least one occasion a *pathera* had 'staged' his confinement by an employer and had called the police in order to pressure the kiln owner. There are also indications that the involvement of lawyers and NGOs has meant that *patheras* have balanced the scales with their employers somewhat. The relationship, which in the past was characterized by employers manipulating police and district government officials, has been changed with the *patheras* being more aware of avenues of redress for themselves.

Even though one partner in the unwritten agreement that leads to the provision of a *peshgi* is uneducated, the *patheras* in this case are not subjected to manipulation by the fudging of numbers. Accounts may be maintained by the subcontractor, but workers are well aware of how much they have borrowed and repaid. There was little or no evidence of accounts not being fairly maintained and *peshgi* amounts artificially inflated by the book-keepers.

Having stated that the inability to pay off a *peshgi* and the subsequent long term indebtedness are problematic—which is how they have been viewed typically—the findings from the fieldwork give a different angle to the picture. *Patheras* in the surveyed districts took *peshgis* not only for expenditure spikes related to health and life cycle events but also for more mundane reasons. Often these advances were demanded from an employer rather than requested and more often than not the *pathera* received his advance. Indebtedness does not appear to weigh heavily on the mind of the *pathera* in Punjab.

It has been reported in the media[17] that the mental strain of incurring large, outstanding loans that in all likelihood would never be paid off forces the *patheras* to take drastic measures, like occasionally selling their kidneys. In Gujranwala, interviews revealed that *patheras* who did sell their kidneys did so without any understanding of what the medical consequences may be. Again, the money obtained was used sometimes for mundane items. Unfortunately, following the removal of the kidney, *patheras* would usually be given a strong cocktail of antibiotics and other medicines that would artificially give the impression that a minor procedure had taken place. The actual implication of the procedure only became clear after the effects of the medicines had worn off.

SUMMARY FINDINGS

We can make the following points about *peshgis* in light of the findings:

- The implications of taking a loan and becoming indebted even for extended periods of time does not seem to be viewed negatively by *patheras*.
- This indebtedness does not appear to bring with it the most serious consequences usually associated with bonded labour—the use of violence to make bondage substantive. There was no evidence of the use of violence or the threat of the use of violence from the kilns in Gujranwala. Instead *patheras* often asked for further *peshgis*.

- Long term indebtedness does not seem to be a burden for *patheras*. It appears that this is accepted as an on-going condition. The ability of the employer to ensure the immobilization of workers through indebtedness is also seriously questioned considering that it was fairly common for *patheras* to move from kiln to kiln and simply take on larger *peshgis* to pay off their existing employers.
- If the *peshgi* is no longer seen as a means of coercing labour into accepting low wages and poor working conditions it needs to be re-evaluated as a facility that workers see as essential to meeting their current needs.
- While the *peshgi* clearly meets a need for the *patheras*, the employers' willingness to advance the sum is linked to the latter's need for a continuous and dependable supply of labour, especially during the functional months at the brick kiln.
- The *peshgi* may not be needed for subsistence purposes but it is still important as a means of meeting 'lumpy' expenditures. Even if higher wages were disbursed, they would not be adequate to cover this area. In sum then, the fact that *peshgis* play crucial functions for both owners and workers is clearly reflected in the interesting fact that *peshgis* do not necessarily hinder labour mobility within the sector. *Patheras* do tend to shift to other kilns on occasions. In these situations, the new employers pay the entire *peshgi* amount to the previous employers, and the workers start a new account of *peshgis* at the kiln. It is clear that owners face the problem of labour-flight even with the *peshgi* system in place, and the removal of the financial obligation to the kiln owner would actually lead to more frequent moves by *patheras*—a fact that would hinder the smooth operation of the kiln. That the new employers are willing to 'take over' the previous *peshgi* reflects their recognition both of the importance of *peshgi* in attracting and retaining the workforce, and of the fact that regular wages do not cater to long-term family expenses. As for the kiln owners, short of providing enough wages and incentives to retain the workforce, *peshgis* remain the only effective means of labour retention and control.

CONCLUDING REMARKS: WHO WANTS PESHGIS?

The fact that *peshgis* cater to important needs of both capital and labour, and tie them in a bond should not be taken to mean that both parties benefit equally from this practice. Or that workers are unaware of the

disadvantages of their position and prefer this arrangement to a more
formal relationship. The *peshgi* system functions—indeed thrives—in the
context of the 'informality' of the brick kilns sector. And by all accounts,
the informal sector disproportionately benefits employers and capital
owners. Recent studies of the resilience and re-emergence of the informal
sector in both developed and developing countries have highlighted how
the informal sector 'frees' the employers from onerous obligations towards
the workers that may be enforced by the state. In the developed world,
several workers' rights were legislated by governments after 1945, and the
rise of informality since the 1970s is a response of capital to the increasing
costs of retaining a permanent workforce. In developing countries,
resistance of business and manufacturing interests is an important factor
in the inability or unwillingness of their governments to legislate or
effectively implement labour-friendly policies. It is this very informality
that has made certain developing countries attractive sites for
manufacturing firms relocating from the expensive labour markets in the
developed world.[18]

The workforce in Pakistan—no less than the workforce in any other
part of the world—is perfectly aware of the disadvantages they incur in
the informal sector. The clearest indication of the workers' preference for
formal employment is the huge number of applicants for government jobs
at all levels. Government jobs in Pakistan—both civilian and military—do
not offer high salaries, but precisely the rights and privileges that the
informal sector does not: job security, a roadmap for career advancement,
pension, health coverage, and return on savings at the time of retirement.
These jobs attract millions of applicants every year—even for positions at
the lowest levels of the ladder like janitorial and manual jobs. The first
priority for the working classes continues to be formal jobs with the
attendant benefits. Given the scarcity of such jobs, they seek subsistence
and job security in the informal sector through whatever mechanisms are
available to them.

In sum then, the *peshgi* system binds and serves both employers and
workers, but has a different meaning and significance for each protagonist.
For the kiln owners, *peshgis* are the price they pay for all the advantages
of relying on an informal workforce. For the workers, *peshgis* are the only
means available to them for earning a livelihood and enjoying a minimal
level of job security. Any discussion of the possibility and desirability of
the elimination of *peshgi*—and bonded labour in general—would have to
take into account the willingness of employers to forego the numerous
advantages they derive from the system and incur the costs of maintaining
a permanent labour force.

Table 1.

	INVESTMENT CALCULATED ON ANNUAL BASIS (with *Peshgi*)*			
	Average 650,000 bricks per cycle, 6 cycles a year			**Rupees**
Fixed Costs	**Coal Cost per Cycle (Rs. 15,000 per tonnes, 100 tonnes per cycle)**			9,000,000
	Estimated Adances to *Patheras*			4,000,000
	Average cost of Electricity for labour (Rs. 20,000 per month)			240,000
	Electricity for Brick kiln (Rs. 6,000 per month)			72,000
	Rent of Brick Kiln (Rs. 252,000 for six months)			504,000
	Land rent for clay making (per 7 acres, Rs. 45,000 per acre)			315,000
	Labour Cost for *Bharaiwala* (Rs. 150 per 1,000 bricks)			585,000
	Miscellaneous cost			1,000,000
	Annual Labour cost for *Patheras* (Rs. 880 per 1,000 bricks)**			3,432,000
	Clay Cost (30p per brick)			1,170,000
	Sand (Rs. 1,250 per trolley, 20 trolleys per cycle)			150,000
Running Costs	**Salary Person cost at Brick kiln**	***Bharaiwala* (Rs. 11,000 each, 2 person)**	132,000	1,358,000
		***Nakasiwala* (Rs. 90 per 1,000 bricks)**	351,000	
		***Munshi* (Rs. 15,000 each)**	180,000	
		***Chowkidar* (1 person)**	72,000	
		***Jalaiwalas* (4 to 5 persons)**	420,000	
		Coal Labor	63,000	
		***Keriwala* (Rs. 10,000 each, 2 person)**	140,000	
		Grand Total		**21,826,000**
		Total Cost in US$		**209,865**

*All figures are in Pakistani Rupees

** This figure includes the commission of the sub-contractor, which ranges from Rs. 20–30 per thousand bricks

Table 2. Weekly *Peshgi* Pattern

Week	Total *Peshgi*	Off-season *Peshgi*	Deductions (repayment of *peshgi* by workers)	Outstanding Loan
0	100,000	2,000	-	102,000
1	102,000	2,000	-	104,000
2	104,000	2,000	-	106,000
3	106,000	2,000	-	108,000
4	108,000	2,000	-	110,000
5	110,000	2,000	-	112,000
6	112,000	10,000	-	122,000
7	122,000	-	2,340	119,660
8	119,660	-	2,340	117,320
9	117,320	-	2,340	114,980
10	114,980	-	2,340	112,640
11	112,640	-	2,340	110,300
12	110,300	-	2,340	107,960
13	107,960	-	3,000	104,960
14	104,960	-	3,000	101,960
15	101,960	-	3,000	98,960
16	98,960	-	3,000	95,960
17	95,960	-	3,000	92,960
18	92,960	-	3,000	89,960
19	89,960	-	3,000	86,960
20	86,960	-	3,000	83,960
21	83,960	-	3,000	80,960
22	80,960	-	3,000	77,960
23	77,960	-	3,000	74,960
24	74,960	-	3,000	71,960
25	71,960	-	3,000	68,960
26	68,960	2,000	-	70,960
27	70,960	2,000	-	72,960
28	72,960	2,000	-	74,960

29	74,960	2,000	-	76,960
30	76,960	2,000	-	78,960
31	78,960	2,000	-	80,960
32	80,960	2,000	-	82,960
33	82,960	2,000	-	84,960
34	84,960	2,000	-	86,960
35	86,960	2,000	-	88,960
36	88,960	15,000	-	103,960
37	103,960	-	2,340	101,620
38	101,620	-	2,340	99,280
39	99,280	-	2,340	96,940
40	96,940	-	2,340	94,600
41	94,600	-	-	94,600
42	94,600	-	-	94,600
43	94,600	-	-	94,600
44	94,600	-	-	94,600
45	94,600	-	-	94,600
46	94,600	-	-	94,600
47	94,600	2,000	-	96,600
48	96,600	2,000	-	98,600

Source: Compiled from the data provided by the Zulfiqar Bricks Company (Registered) in Gujranwala. The table shows *peshgis* increasing off season—weeks 0–6, 26–36, 47–48. Repayments increase during season.

Figure 1: Typical Annual Pattern of Weekly *Peshgis*

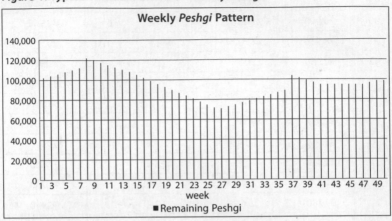

Table shows total remaining *peshgi* increasing to a maximum in the off season months and decreasing in season.

Table 3: Cost of Recovering the *Peshgis*

Brick Kiln No.	Total Families (*Patheras*)	Total *Peshgi* per family	Total Electricity Bill Per Month	Total loss of *peshgis* due to labour flight	Total expense for recovery of *peshgis* (litigation)
1	20–30	125000	12000	650000	175000
2	30	130000	12000	575000	200000
3	30	100000	7000	400000	100000
4	34	147000	15000		
5	25	140000	16000	700000	150000
6	35	200000	20000–25000	900000	600000 (2009–12)
7	28	100000	15000	700000	125000 (2010–12)
8	30	150000	25000	150000	325000 (2011–13)
9	35	137000	10000	450000	125000 (2011–12)
10	25	125000	12000	350000	10000 (2011–12)

REFERENCES

Arif, G. M. (2004), Bonded Labour in Agriculture:A Rapid Assessment in Punjab and North West Frontier Province. Rep. Print.

Bales, Kevin (2000), *Disposable People*. University of California Press.

Breman, Jan (1999), *Footloose Labour*. Cambridge University Press.

Collective for Social Science Research (2004), *A Rapid Assessment of Bonded Labour in Domestic Work and Begging in Pakistan*. Karachi: Federal Bureau of Statistics, Government of Pakistan and the International Labor Organization. *Survey of Bonded Labour in Two Sectors of Pakistan: Brick Kiln Workers (Punjab) and Sharecroppers (Sindh)*. Rep. 2002. Print

Hussein, Maliha H., Abdul Razzaq Saleem, Saira Malik, and Shazreh Hussain (2004), 'Bonded Labour in Agriculture: A Rapid Assessment in Sindh and Balochistan'. Print.

Khan, Ali (2010), 'Peshgi without Bondage: Reconsidering the Links between Debt and Bonded Labour', *Cultural Dynamics*, 22(3): 247–266.

Nasir, Zafar Mueen (2004), *A Rapid Assessment of Bonded Labour in the Carpet Industry of Pakistan*, Rep. 2004.

Nauman, N., Ercelawn, A. (2001), *Bonded Labour in Pakistan*. Geneva: International Labour Organization;. Rep 2001.

Portes, Alejandro, Manuel Castells, Lauren A. Benton (eds.) (1989), *The Informal Economy: Studies in Advanced and less Developed Countries*. Baltimore, MD: Johns Hopkins University Press.

Salim, Ahmad (2004), *A Rapid Assessment of Bonded Labour in Pakistan's Mining Sector*. Rep. 2004.

Tilly, Charles (1995), 'Globalization Threatens Labor's Rights'. *International Labor and Working Class History* 47 (2): 1–23.

NOTES

1. Maliha H. Hussein; Abdul Razzaq Saleemi, Saira Malik, Shazreh Hussain (2004), Collective for Social Science Research, Karachi, G. M. Arif, 2004, Ahmad Salim, 2004, Zafar Mueen Nasir, 2004.

2. See for example Ercelawn, A., Nauman, N. (2001), Ali Khan (2010), Kevin Bales (2000), Jan Breman (1999).

3. Breaking the Bond: Elimination of Bonded Labour in Brick Kilns (EBLIK). A Project for the Elimination of Bonded Labour in Brick Kilns (EBLIK) Labour and Human Resource Department, Government of Punjab. April 2010. Centre for the Improvement of Working Conditions & Environment (CIWCE) in collaboration with the International Labour Organization (ILO)

4. Article 11 of the Constitution of the Islamic Republic of Pakistan deals specifically with forced labour. The Pakistan legal system also has a Bonded Labour System Abolition Act (1992). Moreover, Pakistan has ratified International Labour Organization instruments—Forced Labour Convention 1930 (No. 29) and the Abolition of Forced Labour Convention 1957 (No. 105).

5. See Jan Breman (2013) *At Work in the Informal Economy of India: A Perspective from the Bottom Up*, Oxford University Press; Ali Khan (2007), *Representing Children: Power, Policy and the Discourse on Child Labour in the Football Manufacturing Industry of Pakistan*. Karachi: Oxford University Press.

6. *Survey of Bonded Labour in Two Sectors of Pakistan: Brick Kiln Workers (Punjab) and Sharecroppers (Sindh)*, 2002, Federal Bureau of Statistics, Government of Pakistan and the International Labor Organization.

7. The term 'caste' in the Punjabi context refers to groups tied by complex interaction of professional and ethnic ties. These 'castes' are not to be confused with the Hindu caste system.

8. In areas around Lahore, the wages per one thousand (1000) bricks are in the range of Rs. 650–750 in Gujranwala, 600–700 in Lahore, 700 in Kasur, and 800 in Narowal.

9. *Survey of Bonded Labour in Two Sectors of Pakistan: Brick Kiln Workers (Punjab) and Sharecroppers (Sindh)*, 2002, Federal Bureau of Statistics, Government of Pakistan and the International Labour Organization. Ali Khan (2009), Ercelawn, A., Nauman, N. (2001).

10. In 2014 the minimum wage in Punjab was 12,000 per month for unskilled labourers.

11. See critiques of this in 'Beyond Cash and Carry: Financial Savings, Financial Services, and Low Income Households in Two Communities', John P. Caskey, report written for the Consumer Federation of American and the Ford Foundation, 1997; 'Helping the Poor Save More', Dean Karlan, Stanford Social Innovation Review, Winter 2010; 'Why Don't the Poor Save More?' Pascaline Dupas and Jonathan Robinson, American Economic Review 2013, (103(4): 1138–1171.

12. See for example David Hardiman (1987), 'The Bhils and Shahukars of Eastern Gujarat', *Sulbaltern Studies* V, New Delhi: Oxford University Press.

13. See also 'Beyond Cash and Carry: Financial Savings, Financial Services, and Low Income Households in Two Communities', John P. Caskey, Report written for the Consumer Federation of American and the Ford Foundation, 1997

14. Our informal survey revealed that piece-rates were highest in the Narowal district because of the recent departure of a sizeable number of Afghan refugees who had been working at the kilns. The decline in the available workforce increased their bargaining position, leading to one of the highest piece-rates in the country.

15. De Neve, G., (1999) 'Asking for and giving baki: Neo bondage or the interplay of bondage and resistance in the Tamilnadu power-loom industry'. In: Parry, J. P., Breman, J., and Kapadia, K., (eds) *The Worlds of Indian Industrial Labour*. New Delhi: Sage Publications, 379–406.

16. There was a tragic incident recently when a Christian family was burnt alive at a Kasur kiln in November 2014. But that incident was part of a broader trend of religiously-inspired violence by vigilante groups rather than a strategy used by kiln owners.

17. http://www.irinnews.org/report/28499/pakistan-focus-on-kidney-sales-by-bonded-labourers accessed 1/6/2015, Bricked in by debt, Pakistan's child 'slaves' http://edition.cnn.com/2009/WORLD/asiapcf/11/25/pakistan.bonded.labor/index.html accessed 1/6/2015, Desperation behind Pakistan's kidney trade http://news.bbc.co.uk/2/hi/south_asia/7613235.stm accessed 1/6/2015

18. A comprehensive anthology on the various manifestations and dynamics of the informal economy is Portes, Castells and Benton (1989). For the increasing costliness of labour as a result of state intervention after 1945, see also Tilly (1995).

Copyright acknowledgements

Index